Critical Practice

The WISH List
(Warwick Interdisciplinary Studies in the Humanities)

Series Editors: Jonathan Bate, Stella Bruzzi, and Thomas Docherty

In the twenty-first century, the traditional disciplinary boundaries of higher education are dissolving at remarkable speed. The last decade has seen the flourishing of scores of new interdisciplinary research centres at universities around the world, and there has also been a move towards a more interdisciplinary teaching.

The WISH List is a collaboration between Bloomsbury Academic and the University of Warwick, a university that has been, from its foundations, at the forefront of interdisciplinary innovation in academia. The series aims to establish a framework for innovative forms of interdisciplinary publishing within the humanities, between the humanities and social sciences, and even between the humanities and the hard sciences.

Also in *The WISH List*:

Confessions: The Philosophy of Transparency, Thomas Docherty
The Constitution of English Literature: Ideology, State and Nation, Michael Gardiner
Joseph Cornell versus Cinema, Michael Piggot
Open Space Learning: A Study in Transdisciplinary Pedagogy, Nicholas Monk, Carol Chillington Rutter, Jonothan Neelands, Jonathan Heron
The Public Value of the Humanities, edited by Jonathan Bate
Raising Milton's Ghost: John Milton and the Sublime of Terror in the Early Romantic Period, Joseph Crawford
Reading and Rhetoric in Montaigne and Shakespeare, Peter Mack

Critical Practice

Philosophy and Creativity

Martin McQuillan

BLOOMSBURY ACADEMIC
LONDON • NEW YORK • OXFORD • NEW DELHI • SYDNEY

BLOOMSBURY ACADEMIC
Bloomsbury Publishing Plc
50 Bedford Square, London, WC1B 3DP, UK

BLOOMSBURY, BLOOMSBURY ACADEMIC and the Diana logo are trademarks of
Bloomsbury Publishing Plc

First published in Great Britain 2019

Copyright © Martin McQuillan, 2019

Martin McQuillan has asserted his right under the Copyright, Designs and Patents Act,
1988, to be identified as Author of this work.

For legal purposes the Acknowledgements on p. viii constitute an extension
of this copyright page.

Cover design: Paul Burgess

All rights reserved. No part of this publication may be reproduced or transmitted
in any form or by any means, electronic or mechanical, including photocopying,
recording, or any information storage or retrieval system, without prior permission
in writing from the publishers.

Bloomsbury Publishing Plc does not have any control over, or responsibility for, any
third-party websites referred to or in this book. All internet addresses given in this
book were correct at the time of going to press. The author and publisher regret any
inconvenience caused if addresses have changed or sites have ceased to exist, but
can accept no responsibility for any such changes.

A catalogue record for this book is available from the British Library.

Library of Congress Cataloging-in-Publication Data
Names: McQuillan, Martin, author.
Title: Critical practice: philosophy and creativity / Martin McQuillan.
Description: London; New York: Bloomsbury Academic / Bloomsbury Publishing
Plc, 2019. | Series: The wish list | Includes bibliographical references and index.
Identifiers: LCCN 2018018977 (print) | LCCN 2018028954 (ebook) | ISBN
9781780931005 (ePDF) | ISBN 9781780931012 (ePub) | ISBN 9781780930343
(pbk.: alk. paper) | ISBN 9781780930350 (hardback: alk. paper)
Subjects: LCSH: Criticism–History. | Literature–Philosophy. | Arts–Philosophy. |
Culture–Philosophy.
Classification: LCC PN86.M47 (ebook) | LCC PN86.M47 C75 2019 (print) |
DDC 801/.95–dc23
LC record available at https://lccn.loc.gov/2018018977

ISBN: HB: 978-1-7809-3035-0
PB: 978-1-7809-3034-3
ePDF: 978-1-7809-3100-5
eBook: 978-1-7809-3101-2

Series: The WISH List

Typeset by Deanta Global Publishing Services, Chennai, India

To find out more about our authors and books visit www.bloomsbury.com
and sign up for our newsletters.

Do not all charms fly
At the mere touch of cold philosophy?

Keats, 'Lamia'

'We shudder to comprehend in thought the sphere of Creation … It is as if we were to seek to describe the inner structure and juices of a pomegranate from its outer skin'.

Herder, *Plastik*

In theory there is no difference between theory and practice. In practice there is.

Unattributed

Contents

Acknowledgements   viii

Introduction: Practice Is Not What You Think   1

Part One   In Theory

1   Theory and Practice: From Kant to Plato   25
2   The Last Chapter of the History of the World   53
3   Blindness and Touching   82
4   Prometheus and Pygmalion   113
5   Creation and Innovation   138

Part Two   In Practice

6   1975 to 1871   165
7   Derrida Queries de Man   195

Notes   211
Index   233

Acknowledgements

I would like to thank the colleagues and students at Leeds and Kingston who have provoked me to think about the problem of critical practice. I am grateful to the filmmakers I have worked with and in particular thank Joanna Callaghan and Ken McMullen for the time shared, which I learnt was all about the process.

Sections of this book were read and commented on by Thomas Docherty, Simon Morgan Wortham, John Schad, Sarah Dillon, Nicole Anderson, Willy Maley, and Jean-Michel Rabaté. I am grateful for their comments; any errors contained in the book are entirely my own.

A shorter version of Chapter 6 first appeared in *Derrida Today*, 10(2), 2017, published by Edinburgh University Press.

A different version of Chapter 7 first appeared in *After Derrida: Literature, Theory and Criticism in the 21st Century*, ed. Jean-Michel Rabaté (Cambridge: Cambridge University Press, 2018).

I am grateful to the editors of these volumes for permission to reproduce this work in another context.

This book is for everyone who reads Theory and makes art. It is for Sophie, who saved me.

Introduction:
Practice Is Not What You Think

This is a book about what we call today practice-based research.[1] It has grown out of a twin interest. Firstly, the experience of teaching in art schools and, secondly, working with filmmakers in the cinema of ideas.[2] In both situations, the same problematic imposed itself upon me: does reading theory and philosophy make you a better artist? This is a deceptively simple question with a complex set of answers. If we were to contend that reading literary theory made you a better reader of literature, or at least a different kind of reader of literature, then that would not be the same thing as claiming that reading literary theory made you a better writer. Indeed, there could be a significant period of time in which reading literary theory actually makes you a worse writer. It is telling how many academic authors never escape from that phase of their intellectual development. However, reading literary theory is certainly interesting and gives one a broader vista on literature and culture, making you a more interesting and interested reader than might otherwise have been the case.

Literary Theory is of course one of those gateway drugs into more hardcore philosophical practices. The same is true of the art theory and aesthetics that is taught in art schools. One can take a view on the relative degrees of rigour with which those texts are explored in the literature seminar or the art studio but in both cases the theoretical canon has opened up these disciplines to a broader range of thinking and interests than is defined by their ostensible object of study. In the case of art schools this is more readily reflected at the level of fine art practice than it is in creative writing programmes. Contemporary art, inside and outside of an academic context, has for some time been comfortable with the conjunction of art practice, history, and theory as the basis of its own identity, to the point that the three terms are increasingly indistinguishable at the level of their own practices. This is less true of creative writing programmes in general, although there are heroic exceptions, which much prefer an insistence on craft, structure, and the lone genius of the author, to an engagement with the instability of the signifier. If anything, a creative writing programme that offers a theoretical component is more likely to grow out of an institutional interest in creative criticism and its poetic overspill than it is from a programme staffed by 'professional' writers.[3] Perhaps, this is telling about who makes art and who writes literature and the contexts in which the work emerges.

I am not suggesting that the part-time artists working in our art schools are more committed to their own academization than the part-time writers who supplement their income by teaching on our creative writing programmes. Rather, literary culture outside of the academy is still dominated by an institutional apparatus that privileges the figure of the celebrity author over the challenge of complex thought. To the extent that creative writing programmes themselves, theoretical or otherwise, and the vast majority are otherwise, tend to receive a bad press in the very literary culture they feed. It is thought that writing is something that cannot be taught and those 'studying' on creative writing programmes are somehow deluded fools or idle beatniks putting off the day when they will have to go get a *real* job. We find a similar kind of self-loathing in the media about Media Studies in which commentators cannot imagine their own business to be suitably serious as to merit its own academic study. Suspicion of creative writing degrees by industry professional is a reflection of that industry's own sense of self-worth. The under theorization evident on most creative writing programmes is an indication that those degrees, and those drafted in to teach them, remain semi-detached to the serious business of the Literature department that spawned them as a route to increased student recruitment. The same is not true of the art school where there is a hunger for concepts and the challenge of speculative thought as part of a formation of the student that informs their creative practice.

This is a reflection of the very different histories of the academization of fine art and creative writing. The former, in the United Kingdom at least, emerged from the radical politics associated with the art school occupations of the late 1960s following the publication of the Coldstream Report and the student uprisings across Europe and as part of the civil rights movement in the United States.[4] Key to the demands of the students occupying Hornsey, Guilford, and elsewhere was the demand that an art school education should not be solely a vocational training but should include an emphasis on practice as research and inquiry, explicitly containing a theoretical and philosophical component. Hence a core training in aesthetics and art theory remains the spine of any art school education worthy of the name, despite the ever-increasing pressures to once again utilize the art schools as a service to industry. These art schools can all date their histories back over one hundred years and this contest between utility and theory has constituted their educational dynamic over this period.[5] In contrast, the explosion of creative writing in UK universities occurred at a time of expansion in student numbers and for the most part was initiated by senior managers as a means of maximizing the potential of new student markets. The older programmes can trace their history to the 1970s, but they are very much the exception and were very much places of selection rather than mass participation. This is not to criticize the widespread uptake of creative writing programmes, rather it is to suggest that from the beginning art schools have tilted around the intellectual problematic between theory and practice, while creative writing programmes have been shy even about the seriousness of their own practice as a contribution to academic life. Equally, this is not to insist that in order to be taken seriously or to take oneself seriously it is necessary to be associated with the institutional apparatus of the university. Rather, it is to suggest that there remains in English literary culture a persistent suspicion towards complex thinking that is considered somehow un-literary and un-English and moreover in some way unfortunately 'continental'. The other nations of the United Kingdom are not exempt from this way of thinking either. At least literature departments in England have for the most part opened themselves to theoretical idioms. There are of course exceptions and the history of the reception and dissemination of theoretical thought in the Humanities is complex and is spread across all the regions of the United Kingdom. Precision and scrupulous scholarship would be required to trace that history and to do justice to the relative contribution of the islands of thought make up the absorption of the theoretical tradition into UK universities. That history is not the subject of this book.[6]

However, the basic principle stands that it is in the art school and around art education that we will find a decisive case of the formalization of the problematic between speculative thought and creative practice. The interesting question here is not whether artists should read theory, let us take that as a given. It is no longer the 1970s and I do not propose to expend an excess of energy making the polemic case for the value of theory. If this is not the hot topic it once was, it is because for good or ill, theory has been domesticated by the disciplines of the Arts and Humanities. Whether, this means theory won or not is open to question, but again that is not the subject of this book. Rather, the interesting question for me in working with filmmakers and in teaching creative students is not what does theory contribute to creative practice but precisely what does theory not account for in the process of making? Something happens in creative work that cannot be wholly accounted for by theory. There is a gap that opens, however small, between concept and creation, epistemology and performance, and theory and practice. It is in this crack that, as Leonard Cohen might say, the light gets in and the work takes place and takes its place.

This gap is characterized by a certain kind of unknowing in which thinking is suspended but not absent. It is this *not-knowing* that produces the creative outcome. No creative act – literature, film, drama, dance, or music – is the result of the programmed application of theory. Such work would be dead on the page or on the screen. In fact the only work that could ever be an adequate application of theory would be the book of theory itself, like the hyper-reality of Borges' map that covered the entire kingdom.[7] Instead, something happens in the process of making that derails theory into something else and leaves it stranded in the work of art, no longer the thing it once was but now suspended in another frame of reference. Creative practice perpetually places theory inside inverted commas, making it something other than it once was. We could, and will, read a number of texts, films, paintings, dramas, and performances in which we could demonstrate this othering of theory. However, this is not necessarily to put our finger on the interesting question here. We have a rational discourse to discuss works of art, which are theoretically informed or otherwise, and that discourse is theory itself. So, using theory to describe something that looks like theory will only take us so far, and the object of our study here is not the output itself, although that is obviously something that will claim our attention. Rather, what interests me, as an itch worth scratching, is the gap. How can we know this moment of not-knowing? It is my contention that the process that takes us from theory to practice is not just one in which theory and practice inform one another to their mutual benefit, but one in which this encounter takes place as a radical disruption, in which the epistemological falls into not-knowing as a condition of its performance as creative work. In this sense, the only thing worth knowing is this not-knowing.

Now, this is not to surrender creative practice to the irrational, mystical, or eccentric notions of the divine or even the bodily. Rather, it is to challenge theory to think the moment when theory no longer thinks. By necessity this present account of theory and practice will have to take a theoretical form. It is what I do. This is a book about theory and practice written by a theorist who has worked closely with practitioners but who has never, straightforwardly lost himself in that practice. There are plenty of examples we will look at of where the idiomatic writing of theory edges into another type of creative work, and numerous examples of theorists who are also novelists and so on. I have made films and written screenplays, even won awards for some of them, but in this study as in other domains of my written output, I have retained the position, personae, and intellectual apparatus, of a theorist. On such foundations are academic careers built, and I am not going to start apologizing for it now. However, theory loses nothing from its encounter with practice and equally loses nothing from recognizing within the creative process a moment that theory itself cannot master and is in fact transformed into something other than itself. I am not going to talk in a vague way about the alchemical processes of theatre or writing or some such half-baked mysticism. Rather, this book will deploy the resources of theory to discuss something that is a problem for theory, in a theoretical way. When we say 'problem for theory' we mean a question that is of interest to theory, it is not a problem in the way that having no money is a problem for someone who wants to eat lunch. The problems of theory might seem to some to be of limited importance at this moment in time. In truth they always have been, the issue we might say is academic, in a good sense. However, the astute reader will recognize in the discussion of this book an argument that pertains to the relation between theory and practice beyond the creative writing seminar or editing suite.

When we say that there is a moment of not-knowing or a disruptive gap between theory and practice, we are talking about more than writing a screenplay. It is true that the artist or maker (even the artist who reads theory) must to some degree not know what they are doing in order to initiate creative practice. Equally, it is true that *whatever* practice we seek to inaugurate we must in some important way not know what we are doing. On the one hand, there is the question of what happens to theoretical knowledge when it comes into contact with singular circumstances. Or, as the boxer Mike Tyson put it, everyone has a plan until they get punched in the jaw. The plan is necessary but not sufficient; it cannot survive contact with the enemy, and theory must always be transformed into something other than itself. It becomes practice, that is to say, it becomes the very thing that theory studies. Theory must become its own other. In this sense, practice is profoundly theoretical and what we are calling a problem for theory is just as big a problem for practice. On the other hand, there is the first mark on the page, the initial act of creative practice that is a launch from theory to practice. It is not straightforwardly the case that this is the moment of not-knowing, the unknowing might precede it, or be in advance of it, yet to come in the work that makes the work. However, it is the renunciation of certainty, not the abandonment of theory, which characterizes this disruption. Whether the path from theory to practice results in a film or a political movement is immaterial; the problem of unknowing and the transformation of theory into its own other is the same. What goes for art goes for politics; only the practical outcomes are different.

Equally, this fissure of the uncertain should in no way be understood as a fall into innocence. This cannot be stressed enough. The space where thinking is suspended is not an innocent space; the leap into an abyss can be fully informed. In fact, a fall is rarely innocent, there can be endless reasons for it, including suicide where a fall becomes a plunge, or be the result of a push or a trip, where a fall becomes a drop. Leaping into an abyss might not be a rational thing to do, but then again making art might not necessarily be a rational thing to do either. It is nevertheless something that reason has to account for. There is then nothing innocent about not-knowing, rather this unknowing is the condition for knowing itself. That is to say, the condition for the economic play between theory and practice that makes both possible. It is a black spot for theory in which theory will have to understand its own non-understanding. By definition, while we may be able to approach this black spot by theoretical means, we will not be able to pin it down without the performative picking up the pin and walking off with it. We are looking for the god particle of theory, the thing that is hidden to theory but whose traces are presented to us in the physical universe. Like the search for the Higgs boson, we are approaching this problem from the starting point of a theoretical hypothesis. Theory says this must be true and so we set out from theory seeking to prove the truth of our own theory. If we were to offer a critical reading of our own set-up it would be this, namely, that this investigation into the non-thinking of theory is profoundly complicit with theory's own rational colonialism and its desire to colour another dark part of the map. However, this location cannot be made pink, it is there like the unconscious or dark matter, but it cannot be fully articulated because it is the moment that undoes articulation. To ask theory to understand its own non-understanding is to ask theory to see itself seeing, or perhaps, to see itself seeing blindly.

Now, having established this intention, what will interest us in this book is in fact beyond the grasp of this book and will necessarily escape any attempt to master it through a rational discourse. So, where does this leave the business of practice-based research? Firstly, there is plenty more to concern us in the question of practice-based research than the issues at stake in this book. Other accounts of creative practice as research are available and the industry of practice-based research will not grind to a halt as a result of this book.[8] However, and secondly, if our basic hypothesis is correct, that not-knowing is a necessary condition of making, then what does that mean for the academic, governmental, and institutional discourse of practice-based research that seeks to contain creative practice within the university? The literature on practice-based and practice-led research is, for good reason, deliberately vague on what it actually is.

There are some, by now, canonical examples of this. For example, the 2007 report commissioned by the UK's Arts and Humanities Research Council (AHRC) and authored by Chris Rust, Judith Mottram, and Jeremy Till.[9] Written in the context of a concerted attempt by the AHRC to reach consensus with British universities on a definition of practice as research in order to bring the creative disciplines within the funding regimes of the UK government, this report stops short of defining its erstwhile object of study.

This report emerges from the disciplines of art, design, and architecture and starts from the premise that for academics in these subjects, practice is the normal mode and method of inquiry when learning and scholarship is situated in a setting of professional practice. This immediately opens up the question of two types of practice. When we speak of an architectural practice or a design practice this does not necessarily imply a research content. Indeed, practice in this sense really means the working environment or office of an architect or designer. Practice, then, is what artists do but that is not the same as practice-based research. However, rather than seek to define these uses of practice as a mode of inquiry, the report's authors, following the example of the research council, suggest conditions that have to be met in order for practice to be worthy of the name research. There is a concerted effort not to privilege research over practice, stressing the mutual interaction of both. However, the fundamental point remains in this report, and it defines the whole exercise to understand practice-based research, that if practice can be characterized as research then it can be funded. More accurately, it can then be funded by the Arts and Humanities Research Council and the Higher Education Funding Councils' periodic assessments of university research. Practice as such, practice without research, is more properly the purview of the Arts Council or the commercial sector. The attempt to have practice in a university context recognized as research and to have it funded by the British government is highly commendable. This work has also been undertaken in Australian and North American contexts as well, and it is important that university-based practice be funded.

However, it is possible to see from the very beginning of the writing on practice-based research a series of inclusions and exclusions being set up in order to justify an institutionalization of practice that will allow it to be funded. I am not saying this is a good or bad thing, I am simply saying this is what has happened, and as the idea of practice-based research becomes normalized within the academy these conceptual manoeuvres will be forgotten and these definitions erased with time. The same is true of the Practice as Research in Performance project that the AHRC ran through the University of Bristol in which a deliberately generous definition of practice as research necessarily disguises moves to accommodate practice within existing institutional definitions of research.[10] Accordingly, it is recognized today that practice-based research should define a set of research questions, identify the research context of its inquiry, produce documentable outputs, and so on. This leads to the importance of meta-commentary on practice as one way of satisfying the definition of research. In this sense, writing about your practice is what makes it research as much as the outcome of the inquiry through practice itself. This expectation for documentation in turn takes us to a position that states that practice that does not include such processes is not eligible for support by the research council:

> For research to be considered as practice-led, the [Phd] student's own practice must be an integral part of the proposed project, and the creative and/or performative aspects of the research should be made explicit. The research carried out should bring about enhancements in knowledge and understanding in the discipline, or in related disciplinary areas. Research to provide content is not considered practice-led research in this context. For example, if a film-maker wanted to make a film about refugees, the research questions should be about the process of making the film, not about the experience of the refugees. Work that results purely from the creative or professional development of an artist, however distinguished, is unlikely to fulfil the definition of practice-led research in this context.[11]

Now, to an extent that is a fair definition of practice-led or practice-based, take your pick, research in that it should extend the boundaries of the disciplinary field and that field is practice not refugee studies. On the other hand, it is patently absurd that such a documentary could not be funded on its own terms by the research council. It would mean that films about asylum-seekers should be funded by commercial partners, but research projects about lens depths and shutter speeds can by funded by the government. Or, if you want to make a film about refugees you darn well better be documenting the impact of the camera angles you are using. This probably was not the intention of those early pioneers of practice as research who penned those reports for the research council. It hardly makes for a vibrant research culture in our university departments of film and media.

I have no investment in dismantling the edifice of practice-based research and its institutional funding arrangements. However, it must be said that something that we now take for granted as part of the academic landscape has a fairly recent history and that this history is characterized by a number of conceptual elisions that are about the institutionalization of art forms within the framework of research funding and so the political priorities of the nation state. This places practice as research in the landscape of what Schiller calls the aesthetic state (*Aethetischer Staat*).[12] That is to say a situation in which the state accords a principle of political value to the aesthetic and claims an authority for it, and over it, to shape the possibilities and limits of freedom previously safeguarded by art. We might think this is quite mild in the case of the Arts and Humanities Research Council or even a price worth paying to ensure funding for practice in our universities. However, it introduces into the very idea of practice-based research a foundational compromise with the powerful ideological drive that accords a political force to the aesthetic and which in alternative locations has produced quite different historical outcomes.[13] What makes this significant is the way that the formulations of practice-based research repeat the historical gesture of giving the aesthetic an institutional agency and so a practical, political impact by linking it to knowledge production. That is to say, practice-based research introduces a mode of formalization to art.

Without formalization there could be no funding, no research council for the arts, no university setting and no teaching programme. Aesthetic formalization is essential to the universitification of creative practice. That is not a criticism; it is fact as old as Schiller. The categories of practice-based research are those of our aesthetic modernity, they are Schillerian through and through and run deep in our pedagogical institutions.[14] The reason one should be wary of such formalization without due critique is, to borrow a phrase from Paul de Man, that 'it stages a loss of hermeneutic control over art as a scene of hermeneutic persuasion'.[15] It is the hermeneutic excess of art that must be brought within the institution and there is no better way to place a limit around that excess than by becoming its paymaster. It is precisely because the research paradigm cannot account for the hermeneutic overspill of creative practice that practice must be brought within it. And, as de Man says, 'when a persuasion has to become a scene of persuasion one is no longer in the same way persuaded of its persuasiveness' (p. 269). It is wise then that most of us remain wary about placing a definition of practice-based research to avoid a formalization falling into a schematization that quickly becomes a technique. What remains problematic is whether the research function can remain compatible with aesthetic effect. That is to say, can a funded programme produce art that is worthy of the name? Practice-based research can produce an institutional scene of education, the aesthetic state requires this, but it cannot programme, even if it produces, aesthetic effects. To be precise, the formalization of practice-based research cannot account for the gap, the not-knowing and uncertainty essential to making, because practice-based research is an epistemological overlay onto something that cannot be mastered by knowledge. Practice-based research says that practice can be productive of knowledge. But practice is not epistemological, it is a matter of affect. To not know is to practice, without not-knowing practice would never get started. This is not an argument for defunding art programmes or for suggesting that creative practice cannot result in new forms of inquiry. Rather, it is to say again that there are genuine conceptual lacunae in the founding premise of practice-based research that need to be explored further and understood better if it is not to repeat the historical errors of research as an activity of the nation state.

But how can it ever do otherwise? All governmental policies on science and culture attempt to programme creativity. Any research programme attempts to include within it the benefits of contingency within the order of the measurable, calculable, and accountable. For research to be research as such, and not just practice (the sort that the advice to doctoral students quoted above says should not be funded) the aleatory must reside in the order of the same, within the conceptual frame of the programmable. This results in a creation or invention of the same, not something different at all.[16] Practice as research places limits around practice that requires the outcomes of that practice to reside within a recognizable, knowable, and measurable set of possibilities. Even where a practice embraces serendipity, in order for it to retain the name of research it must be subject to a probabilistic quantification. That is to say, nothing can truly be invented, nothing that is wholly other to the frame of the research calculus, as a result of practice-based research. And yet invention and creation still take place. The other is not entirely absent from this process. How can it be? Despite the desire to recuperate the value of the aleatory, the gap of uncertainty or the moment of not-knowing, this dehiscence, still initiates any practice and in so doing opens up any attempt to measure the abyssal. In other words, practice ruins practice-based research from the very beginning and practice-based research would lose nothing by recognizing from the start its own impossibility.

This might not be welcome news over at the research council but is a necessary condition of the very activity that the institutional edifice of the academic arts and humanities is built upon, whether to facilitate creative practice or to support its study and criticism. In fact, the invention that practice-based research gives rise to is its own institution: the research council, that post hoc seeks to define and measure the very thing that brings it into being. Inventions that have status conferred upon them are always institutions, as Derrida says.[17] It is not the university that gives practice-based research its identity; it is the other way round.

Without practice there would be no humanities and without the humanities there would be no university. The invention of practice-based research, very late in the day, is a rationalization of the inventive possibility of practice. It is an attempt to persuade that practice can be brought to account. That is to say, that creativity can be measured. There is a kind of madness in that, a folly that is just as recognizably human as it is doomed to failure, no matter how much money a research council throws at it. In response to the articulation of the frameworks of practice-based research one must be aware that the only possible thing to create, the only thing worth creating, for creation to be worthy of the name, is the impossible, that which does not exist. But creating the impossible is impossible, you might say. For sure, but it is still the only possible creation, creativity must announce itself as that which brings into existence that which did not exist before and did not appear to be possible, otherwise it is merely formalizing something that already sits as part of a set of possibilities within an economy of the same. Practice then has to be a passage towards the arrival of the impossible; it is a preparation for the chance encounter, the expectation of the unexpected. Practice itself involves a process, a formalization as technique of something that can be taught, repeated, and captured. But creativity is the name we give to the disruption of that process by the wholly other of the aleatory in the moment of not-knowing. In this sense, creativity must be incalculable, something no longer consistent with the calculable. Is such a thing possible? Of course not, and that is why it is the only possible creation, the only thing that creativity could create that would be an actual creation.

***

In this book we will take as our object of study something that we will call Theory-Practice. This is different from 'Theory' proper, that is, written works of a philosophical nature that constitute a body of knowledge concerning modern thought. It is also different from 'Practice' as such, which can either be a purely professional enterprise (playing first violin in a symphony orchestra does not require a familiarity with the work of Michel Foucault) or be an exercise in practice-based research that did not seek an explicit relationship with theoretical texts, for example, one could base a musical composition on a mathematical sequence rather than a text by Walter Benjamin, and still be of interest to the AHRC or the Research Excellence Framework (REF) panel. Theory-Practice by contrast refers to those texts, works of art, films, architectural outcomes, performances, or sonic pieces that not only bear a close and determining relation to the canon of Theory, but open themselves up as theoretical endeavours in their own right. Theory-Practice, however, retains its own singularity in the continuum of idiomatic approaches to humanist study. It is both fully Practice and fully Theory and neither only Practice nor simply Theory. As one might expect in this scenario Theory-Practice pushes at the boundaries of what constitutes theory proper and what can be identified as practice. Theory-Practice happens around the limits of philosophy, where disciplinary philosophy most actively polices its boundaries.

For example, we might take the 'Envois' section of Jacques Derrida's *La Carte Postale* as an exemplary case of Theory-Practice.[18] It is at best an autobiographical text, at worst a total fiction, situated at the core of an otherwise formal work of philosophical scholarship. It is the fragments of a one-sided correspondence that relates the story of a love affair between the narrator and the addressee.[19] However, it also contains often long and detailed passages of a philosophical nature. They are not just a reflection on or expository of the action of the love story, but are an essential part of the written fiction. The various fragments of letters, or '*envois*' [postings or sendings] are individually and collectively the performance of a central thesis in the text of 'Envois' concerning the errancy of meaning. They cannot be separated from this context or their performative role. Equally, the rest of *La Carte Postale* cannot be read independently of the 'Envois'. The extended reading of Freud in the second half of the books refers to and depends upon everything that has gone on before in the 'Envois'. The narrator of the letters for example is writing a lecture called 'The Legs of Freud', which then turns up later in the formal philosophical text. In this sense, we would struggle to restrict the designation Theory-Practice just to the 'Envois' because the whole of *La Carte Postale* initiates, depends upon and cannot be separated from, the performativity of the letters as Theory-Practice. Derrida more so than other philosophers is quite deliberately experimenting with another type of writing that seeks to outflank the policing and policed borders of disciplinary philosophy. He speaks at the end of his 1968 essay 'The Ends of Man', of a 'change of terrain' and a 'new writing [that] must weave and interlace' the two persistent modes of deconstruction, firstly attempting an exit by using the resources of the tradition against itself without consolidating it, and secondly, affirming an absolute break from and difference to that tradition, while retaining an awareness of the textual effects that run the risk of naively repeating the ground that is said to be abandoned.[20] The 'Envois' would seem to be an attempt to capture something of that ambition in a daring confessional text that tells the story of a love affair in the context of public philosophy while disavowing it in the form of a fiction, which would have every and no relation to the facts of Derrida's own life. If the 'Envois' is Theory-Practice then it is because it is trying to do something that neither Theory nor Practice can do on their own. It is being both Theory and Practice at the same time, while expanding the limits of both.

As an example of another writing that extends the idiomatic boundaries of speculative thought, we might consider the oeuvre of Hélène Cixous who would be labelled in the Anglophone world as 'a feminist theorist'.[21] However, she has a considerable writerly practice that runs across genres, including drama, novels, autobiography, and literary criticism. It is importantly and increasingly undecidable in the case of Cixous where the borders of her idioms lie, her 'theoretical' books of mourning for Jacques Derrida, such as *Insister* and *Portrait of a Young Jewish Saint*, are every bit as writerly, transgressive as the novels that have won her the premier prizes of the French literary institution, such as *Manhattan* and *Hyperrêve*.[22] These texts are theoretical, autobiographical, critical and fictional all at the same time, and this is also true of those earlier works such as 'The Laugh of the Medusa', which when received into English earned her the name of a theorist.[23] Derrida occasionally took on the rules and borders of formal philosophy, Cixous does it all the time and it has gone from being a strategy in the case of Derrida to being an established new frontier for writing in French in the case of Cixous. For example, and in contrast to *La Carte Postale*, one could look at Cixous' so-called novel *Love Itself: In the Letter Box* [*L'Amour même dans la boîte aux lettres*].[24] A text that treats poetically the history of literary and philosophical love letters, whose provenance and destinations are uncertain but nevertheless they continue to arrive, from Athens, Napoleonic Egypt and other unexpected locales, from Proust, Artaud, Derrida, and so many others. This work, however, is more than a novel of epistolary anthology. It is also a counter signature to the 'Envois', performing a contribution to the errancy of letters, raising that analogue argument into another writerly sphere in which address and language combine to create a certain deafness in love, in which it is only capable of speaking to itself. This is identifiably a novel, more so than the 'Envois', but one that would not be possible without a rich philosophical culture, to which it makes its own sustained contribution.

However, despite the claims of the gatekeepers of disciplinary philosophy it is not Cixous or Derrida who are the exceptional cases with respect to inventive writing and the philosophical genre. As soon as one begins to look at the history of philosophy, one can find, time and time again, the most interesting of speculative work taking places at the borders of the discipline, both inside and outside of philosophy, constructing philosophy just as it is excised by philosophy. We will see in the next chapter the ways in which the text of Plato, the heavily structured and artificial dialogues of Socrates, should and must importantly be considered as fictions. In other words, philosophy begins in a consideration of style and genre. The normative idiom of philosophy today is simply the winner in a contest of genre that constitutes the philosophical tradition since Plato. For example, who would have the resources to seek to disentangle the literary dimension of Augustine's *Confessions* from its philosophical importance? How can its contribution to Christian theology be disentangled from *The City of God*, with one marked on a shelf designated for literature and the other earmarked for philosophy?[25] Similarly, Marcus Aurelius, Boethius, and Thomas More, all explicitly open up the philosophical genre to literature. While Teresa of Avila, John of the Cross, and so many others of the mystic tradition, make it difficult to distinguish between poetry, philosophy, and the theological in their writing. Machiavelli was a poet, dramatist, author of novellas and a translator. Erasmus writes as part of a genre-bending tradition of philosophical-social satire. Francis Bacon wrote across genres, while Hobbes translated Homer. Pascal was responsible for notable experiments in philosophical style as was Spinoza. It would seem much easier to consider polymaths such a Leibniz, Descartes, and Francis Hutchinson to have retained a philosophical purity in their systematic exposition of multiple idioms than it is to accept the novel writing of Montesquieu or Voltaire. How shall we understand the complex writing of Rousseau if we were to seek to detach form from content or to raise one genre of writing over another? The same holds for Diderot, Lessing, and William Godwin in different national traditions. Schiller, Madame de Staël, and Thoreau are equally at home across philosophical and literary genres. Alexis de Tocqueville was a diarist, memoirist, and travel writer as well as a political philosopher. Kierkegaard wrote *The Seducer's Diary* as a supplement to the dialogue *Either/Or*.[26] Nietzsche's experiments in style define his opening in philosophy. One might say that it is not the case that Theory-Practice today is a peculiarly modern contribution to philosophy but that rather the erasure of questions of style and genre as constitutive of philosophical work is itself a deadening effect of the rise of systematic philosophy in the Modern period. In this sense, Theory-Practice has much more in common with the epistemological tradition it opens up than it does with the conventions of institutional academic philosophy that might view it with suspicion.

However, the twentieth century also presents us with a rich vein of Theory-Practice, an almost subterranean tradition in which the constative and the performative open one another in a chase across the philosophical canon. Santayana was also a novelist and essayist, Bertrand Russell was a prodigious autobiographer, Gaston Bachelard's prose reaches the highest orders of poetry. One could cite Walter Benjamin's collected fictions in *The Storyteller*, which provide evidence of a theorist who was always on the furthest shores of philosophical style.²⁷ However, in terms of his experiments in writing he is a long distance from the mature work of either Maurice Blanchot or Georges Bataille, who are both comfortable working across the genres in which philosophy and fiction irreducibly pollute one another as a performance of thinking within a wider configuration of writing. Both Jean-Paul Sartre and Simone de Beauvoir are similar figures who offer a complex writing practice in which works of philosophy and theory sit alongside texts covering a range of literary genres. It would be quite irresponsible to seek to understand the thinking of either by compartmentalizing the constantive and the performative in their respective outputs. Albert Camus is cut from the same complex textual cloth, as is André Malraux, while the writing of Roland Barthes moves from the systematic and theoretical to poetic texts such as *A Lover's Discourse* and the posthumously published autobiographical texts of the *Mourning Diary*.²⁸ Philippe Sollers and Julia Kristeva both combine theoretical speculation and novel writing across a range of texts, which cannot be separated one from the other without damaging a just estimation of either's contribution to thought and art. Franz Fanon wrote dramas alongside his theoretical work, Louis Althusser, like Freud, provides us with a detailed autobiography, while much of Jean Baudrillard's output might be classified as experimental in style in its reflections on art, photography, and memoir. Didier Eribon's memoir *Returning to Reims* combines theoretical investigation with life-writing, much like Guy Debord's autobiographical books *Mémoires*, *Panégyrique*, and *Cette Mauvaise Réputation*.²⁹ Geoffrey Hartman's *A Scholar's Tale* is similarly part of the genre of theoretical autobiography, while Bernard Stiegler *Acting Out* is a genuine example of theorized life-writing.³⁰ Alain Badiou is both a novelist (*Portulans*, *Almagestes*) and playwright (*Ahmed the Philosopher*).³¹ Jean-Luc Nancy's text on Mary Magdalene in *Noli Me Tangere* is an example of theory-poetry.³² While Gayatri Spivak combines her theoretical writing with translating the stories of Mahasweta Devi.³³ There is, then, a rich history of work that one might reasonably identify as Theory-Practice, that critical practice which contributes to philosophical culture through the expanded idioms of writing as inquiry. This is before we even consider the opera of Rousseau (*Le devin du village*), the music of Nietzsche, the compositions of Adorno, the drawings of Paul Valéry, or the film collaborations of Slavoj Zizek (notably the two excellent *Pervert's Guides*, with Director Sophie Fiennes, which move beyond documentary and illustration to stand suggestively as a contribution to both film and theory).³⁴

There are also a number of academic theorists in the Anglophone sphere who have combined speculative work with writing that could equally qualify under the rubric of critical practice. Nicholas Royle is the author of several studies on Derrida and more recently two novels (*Quilt* [2010] and *An English Guide to Birdwatching* [2017]) both of which reflect a post-structuralist sensibility through the form of the English novel.[35] Susan Sellers is both a scholar of feminist theory (notably Hélène Cixous) and is author of theoretically inclined fictions, *Vanessa and Virginia* (2008) an account of Virginia Woolf, later adapted as a play, and more recently *Given the Choice* (2013).[36] David Farrell Krell is a significant interpreter of Heidegger as well as an accomplished novelist. He has authored fictional texts such as *Nietzsche* (1996) and *Son of Spirit* (1997) on Hegel.[37] His theoretical fictions that work in and around the philosophical tradition are quite different from the genre writing of Kelly Oliver. While Oliver is the author of noted works of philosophy and media analysis, her fictional writing in the Jessica James, Cowgirl Philosopher Mystery Series, is for those who prefer their theory hardboiled.[38] These detective novels, if they can be called that, rely entirely on a philosophical sensibility and work remarkably well by simultaneously nuancing and undercutting the seriousness with which academic philosophy treats itself. Frank Lentricchia is remembered for his early accounts of the theoretical scene in *After the New Criticism* (1980) but is now most active as a writer of detective fiction (the Eliot Conte novels) and tales of professors in peril such as *Lucchesi and The whale* (2003) or *The Sadness of Antonioni* (2011).[39] Patricia Duncker is now more successful novelist than theorist but her first novel *Hallucinating Foucault* (1996) betrays her origins in the academic study of post-structuralist writing.[40] Terry Eagleton has successfully combined an engagement with theory and writing for the theatre (*Saint Oscar* [1989]) and screen (*Wittgenstein* [1993]).[41] Similarly, Willy Maley writes across theoretical, critical, and literary genres, although one might say that his creative writing is influenced by a theoretical tendency rather than explicitly reflects one.[42] This is in contrast to Lars Iyer whose trilogy of short novels *Spurious* (2011), *Dogma* (2012) and *Exodus* (2013) are an account to what it means to have been a humanities academic in the UK since the 1980s and how theory has circulated around the lives of scholars and in the new university of 'excellence' and human capital.[43] In this sense, these novels are not mimetic but are inculcated within the institutions and discourses they describe, leaving their own mark within them, consciously philosophical, and opening the topic in the manner of speculative inquiry. John Schad's *Someone Called Derrida: An Oxford Mystery* (2007) is an exemplary instance of academic autobiography (a dying father) inventively interweaved with a reading of theory (Derrida's *La Carte Postale*), which in turn theorizes what it means to write both biography and theory.[44]

However, is there a difference between professors who write novels and novelists who write about philosophers? Here, I am not referring to the novel of ideas such as *Middlemarch* or *War and Peace*,[45] rather there are numerous examples of literature that takes theory as its object, for good or ill, as in the several fictional accounts of Paul de Man which find rich material for fiction in the scandalous event of a seemingly fraudulent professor with a secret Nazi past (Gilbert Adair's *The Death of the Author* [1992], John Banville's *Shroud* [2003] and *Ancient Light* [2012], and Bernhard Schlink's *Homecoming* [2008]).[46] None of these novels contribute to knowledge of figurative reading, nor do Henri Thomas's *Le Parjure* (1964) or Mary McCarthy's *The Groves of Academe* (1952) that fictionalize de Man's earlier life on arrival in the United States, significant resources as they are.[47] These novels draw on the narrative reserves of philosophy and theory, and because of that are important in their own right, but they neither engage with nor add to the thought that theory and philosophy encapsulates. They are similar in this sense to the large number of novels, dramas, and screenplays that feature Freud. Some are more informed about psychoanalysis than others, like Jed Rubenfield's engaging detective mystery, *The Interpretation of Murder* (2006) or Irving Stone's *The Passions of the Mind: A biographic novel of Sigmund Freud* (1971) which treats fiction as another way of disseminating the principles of analysis.[48] Terry Johnson's drama *Hysteria* (1993) plays a fictionalized version of the genuine meeting between Freud and Salvador Dali for broad laughs.[49] Brenda Webster's *Vienna Triangle* (2009) is a more sombre take on the Freud as mystery adventure, Selden Edwards' *The Little Book* (2008) involves a time-traveller who meets Freud in fin-de-siècle Vienna, while Angela von der Lippe's *The Truth about Lou* (2006) is an attempt to write a biography of Lou Andreas-Salomé in the form of a fiction, Freud appears as a significant character.[50] The same relationship is central to Irvin D Yalom's *When Nietzsche Wept* (1992), one of several fictionalizations of theory by the author (a Stanford professor of psychiatry) including *The Schopenhauer Cure* (2006) and *The Spinoza Problem* (2012).[51] In *Freud's Sister* by Goce Smilevski (2012, translated from the Macedonian 2011 edition) the author asks in the form of a fiction whether Freud's disregard for his sister resulted in Adolfina's death in a Nazi concentration camp ('based on a true story', as they say).[52] All of this is just a sample of the figuration of Freud in popular and literary culture. It is not the same thing as a Theory-Practice encounter with psychoanalytic work, of the sort that characterize the artistic engagements of the Centre for Freudian Analysis and Research in London, or even the thoughtful questioning of the history and practice of analysis we see in Cornelia Parker's art works based on the dust and fibres of Freud's belongings. No doubt a case could be made for how well informed these various Freud-novels are concerning psychoanalysis; the de Man novels are distinguished by their ignorance of deconstruction. There are other novels that are extremely well informed about analysis, such as Hanif Kureishi's *Something to Tell You* (2008) and Salley Vickers' *The Other Side of You* (2006) which both demonstrate a deep engagement with the therapeutic dimension of analysis but which do not proceed to advance psychoanalysis as a research question within the writing.[53] These are novels that reward the reader for knowing something of theory but do not contribute to the speculative endeavour, there is not necessarily an interrogative principle or research question to such writing. In the same vein Lauren Binet's conspiracy thriller about the death of Roland Barthes, *The 7th Function of Language* (2015), is an erudite and engaging read, but it is not scholarship in any conventional sense, any more than Philip Kerr's serial killer novel, *A Philosophical Investigation* (1992), contributes to an understanding of Wittgenstein.[54]

There is then a continuum at work here across writing about philosophers and the stories of philosophy to works which engage and open the texts of philosophy as a contribution to advancing theoretical work. Equally, there is a question to be asked about philosophers who write novels and how far the form of the novel is advanced by the choice to pursue this idiom rather than a more formal genre of philosophical writing. Alain de Botton, Plato scholar and popular philosopher, adopts the novel form in *Essays in Love* (2006) a romance that leans towards Barthes' *Fragments d'un discourse amoureux* with chapters on the philosophical history of love.[55] It is neither groundbreaking literature nor innovative philosophy but its hybridity leaves its own mark in the traditions of both. George Santayana's *The Last Puritan: A Memoir in the Form of a Novel* (1935) wants to make a philosophical case about the predestination of experience and looks to the history of the novel form to achieve that (it was the second best-selling novel of 1936 after Margaret Mitchell's *Gone with the Wind*).[56] The fictions of Iris Murdoch often fall between novels too crowded by philosophy and philosophy that is distracted by novel writing. She is the author of several studies of formal philosophy, but in her novels there is always a balance to be struck between theoretical exegesis and the comic potential of the English middle class sleeping with one another. Her contribution to the form of the novel in works such as *A Severed Head* (1961) might be despite her philosophical interests rather than because of them.[57] Perhaps, the point of reading her philosophical writing would be to better understand her work as a novelist. In contrast Umberto Eco's labyrinthine novels have a more obvious connection to his theoretical writing as a semiotician and scholar of medieval literature. From *The Name of the Rose* (1980) to *Numero Zero* (2015) Eco treads a thin line between scholarship and conspiracy theory but as a contribution to the European novel it is possible to discern a red thread that links Eco's academic research and formal expansiveness as a writer.[58] Christine Brooke-Rose is an even more experimental writer, a true, ascetic modernist in contrast to Eco's crowded post-modernism. She was also a scholar of structuralism and narrative theory, her later novels such as the autobiographical *Remake* (1996) sit somewhere between the nouveau roman and narratology.[59] Raymond Queneau was an editor at Gallimard, publishing work by Kojève and Hegel, his contribution to the nouveau roman takes both a philosophical inflection, The *Sunday of Life* (1952), and a linguistically innovative turn, *Zazie in the Metro* (1959).[60] Comfortable across a range of genres, including screenplay and essays, Queneau is not Hegel but is as worthy of any of his generation of French writers of the epithet philosopher-novelist. The South African novelist Zoë Wicomb and the English author Tom McCarthy have significant personal investments in reading theory, Wicomb was very many years a professor of English at Strathclyde University in Glasgow and McCarthy demonstrates his skill as a semiotician in his collected essays. However, it is less obvious how this theoretical sensibility is played out in novels such as Wicomb's *Playing in the Light* and McCarthy's *Remainder*.[61] Drusilla Modjeska's *Poppy* (1990) is another autobiographical reflection that looks to theories of life-writing and offers a bold and poetic contribution to the Australian novel.[62] Before a career in editing she was a Senior Research Fellow in race and gender in the post-colonial arts. The theoretical inflection and speculative inquiry jump out of every page; *Poppy* does not fall into the category of Wittgenstein as serial killer or Freud as amateur detective.

One could spend an entire book-length study working a path through this considerable reading list, seeking to show the difference between the philosopher who writes novels and the novelist who mobilizes philosophy in order to advance story telling or the literary avant-garde. The taxonomy would be encyclopaedic and the differences would become increasingly difficult to sustain as a systematic set of categorizations. The question is not whether one novel is more serious than the other, the solemnity of philosophy is perhaps its most amusing characteristic, but whether the writing in question is compelled by an understanding of itself as an inquiry into its own status as critical. Equally, there is a difference between films that tell the stories of philosophy (Derek Jarman's *Wittgenstein* [1993], Liliana Cavani's *Beyond Good and Evil* [1977], or, Roberto Rossellini's quartet *Socrates* [1971], *Augustine of Hippo* [1972], *Blaise Pascal* [1972] and *Cartesius* [1974]), films that feature philosophers (Astra Taylor's *Examined Life* [2008] and her *Zizek!* [2005], or, Kirby Dick and Amy Ziering Kofman's *Derrida* [2002]), films with philosophical content (David O Russell's *I Heart Huckabees* [2004], or, Spike Jonze's *Being John Malkovich* [1999]), the European cinema of ideas (Bergman, Ackerman, Rohmer, Goddard, Tarkovsky etc.), and films that engage cinematic form as its own speculative idiom (Barison and Ross's *The Ister* [2004], Safaa Fathy's *D'ailleurs Derrida* [1999] or Sophie Fiennes' *The Pervert's Guide to Cinema* [2006]). A just understanding of critical practice does not lie in determining the detailed classification of such a catalogue, or, in asking who has the institutional right or qualification to speak in the name of philosophy and theory. Rather, film as film, like the novel as literature, must stand on its own as film, or literature, otherwise it is worth very little. If it is nothing more than an illustration of philosophy, why mobilize the possibilities of such creative forms only to subjugate them to the authority of philosophy? Theory-Practice would be a form of critical reading as making that consciously pushed and interrogated the singularity of its medium as a speculative idiom.

Equally, one must not imagine that Theory-Practice can easily escape the trap it seeks to outflank. As writing, or film, no one text can be innately more philosophical than any other: this is a matter of reading. There might be nothing philosophical at all about Rossellini's quartet and everything to be said philosophically about a film by Katherine Bigelow. The most theoretically important work might well happen in the complete absence of theory, while conscious attempts to engage theory might result not in singular enquiries but a reduction of philosophy to a question of style. We see this in so-called 'deconstructivist' architecture in which a sustained reading of philosophy by critical practitioners (Eisenman, Tschumi, Libeskind, etc.) leads to stylistically similar buildings, and architecture that is as much defined by economic and social considerations as it is by theoretical enquiry.[63] As with any text, such works of Theory-Practice, and there is nothing more textual than architecture, will be judged on the merits of the affects they produce and will be studied in the context of their historical and social making. It is not quite enough simply to ask of Theory-Practice, is it any good as art? The truth is that it is not homogeneous and will produce varying results with different degrees of success. Rather, in this study we will ask what are its merits and why is it interestingly different from other approaches to creative practice. If Critical Practice is above all a compulsive predisposition and vigilant attitude to self-analysis and speculative thought through creative idioms, then it will require its own degree of self-understanding. The first five chapters of this book seek to draw out the threads of Critical Practice through reading philosophical and theoretical texts as a way of understanding what happens when theory and practice come into contact in the ways that occur in the texts cited above. The final two chapters look at two necessarily brief examples of the textual play of Theory-Practice, not to judge them exemplary or to promote them as pre-eminent but to understand the difficulties that ensue when we read our knowledge of Critical Practice back on to creative texts.

Part One

In Theory

1

Theory and Practice: From Kant to Plato

Critical Practice in the creative arts defines a productive relation between speculative thought and the making of art objects. It does not necessarily lie in the objects themselves but in the process and attitude by which philosophy and art speak to one another in a dynamic that is neither dialectical nor a privileging of one over the other. Critical Practice is living with aporia as the condition of being able to think or make anything at all. While the relationship between theory and practice in our art schools and on our university courses for the creative arts may seem a relatively recent occurrence, this chapter looks at the deeper philosophical roots of the divide between these terms. That is to say, the contrast between philosophy and creative art (theory and practice) is itself a philosophical issue and has a long conceptual inheritance that comes into play every time we approach the task of engaging with Critical Practice. The place of art in the philosophical inheritance is complex and is one that can be traced back to foundational moments in the speculative tradition. It is not the case that philosophy can be made to account for art because art is a philosophical problem. Equally, art does not come after philosophy as a by-product of thinking. Rather, art and philosophy open up one another at decisive moments, preventing the foreclosure of thought in philosophy or the possibility of rest in art. Similarly, Critical Practice is not a late, aberrant idiom of the more normative genres of art and philosophy. Rather, in the beginning was Critical Practice and neither art nor philosophy will ever get over it.

Practical philosophy

Kant was a great defender of the prospects of Theory. He offers us a distillation of his position in the archly titled essay, 'On the common saying: That may be correct in theory, but it is of no use in practice'.[1] He opens it by defining his terms.

By 'theory' he means a collection of rules, 'if those rules are thought as principles having a certain generality, so that abstraction is made from a multitude of conditions that yet have a necessary influence on their application' (p. 279). This is not quite what we mean by Theory in this book but the description will help us understand the set of relations we are trying to draw here. Theory as a term used in the contemporary humanities describes a canon of texts more or less derived from a tradition of modern European philosophy, related to questions of culture and politics. Every book of Theory is in its own right a singular account of a distinctive topic and the canon is often in contradiction with itself. In this sense, it would be inaccurate to describe Theory in its latest sense to mean a set of rules that are applied in the study of the arts and humanities. However, it would be fair to say that Theory helps to form a way of thinking about and questioning the world. It is then more of a framework, or, intellectual scaffolding rather than a body of rules. When *used* by naïve readers it can easily become an application, of the order, say, of 'a Freudian account of something' or a juxtaposition, of the order of, say, 'Deleuze *and* animals/art/music/gardening etc.' Theory in this context can indeed have a quantum of utility and so must involve as Kant defines it a certain generality that has a necessary influence on its application. What Kant is in fact defining in his easy is philosophy itself, which in its most formal aspect attempts to produce universal axioms from the examination of singular case studies. This transcendental gesture is both the defining characteristic of philosophy, its main muscle as it were, and that which distinguishes it from other idioms of reflective thought such as, say, literary theory that would work according to a principle of reading or textual explication that was more hesitant about, if not entirely free from, deriving abstraction from singularity.

Kant's definition of practice is just as illuminating, 'not every doing [*Hantirung*] is called practice, but only that effecting of an end which is thought as the observance of certain principles of procedure represented in their generality' (p. 279). This is perhaps a stricter definition of practice than the one intended in this book. Kant seems to want to reserve the name of practice only to those activities that are the result of application of general principles, as when we speak of 'clinical practice' to mean following the rules of best procedures for health care. We speak of best practice in treating a wound, of a dental practice, or of a 'general practitioner' as someone 'in practice'. This sense of 'practice' would seem to exclude the idea of practice as making mistakes, as a learner does when practicing a musical instrument or as in the old joke that the young Augustine would be considered an example of a practicing Catholic because he had not got it quite right yet. Practice may make perfect but it can also involve a degree of experimentation or pushing at the boundaries of what is possible in a sport or discipline. Practice in that sense can also be repetitive and dull, a form of training in the execution of technique. In the mode we wish to use it in this book, and in the sense it is employed when we speak in the academy of 'practice-based research', we mean the work of creative artists across art, architecture, design, film, drama, dance, creative writing, and music. When we talk of practice in this context we are speaking somewhat tautologically of the stuff that practitioners do.

This is in contrast to so-called non-practitioners, such as say a critic or a philosopher, who does not have a practice but instead writes criticism or philosophy. Writing either philosophy or criticism of course requires practice and can rightly be thought of as a practice as much as any occupation. Blurring the lines between what does and does not constitute practice will be a considerable stake for us going forward. As a text a work of formal philosophy is every bit as figurative as a novel, the fact that one narrates concepts and the other narrates characters is neither here nor there when it comes to composition and reading.[2] The difference comes in the type of truth claims that the novel and the work of philosophy wish to make, the former not necessarily being less true than the latter. The truth of a novel does not necessarily lie in its reference to supposedly real things. However, practice in the sense of the creative arts, and in particular the creative arts as a medium for research in a university context, depends more upon the sense of practice as serendipity and experimentation than it does on practice as the repetitive application of rules. Nevertheless, we can accept the notion that practice in the university-based creative arts can have a notable relation to Theory in the sense of the philosophical culture of the humanities. Indeed practice as an academic practice, practice worthy of its place in the academy, often requires an essential relation to Theory in order to justify its status a 'serious' university discipline. This sort of practice, in so far as it has been welcomed into the university, must give itself up to be measured and evaluated. At this point, practice is keen to point to its capacity for abstraction or its determined application of general principles. Again such attempts to determine the value of practice can lead to a utilitarian approach to Theory in which one might have a 'Deleuzian art practice', for example. Practice in order to be research must have a research element or address a research question. Simply being good at playing the piano will not cut it in the university, as compared to the conservatoire, which is concerned with the training of artists. That requires a different kind of practice. Practice-based research often derives its research content from the Theory it adopts or misprisions. In such scenarios Theory remains the privileged term and practice runs the risk of subordinating itself in order to claim legitimacy through the written idiom that it supposed to displace.

If Theory can legitimately lay claim to be a modality of practice itself, and if practice can be a complex and unpredictable phenomenon, then it is clear enough that the hard borders of any definition of either is bound to come under pressure when we look at specific examples. The difference between Theory and Practice and the ways these two terms rely on and define one another will be of considerable interest to us in this study. It will be difficult, even if it were desirable, to hold fast to any rigorous differentiation between the two as they are understood in an academic sense at this present moment. However, one cannot speak about Theory and Practice in that sense without partaking of an entire history in which the two terms have been opposed to one another, with a privilege accorded to the manly action of practice. This is the situation summed up in the title of Kant's essay, with the philosopher setting out to make a defence of theory, or speculative thought, in face of the value accorded to utility and achievement. Rather, than simply take the side of theory over practice and so repeat the gesture that wants to seek a winner between the two terms, Kant proposes a third term that joins theory and practice in a more complex relation. He writes that this middle term provides 'a transition from one to the other' because 'no matter how complete a theory may be … a concept of the understanding, which contains a rule' also requires 'an act of judgment by which a practitioner distinguishes whether or not something is a case of the rule' (p. 279). The passage from theory to practice is not a simple application or initiation of predetermined rules. This would not be practice but a programme, pre-ordained in advance without the prospect of unexpected outcomes. It would be computational and inflexible, hardly worth bothering with as a practice. Indeed no practice would be involved as there would be no possibility of failure, experimentation, or surprise. Instead of the application of principles, Kant gives us the exercise of judgement as the bridge between pure and practical reason, or, between theory and practice.

Judgement in Kant is sticky, regulated by the framework of the unconditional imperative of duty but not teleological, or, at least not teleological in any sense that Kant can adequately explain. It is in the realization that there can be no satisfactory delimitation of the conditions of judgement that the *Third Critique* comes up short and ruins the project of critical philosophy.[3] However, this is not to say that Kant is not on to something here. The passage from theory to practice is not straightforward and requires a transitional element that is neither a strict comprehension through rules nor an unreflective process or action. That which joins theory and practice needs to be something that is neither wholly theoretical nor entirely practical. Kant identifies this lubricant as judgement, which cannot be reduced entirely to an act of cognition but is a necessary step in order to embed the principles of theory into a material action. Judgement is a sensibility, something learnt by experience through a historical and subjective formation. It has then a relation to the practice it enables without being reducible entirely to action. It is an excess of judgement that stays the hand of Hamlet, but it is judgement finally that compels the name of action. Judgements are made for reasons that cannot always be confined to available evidence, data sets, or algorithms. There always remains a gap in judgement, which makes it something other than pure thought.

Kant suggests that the theoretician who lacks judgement will never become practical. Equally practice can prove itself a failure when new circumstances demonstrate a prior theory to have been inadequate. In such a scenario, Kant says the problem is not theory but a lack of theory, the new circumstances requiring further abstraction and a more robust set of general rules to expand our understanding of the scene that caused the failure. The example he gives is general mechanics in which it would be foolish for an engineer to dismiss a mathematical theory of ballistics before fiddling with heavy artillery. The rejection of theory in this instance comes from a preference for experience. The veteran canon operator knows more about how his gun works than the mathematician. The solution for theory is to have more information from the artillery man so that an adequate theory can be developed that better understands the effects of friction and wind speed so as to accord better with the experience of the soldier. Where theory is of a more speculative order, dealing with concepts rather than cannon balls, it is harder to calibrate their practical value. However, Kant's interest lies in a theory based on the concept of duty that would immediately remove any concerns about the empty ideality of concepts because the effects of such a theory would be directly relevant to experience. The point is not to change philosophy through an exposure to experience but to move beyond a dull understanding of experience as the justification for an unreflective preference for the practical:

> For, to the scandal of philosophy, it is not uncommonly alleged of this theory that what may be correct in it is yet invalid in practice; and this is said in a lofty, disdainful tone, full of the presumption of wanting to reform reason by experience even in that in which reason puts its highest honour and in a wisdom that can see farther and more clearly with its dim mole's eyes fixed on experience than with the eyes belonging to a being that was made to stand erect and look at the heavens'. (p. 280)

Kant would seem to be a believer in Oscar Wilde's maxim concerning lying in the gutter but some of us looking at the stars. His defence of Theory is commendable and fierce, philosophy's dim mole eyes can still tell us more about experience than the empiricists can.

In this context (that of morality and duty) the only value of actions is for them to accord perfectly with theory. Some of us on this topic, however, would prefer to be in the gutter with the moles, innately suspicious of Kant's call of duty and more open to the experiences of the world than the demands of the starry heavens above. For Kant, it has to be this way, 'all is lost if the empirical and hence contingent conditions of carrying out the law are made conditions of the law itself, so that a practice calculated with reference to an outcome probable in accordance with previous experience is given authority to control a self-sufficient theory' (p. 280). The law transcends experience and must regulate it, experience should not be that which shapes and transforms the law. We might begin to sense a flaw in Kant's argument, noting that this in fact is not how law works. The law is made and shaped by experience, changing with governments and as new facts emerge, and not always for the better. However, Kant is talking about the moral law, which for him would fall into a different category than civil law. Nevertheless the bridge of judgement would be common to both. While it is a hard sell to imagine that a perfect judgement is possible that will accord the moral law with the actions of humanity, it is entirely plausible that an imperfect judgement, flawed, and necessarily capable of error, is the mechanism by which theory arrives in the misshapen form of practice. It is down here in the gutter of practice that philosophy needs to train its mole like vision.

Kant goes on to run his thesis, this theoretical argument about theory, through the three practical examples of the morals of individuals, the right of the state and the right of individuals. In this way he risks his theory against the practical, even if his account never leaves the ambit of a theoretical text of formal philosophy, although one which could rightly be called entirely practical. Even here in the most canonical spaces of philosophy, in the founding texts of the critical tradition, we can find an opening to the practical that results in a trembling within the genre of philosophy. 'Practical Philosophy' in the Kantian sense ought to be an oxymoron, or at least something other than philosophy proper, the ideation of theory that Kant identifies in this essay as the object of scorn by worldly-wise practitioners. Working at the frontiers of philosophy, expanding its horizons, and working in an entirely philosophical way, using the resources of the philosophical tradition, Kant imagines a new idiom of philosophical inquiry, one that is opened by and to practice. In so doing, Kant demonstrates that all philosophy has always had this orientation and that the boundaries between theory and practice are considerably porous. Something like 'practical philosophy' would surely merit the name of both a practice and a theory? It very much depends upon what one means by 'theory' and what is meant by 'practice'.

What holds for Kant surely holds elsewhere, and there will be no secure position from which to take up an easy opposition between these two terms. Kant's essay ends with a rousing defence of theory but it also a commentary on the difficulty of extracting theory from practice. He writes:

> For my own part, I nevertheless put my trust in theory, which proceeds from the principle of right, as to what relations among human beings and states *ought to be*, and which commends to earthly gods the maxim always so to behave in their conflicts that such a universal state of nations will thereby be ushered in, and so to assume that it is possible (*in praxi*) and that it can be ... (p. 309)

That is to say, that despite the flawed behaviour of politicians and kings, theory is there as a horizon to be aspired to, of how the world ought to be. One needs to hold on to the possibility that in principle the world is perfectible according to theoretical principles. However, Kant continues: 'But at the same time I put my trust (*in subsidium*) in the nature of things, which constrains one to go where one does not want to go (*fata volentem ducunt, nolentem trahunt* [the fates lead the willing, drive the unwilling])' (p. 309). His focus is also on the world as it is, not as he would like it to be; Kant is a very practical philosopher. The interesting word in this paragraph is 'trust', *Vertrauen* in German, whereby Kant says he trusts in theory but also in the world of humanity. This act of trust, like judgement, is something that cannot be reduced to pure cognition. This trust in trust comes as much from experience as it does from theoretical principle, and it is neither strictly an applicable rule nor an action in itself. Trust is another bridge that connects the practical to the theoretical:

> In the latter [the nature of things], account is also taken of human nature, in which respect for right and duty is still alive, so that I cannot and will not take it to be so immersed in evil that morally practical reason should not, after many unsuccessful attempts, finally triumph over evil and present human nature as lovable after all. Thus on the cosmopolitan [world] level too, it can be maintained: What on rational grounds holds for theory also holds for practice. (p. 309)

In morality we trust, says Kant. This is a trust not based on evidence but on a faith in the judgement of humans. It is undoubtedly a trust in Kant's own theoretical position but it is also not something that can be strictly called theoretical: belief or faith cannot ground itself in theory, nor does it require empirical evidence. Experience can shake faith but equally for the true believer no evidence is required or ever enough. No one would ever accuse Kant of being a people person, but at least in theory he does not believe that people suck. This is a remarkable position for a practical philosopher to take. Whether it is true or not should be left for the reader to decide but what it demonstrates, as a position, is that theory and practice are not binary terms, and that the economy between them is determined by something other than the theoretical or practical *stricto sensu*. Judgement, trust, faith are all philosophical concepts of course but they describe something that philosophy may not be able to account for. That is to say, dominate in an entirely theoretical way, which is not to say that this will not stop philosophy from trying. This is its practical nature.

Ethical dilemma

The metaphysical distinction between theory and practice has longer roots than the ones that Kant seeks to pull up. However, a familiarity with the origins of this opposition will show us that philosophy has always had a problem with containing the conceptual overspill around the borders of theory and practice. For example, in Book VI of the *Nicomachean Ethics*, Aristotle makes a famous distinction between *episteme* and *techne*.[4] This differentiation between 'knowledge' and 'craft' is frequently taken to define an opposition between the theoretical and the practical. However, the text of Aristotle intends no such easy distinction and in fact lays out a problematic, without resolution, that demonstrates the conceptual excess at play in any attempt to fence off theory from practice and vice versa. This section of the ethics is a discussion of *arete* [intellectual excellence/virtue] and *dianoia* [thought]. Here, thought in the context of the discussion of human good in the Ethics, refers to a faculty of the soul. That is to say, the discussion pertains to how intellectual excellence or virtue pertains to moral excellence. In order to set out this argument, Aristotle deploys a number of terms that while seemingly producing clarity within his exposition, presents a reader concerned with Theory-Practice with less certainty.

Firstly, there is a division between 'practical wisdom' [*phronesis*] and 'theoretical wisdom' [*sophia*]. *Phronesis* is one of the intellectual virtues, and so moral virtue requires a degree of practical wisdom in order to enact the choices that would lead to moral excellence. *Sophia* is also an intellectual virtue but relates to thought that is not straightforwardly useful or pursued for practical application, such as mathematical formula. In English-language translations of Aristotle these two terms look as if they form an easy dichotomy or are two varieties of the same thing. In the Greek the terms are not related, '*sophia*' is often translated simply as wisdom, as in the etymology of 'philosophy', the love of wisdom. In fact, philosophy would seem to contain within its very roots an attachment to the theoretical, abstract, and the non-instrumental. Equally, there is no etymological connection between *sophia* and *theoria* [contemplation or theoretical knowledge]. The terms obviously have a connection but they are *sui generis* in Greek and are intended by Aristotle to define separate virtues.

Now, while *sophia* describes an intellectual virtue that is abstract there is clearly some of this 'theoretical wisdom' that is of practical value. Knowledge such as the higher mathematical formula are essential in the exercise of engineering or architecture. Kant identified them in relation to the arc of an artillery shell. There is nothing more practical than theoretical physics, which moves over time from the lecture hall to the destroyer of worlds. The distinction that Aristotle wants to make is between theoretical knowledge that concerns 'unchanging realities' and making reasoned choices, *boulesis* [deliberation], concerning what can be changed with our actions as the exercise of intellectual and moral virtue. It is necessary to understand the difference between what can be changed and what cannot in order to exercise moral virtue. Hence, *sophia* is essential to the *arete* of *dianoia*. As is the activity of the mind, *nous*, usually translated as intelligence. It is of course difficult to separate this virtue from either practical or theoretical wisdom. In Book I of the Ethics, Aristotle has suggested that the human has an *ergon* (function or work) that would seem to have something to do with the exercise of reason. Book VI is an attempt to unpack that *ergon* of human reasoning. He notes, 'truth [*aletheia*] is the function [*ergon*] of both intellectual parts of the soul [i.e. *nous* and *orexis*, desire]. Therefore those characteristics which permit each part to hold truth most will be the *aretai* of the two parts' (1139b; Book VI, Chapter 2). *Aletheia* in Aristotle means more than truth in its conventional modern sense, rather it refers to the unveiling of reality or disclosing the genuine. That is to say, the function of the intellectual part of the soul is to work out and desire the genuine or real, i.e. to distinguish between the true and the false. One should desire what is real and obtainable not false dreams if one is to excel in moral virtue. For the moral person, intelligence should lead them to desire real things, 'reasoning must affirm what desire pursues' (1139a25).

Knowing what is good and what is real then requires, *sophia*, the theoretical wisdom that tells us what is unchangeable and what can be otherwise. Truth, according to Book VI Chapter 3, can then be attained by a five faculties of the soul: *phronesis, sophia, nous, techne* (art, skill, craft) and *episteme*, often translated as 'scientific knowledge' but more generally means demonstrable knowledge. Episteme, here, does not mean scientific in the sense of theoretical physics, rather 'what we know through *episteme* cannot be otherwise than it is' (1139b20). This is knowledge that can be taught by demonstration, i.e. not through what we would now call 'practical demonstration' but through argumentation or by showing a valid reasoning that leads to a certain conclusion. In particular it involves demonstrating the truth of a proposition or hypothesis that might begin by being not well understood but which through reasoning can be shown to be true. The proof of a mathematical theorem would be a matter of episteme, for example. Hence, we can see that *episteme* would have a close relation to *sophia*. It is key to an attempt to gain the theoretical wisdom essential to the exercise of moral virtue and is required for deliberation. *Episteme* would then seem to be an extremely practical virtue and not easily bracketed off as a mode of abstraction. It is absolutely necessary in the definition of the function of the human.

Techne, by contrast, as detailed in Chapter 4, is a 'trained ability of rationally producing' (1140a). In other words, it is the ability to exercise reason under different conditions to produce reliably an outcome. It is variously translated as 'applied science', 'skill', or 'art'. This would be 'art' in the sense of the craft of production, like the art of captaincy or the art of the deal, as it were. The figurative shift that displaces *techne* as art into the sense of fine art, and episteme as reasoning into episteme as abstraction, clouds the conceptual tradition that follows from Aristotle. This move, however, while not apparent in the text of Aristotle itself, does owe much to Aristotle's own inability to control the ambiguity of his terms. For Aristotle, *techne* and *episteme* are not mutually exclusive terms. He cites architecture as an example of *techne*:

> Now architectural skill, for instance, is an art, and it is also a rational quality concerned with making; nor is there any art which is not a rational quality concerned with making, nor any such quality which is not an art. It follows that an art is the same thing as a rational quality, concerned with making, that reasons truly. (1140)

So, episteme is inescapably involved in techne. In architecture or artillery, there must be reference to the stable principles of geometry, for example, that are familiar to theoretical knowledge. In order to produce results under the guidance of reason then it must be necessary to refer to those reliable principles. *Techne* is required for moral virtue because under certain circumstances it will be necessary to have the technique of reasoning to produce the appropriate outcome. *Techne* and *episteme* lean on each other just as they rely on *phronesis*, *sophia*, and *nous*, as they all pertain to the achievement of truth, or, *aletheia* as the disclosure of the reality of things.

For Aristotle, there is no easy distinction between the practical and the theoretical, and both are required for a pursuit of truth, which in Aristotle's terms is a material experience:

> All Art deals with bringing some thing into existence; and to pursue an art means to study how to bring into existence a thing which may either exist or not, and the efficient cause of which lies in the maker and not in the thing made; for Art does not deal with things that exist or come into existence of necessity, or according to nature, since these have their efficient cause in themselves. But as doing and making are distinct, it follows that Art, being concerned with making, is not concerned with doing. And in a sense Art deals with the same objects as chance, as Agathon says: 'Chance is beloved of Art, and Art of Chance'. (1140a)

Techne pertains to the artificial, things that do not come into existence through natural means. However, it is concerned with making rather than doing. That is to say, if anything, *techne* would seem to sit on the edge of the practical. Equally, this not a question of programming an outcome from first principles or of *techne* as something algorithmic. Rather, *techne* works in the same realm as chance. Risk and serendipity attach themselves to *techne* in a way that would be different from the stable principles of theoretical knowledge. *Phronesis* also relates to that which is subject to change but it is not an art because doing and making are, for Aristotle, generically different, '*phronesis* is an excellence or virtue, and not an Art'. Practical wisdom then, while the basis of deliberation, looks to be the supplement that *episteme* and *techne* require to contribute to the uncovering of truth and the achievement of moral excellence. However, the same could be said of *nous* and *sophia* as terms within Aristotle's classification. There is no simple division between the practical and theoretical in this schema, and *episteme* and *techne* cannot be separated from the context of the other three virtues. Equally, the five terms in total are overlapping and mutually dependent.

If there is no clear distinction in Aristotle, how are we to account for the unbundling of *episteme* and *techne* as the progenitors of a binary division in the conceptual heritage that follows? We should note the distinction Aristotle makes between making and doing. Here the important term in the Ethics is *praxis*, as derived from the Greek verb *prattein*.⁵ Praxis, as one might suspect, has several operational meanings in Greek and in the text of Aristotle. It can refer to action and agency. In the opening lines of the Ethics, Aristotle says, 'every art and every kind of inquiry, and likewise every act and purpose, seems to aim at some good: and so it has been well said that the good is that at which everything aims' (1.1). The Ethics speak of 'good living and good acting' as well as 'men of culture and me of action', where *praxis* is synonymous with political action. Action here is opposed to an inactive and speculative type of existence. In all of these senses, *praxis* involves the exercise of virtues that result in outcomes for the human good. Accordingly, while it might seem that *praxis* might be opposed to knowledge or speculation, it in fact involves and implies these undertakings as the means through which action takes place. Intelligence, practical wisdom, craft, and so on are all required and find their form in action, the praxis that leads to the good life. This praxis can connote both ethical behaviour and political interaction, the way in which people act towards one another within the polis, the city. These two senses of praxis come together in the notion of 'making oneself' by acting for the common good in accordance with the five virtues we have previously identified. This results in *autarkeia* or the ideal of self-sufficiency that pertains not to a 'solitary animal' but to the human who is 'political by nature' (1079b8-11). The classic distinction between man as 'a political animal' and other beasts, then owes its formation to this classification of *praxis* and *autarkeia*.

Praxis is an important third term in the division between *episteme* and *techne* as *poiesis* (making, poetry) in order to determine the value of *phronesis* as part of the argument of Book VI. *Praxis* triangulates *techne* and *episteme*. However, by Book X of the Ethics, Aristotle has replaced *episteme* with *theoria*, which seems to take on the previous values of this term as well as having its own theological dimension in which *theoria* operates at the limits of the human and in contact with the divine. Only a god can operate at the level of pure *theoria*. What we see in later accounts of theory and practice or thinking and making, is an erasure of this important ternary structure in Aristotle's thinking and a figural substitution in which *theoria* takes the place of *episteme* and also loses its theological connotation, resulting in a division between theory and practice that has lost all of the conceptual caveats of the Aristotelian schema.

The triad between *praxis-poiesis-episteme* is there in the opening lines of the Ethics, 'every art and every inquiry, and similarly every action and pursuit' [*pasa techne kai pasa methodos, homoios de praxis te kai proairesis*]. A few lines later Aristotle speaks of 'actions, arts, and sciences' [*praxeon kai technon kai epistemon*]. Here *poiesis* and *praxis* belong to the faculty of making and the faculty of acting. But as we have seen art is not separate from chance, even if Aristotle insists that *poiesis* and *praxis* are part of the realm of the rational, as necessary to the true course of reasoning, one to produce the other to act. Interestingly and importantly, while episteme refers to the necessary and general, the element of contingency in *poiesis* and *praxis* means that they work on a case-by-case basis, what we would now term 'singularity'. This sort of making brings material into the world through chance rather than as a result of a programme or calculation. Equally, in the Ethics *praxis* forms a significant coupling with *episteme* in contrast to *poiesis*, whereby the shaping of the morally excellent human is a *praxis* that is guided by *phronesis*, practical wisdom, which leans on the unvarying nature of *episteme* in necessary ways. However, *praxis* is said to approach *episteme* through a relation to singular cases, drawing upon it on a case-by-case basis as well, 'nor is practical wisdom concerned with universals only – it must also recognize the particulars; for its practical, and practice is concerned with particulars' [*praktike gar, he de praxis peri ta kath' hekasta*, 1141b14-15]. *Praxis* then in some way exceeds *episteme* and *praxis* is importantly related to the individual circumstances of the political, 'political wisdom and practical wisdom are the same state of mind', says Aristotle, (1141b23).

Political praxis is by this point of the Ethics close to the ideal of self-sufficient *autarkeia*. This is the classical formulation of practice that passes through the Western philosophical and political tradition in which *praxis* is the means by which moral excellence is realized, as the compulsion beyond abstraction and theoretical knowledge. However, it is a model that Aristotle himself goes on to challenge in Book X of the Ethics in which, during a discussion of pleasure, he uncouples the necessary link between living well and acting well implied by *praxis* as politics. In this later section of the book, Aristotle recognizes the life of the mind (speculation, theory) as an acceptable basis for *autarkeia*, 'the self-sufficiency that is spoken of must belong most to the contemplative activity' [*legomene autarkeia peri ten theoretiken malist an ete* 1177a27]. This later revision of Aristotle's earlier conclusion seems to have fallen away in the transmission and translation of *The Nicomachean Ethics*. In Book X, ethical and political praxis still relies on *poiesis* because it does not produce objects but effects in the relations of humans. Consequently, *theoria* must be a verifiable *praxis*, 'nothing arises from it [excellence in theoretical thought] apart from contemplating, while practical activities [or excellences, *aretai*] we gain more or less apart from the action' (1177b1-4). *Theoria* then takes its place in the accomplishment of moral excellence through its own praxis. Equally, a subtle shift has occurred here in which excellence in virtues is achieved not by the shaping of humans through their interaction with other humans, but through the contemplation of first principles. Excellence can then be achieved through the life of the mind, because in *theoria* we approach the status of the divine.

This might look like something of a *deus ex machina* as a final twist in the text of Aristotle, which places the good life beyond the reach of the actual life that humans lead. However, it is Aristotle's contention here that speculative thought is a transcendent activity that raises the human world beyond the opposition between action and predisposition, 'it is not insofar as he is a man that he will live so, but insofar as something divine is present in him' [1177b27-28]. Equally, it is this aptitude for transcendence that is specifically human, 'that which is proper to each thing is by nature best and most pleasant for each thing; for man, therefore, the life according to reason is best and pleasantest, since reason more than anything else is man' (1178a5-7). That is to say, *theoria* is the best means to uncover the actuality of things, the best path to the truth and moral excellence, because it is, according to Aristotle, the nature of what it means to be human. On this estimation, *theoria* would be more essential to the human condition than *praxis*.

This is quite a different version of the relation between theory and practice than the one that is handed down to us today. Our modern sense of praxis has of course passed through the Marxist tradition, and Marx's transliteration of Aristotle's term based on his own familiarity with the Ethics as a commentary on practical philosophy. In this tradition the divine or even mystical aspects of *theoria* are dropped as a form of idealism and an inversion takes place that once again privileges praxis, grounded in political circumstances. In this scenario, self-sufficiency and moral excellence are replaced by humanity's self-realization and transformation through the historical dialectic. As the eleventh theses on Feuerbach says, 'philosophers have hitherto only interpreted the world in various ways [*verschieden interpretirt*]; the point is to change [*andern*] it'.[6] However, several of the other previous theses explicitly invoke the term praxis, as if it were a German word and not an adaptation from Aristotle. For example, the second thesis states, 'The question of whether objective truth can be attributed to human thinking is not a question of theory but is a practical question [*eine Praktische Frage*]. Man must prove the truth, that is, the reality and power, the this-sidedness [*Wirklichkeit und Macht Diesseitigkeit*] of his thinking, in practice [*in der Praxis*]. The dispute over the reality or nonreality of thinking that is isolated from practice is a purely scholastic question'. The mobilization of the same concerns as Aristotle with respect to thinking and the human good is evident but the conclusions seem to be different. The third thesis reads, 'the coincidence of the changing of circumstances and of human activity or self-change can be conceived and rationally understood only as revolutionary practice [*revolutionare Praxis*]'. In Marx, the Greek word has not been translated at all but the concept it named has been shorn of the meanings that attended it in its original form. The eighth thesis says, 'all social life is essentially practical. All mysteries that lead theory to mysticism find their rational solution in human practice and in the comprehension of this practice [*in der menschlichen Praxis und in dem Begreifen dieser Praxis*]'. There is a literal way of reading all this, namely, to imagine that the inversion of *theoria* and *praxis* is of a piece with the reversal of idealism in Marxian thought specific to the philosophical conjuncture of which the *Theses on Feuerbach* would be a part. However, this reversal in Marx is only ever a provisional change in emphasis while historical materialism establishes itself. It is not a refutation or dismissal of the conceptual inheritance.

In Kant's practical philosophy, like Aristotle, moral goals are attached to the exercise of reason. Throughout his writing he makes systematic use of the term *praktisch* in his designation of practical reason and pure practical reason. His only use of the word praxis comes in the essay with which we began, 'On the Common Saying: This May be True in Theory but it Does Not Apply in Practice [*Praxis*]'. Elsewhere, Kant will speak of *das Praktische* [the practical or the practical element] but in this essay adopts the substantive Praxis in his title as a common saying. In this sense, he is adopting the term used by the writers he is opposing in his essay, the 'popular' philosophers of the eighteenth century who oppose the radical implications of the Enlightenment and the French Revolution and who imagine institutional tradition and inherited privilege to be the reservoir of political wisdom [*Staatsklugheit*]. For Kant the moral achievement of practical philosophy does not lie in *phronesis* or technical skill but solely in morality as principles that define the categorical imperative. His is a *moralisch-praktisch* rather than a *technisch-praktisch*. The path from the laws of practical reason to action and experience is a matter, for Kant, of the pragmatic and of managing the pathological element introduced by the vicissitudes of human nature. The pragmatic task of practical philosophy is to put morality at the centre of relations between humans and so to transform the world. We can see how that inheritance plays out in Marx, even if it is realized in a quite different way.

However, it is Kant's three critiques that place the question of the practical at the heart of theoretical discourse. In so doing, he does not easily separate outcomes in the material world from a speculative principle identified with reason, and accordingly neither do Marx and Engels even if their own extensive theoretical accounts wish to put a pin in *theoria* to further the cause of *praxis*. Other traditions are available, and we could follow the transmission of Aristotle's ethics through a French line that would suffer equally from the failure of the *translatio philosophiae* from Athens to Rome and into European vernacular languages to render an adequate Latin translation of the Greek word *praxis*. The point here is not to prefer one tradition to another or to prefer *theoria* to *praxis* or vice versa, but to recognize that the relation of one to the other is complex and runs to the very roots of the philosophical tradition. Art cannot hold this philosophical tradition to account on this point, because 'art' in this sense, as we saw in *The Nicomachean Ethics* and in Kant's *Third Critique*, is also a product of that tradition. We are not dealing with an easily dichotomized academy between the theoretical and the practical, between the humanities and the creative arts. Instead, we are looking at a set of relations, conceptually and historically overlayed, from which a complex object of study begins to emerge as a decisive index of some of the most compelling questions raised by human experience.

Plato's Other Republic

Theory-Practice is not the same thing as philosophy. The former has a clear relation to the latter but philosophy designates an idiom of writing and a register of thought, a training, and discipline, which cannot be reduced to other related genres. However, it is our contestation here that as a genre philosophy has its limits, and it is precisely at these borders that philosophy is opened up, presenting us with the most decisive indices of what philosophy might be and performing its differential relation to other idioms. The border between philosophy and literature, for example, is of particular interest to us. It is increasingly difficult to determine the exact nature of that boundary as soon as one considers the history of philosophical writing. For example, how are we to determine which aspects of Augustine's thought in *Confessions* amounts to 'life-writing' and which to philosophy?[7] How are we to read across the corpus of a Rousseau or a Sartre and decide which text can be designated as novelistic and which earns the name philosophy? Is the *Emile* a treatise on the philosophy of education or is it a bildungsroman that recounts the story of a student and his tutor?[8] Is *The Age of Reason* a commentary on existentialism or a story of 1930s Paris?[9] From Boethius to Abelard, from Thomas More to Pascal, from Voltaire and Diderot to Schiller and Wollstonecraft, from Madame de Staël to Kierkegaard, from Thoreau to

Nietzsche, from Benjamin to de Beauvoir, from Bataille and Blanchot to Derrida and Cixous, how can one draw a line through a body of texts and determine where literature ends and where philosophy begins? In these examples, and across the tradition of Western thought, literature, and philosophy bleed into one another across idioms of writing that cannot be easily disentangled. And of course, philosophy itself begins, with Plato and with writing that cannot be said to be straight forwardly or purely 'philosophical'. Philosophy begins in writing and never escapes it. While it may be important politically and pedagogically to defend the borders of philosophy and to maintain the institutions of philosophy in order to preserve a disciplinary training in a properly philosophical space, this should not be at the expense of recognizing the artificial nature of those borders. It is not possible, under any degree of readerly pressure, to separate the philosophical from the other genres of writing, as if it were, to not subject to the same rules of figuration and composition to be found elsewhere. Accordingly, while we might wish to retain an institutional distinction between Theory-Practice of the sort exemplified by *Delphine, Candide* or *La Carte Postale*, and philosophy proper, such a categorization falls away at first point of contact with these texts.[10] Theory-Practice as the near neighbour of philosophy opens philosophy up and restores it to the wider terrain of writing that is its inescapable home.

This is not to say that philosophy thinks in the same way that Theory-Practice does. In the case of filmosophy (films that exhibit philosophical content) for example, the sound-image of cinema does not operate on the same level of conceptualization and critique as idiomatic philosophy, despite all the claims to the contrary by writers who have read their philosophy but never made a film.[11] If we are to account for the question of film there must be a reckoning with the material difference of film to philosophy, a materiality that cannot be abridged as the thematic or illustrative. Theory-Practice can do its work across a range of genres and media, visual art for example does not operate in the same way as philosophy does. However, it can perform an idea with its constative dimension inseparable from its performative element. Conceptual art remains irreducibly conceptual and irreducibly art. While the constative and performative dimensions of philosophy are equally inextricable, it is in that part of Theory-Practice that grafts philosophy to art that it accepts another logic to philosophy, namely, that of contradiction.[12] It is the purpose of philosophy to seek to establish a principle of truth, while it is the nature of art to embrace a principle of ambivalence. The literary text, for example, is free to work within a double resonance at once accepting no referential relation to the real world and relying entirely on this suspension of reference as a means of presenting the truth of the world. The work of literature and its fundamental difference from philosophy is that in order to be literary the text must accelerate and heighten that ambiguity as a condition of its own status a literature. Philosophy, by contrast, seeks to repress that element of uncertainty within its position as writing. Philosophy as an idiom and a discipline proposes a logic of non-contradiction as the basis of its rational discourse and the condition of all ontology. Literature by contrast requires a logic of ambivalence, in which equivocality puts in play an essential non-resolution of polarities. Philosophy accepts the logic of the logos, while literature departs from it and seeks another mode of comprehension. In this sense, philosophy and literature are not the same thing, even if we struggle to separate them in the textual history of Western thought. However, as we can see from the example of Plato, philosophy's law of non-contradiction emerges from the ambiguous pages of a formal equivocality. The genre of the dialogue and the frequent use of myth and narrative illustration by Plato places his work firmly in the category of 'writing' and to all intents and purposes in the realm of fiction. Philosophy then begins in fiction, one might even say that Theory-Practice precedes philosophy. In the beginning was Theory-Practice and philosophy has never recovered.

It is appropriate then to look to the text of Plato for an indication of the difficulties of creativity and the aporias of Theory-Practice. We might turn with advantage to one of Plato's most significant texts on the question of creation, the *Timaeus*.[13] It is notable that Plato's account of the origin of the universe is embedded within a series of narrative frames, in which we pick up the dialogue the morning after the discussion on *The Republic*.[14] Seeking alternative 'entertainment' Socrates wishes to hear an account of how the ideal state engages with other states. Critias then tells the story of Solon's journey to Egypt where he in turn hears the tale of Atlantis and its war with Athens. We will return to this particular issue in a moment, as it is by no means the least interesting aspect of the *Timaeus* even though it is one that attracts little attention within the philosophical commentary on Plato's text. Even Critias interrupts his own account of Atlantis to note that he is getting ahead of himself and inviting Timaeus to offer an account of the origin of the universe, folds his own diegetic level onto that of the eponymous interlocutor. Critias will pick up the story of Atlantis in the subsequent dialogue that takes its name from his own and which remains incomplete or lost, ending the text of Plato in fragments and fiction. All of this works on a level of considerable textual sophistication and narrative complexity, introducing the logic of ambivalence into the text of philosophy with every narrative twist and turn of character. In this dialogue we have both the use of *mythos* as a predicate for *logos*, and a philosophical text that puts on display its figurative dimension in an extended performance of its own textuality. And yet such a text is taken by the institutions of philosophy as the edge at which *philos* breaks from *mythos*, and the idiom buries its own status as writing. The text is in fact Theory-Practice that aspires to the condition of philosophy through the repression of its own performativity. We might equally say that philosophy is Theory-Practice that denies its own figurative dimension.[15] This will take a little unpicking.

Here, it would be advantageous to attend to Jacques Derrida's reading of the *Timaeus* around the Greek word 'khora' [χώρα] which in its most common usage names the territory of the polis outside of the city proper.[16] In the text of the *Timaeus* to mean a 'third kind' [*triton genos*, 48e4] of space in the creation of the universe that is neither that of being nor non-being but a material substratum through which *eidos* [form] enters into existence.[17] As such khora presents another logic to that of non-contradiction, to the binary of yes or no. It is described by Timaeus variously as a receptacle, mother, or a midwife, operating as a concept through a figurative chain of metaphorization to denote a place beyond categorical oppositions. Khora, then names another logic than goes beyond that of the *logos* but which is at the same time does not belong strictly to *mythos*. It is a philosophical concept that emerges from narrative fiction, denoting as it performs, creating as it describes creation. Khora is a figure that, in Derrida's terms, 'oscillates between two types of oscillation: the double exclusion (neither/nor) and the participation (both this and that)' (p. 91). The philosophical commentary on khora notes the metaphorical nature of the term without necessarily mobilizing the resources of rhetorical reading to consider it further.[18] Philosophy is also blind to the translation that seems to be integral to khora as a term that begins as a reference to one thing but must necessarily move through a transformation to refer to something else. At the same time, khora as a concept describes a place that is beyond the polarity of structures such as metaphor or translation. Khora itself would make tropology inevitable but not something supplementary to denotation or a provisional or accidental state. The naming of khora itself is an effect of khora, the form by which khora is formed. At the same time, khora itself is neither of the order of *eidos* nor that of *mimesis* (the image of forms). The non-being of khora cannot be rendered by the anthropomorphic schemas that are used to translate it. It is something that is not a thing, escaping the order of meaning it puts into play. It is not then subject to or of an ontology, to an order of the intelligible or sensible. That is to say, khora may be that which initiates a certain philosophical idiom but which cannot be submitted to its logical regime. Khora is the formalization of the unformed as well as the formalization of formalization.

Derrida's reading of Plato takes a route through Hegel and for good reason. Hegel notes, following Aristotle, that 'those who philosophize with recourse to myth are not worth treating seriously'.[19] This would seem to place Plato's presentation of the origins of the universe in a difficult position given that it seems to explicitly rely on myth and moreover figuration and fiction. Hegel also suggests that 'the value of Plato, however, does not reside in myths'.[20] That is to say, for Hegel, there is a 'seriousness' in Plato that allows the Western tradition to extract his thought from its fictional and figurative setting. In this sense, Hegel sets up his own binary opposition between the serious and the non-serious that maps onto that between *philos* and *mythos*, rescuing a logic of non-contradiction from a context of originary ambivalence. Hegel is of course privileging the content of Plato, while subordinating the form of Plato in order to justify the seriousness of Plato and so the origins of philosophy and accordingly his own dialectical method, which in this way operates as both the sublation of philosophy and philosophy as sublation. In this way, the text of Hegel offers an exemplary 'Platonism' in the way it extracts content from form, removing an ideal Plato from the actual text of Plato. The philosophy of Plato comes at the expense of Plato the writer, and Platonism is something that Hegel applies to Plato himself. In contrast, khora would be a place inimicable to this logic of opposition, a place without place, that is the threshold of place and an undiscoverable place. In so far as philosophy then extracts khora from the text of Plato, we have the becoming philosophy of myth, in which the non-serious becomes serious by removing it from its own place, enacting a reductive violence on khora that as a term designates another kind of logic.

The place of khora is the place of Theory-Practice, a place of creativity that is both theory and practice, and neither fully theory nor solely practice. Theory-Practice is the place of Plato the writer, a place that is not fully recognizable to philosophy or as literature. It is a place without place that can address the place of philosophy and the place of practice, both from the outside and as a receptacle for philosophy and the creative arts, while generative of both. Theory-Practice occurs in a third genus and in the 'neutral' space of place without place. As Roland Barthes tells us the *neutre* is not a simple splitting of the difference between two binaries, rather it is its own space, which is marked in its own distinctive and singular way just as it appears to be unmarked.[21] Theory-Practice is not neutral in the sense that word often has, meaning uncommitted or disinterested. It is *le neutre* in the contradictory sense that Barthes suggests, a commitment to both theory and practice, from a space that is neither strictly theory nor practice. To reduce the outcomes of Theory-Practice to an identifiable truth of philosophy would be to do considerable violence to the mis-en-abyme of the scene of Theory-Practice and to ignore the materiality of the practice that structures that scene. It would be to enact the abstraction of Platonism on Theory-Practice, reclaiming it for philosophy in a universalizing gesture that philosophy finds second nature. This extraction and reduction constitutive of philosophy itself would then be an effect of Theory-Practice itself. Derrida suggests that Platonism 'is not only an example of this movement, the first 'in' the whole history of philosophy. It commands it, it commands this whole history' (p. 121). That is to say philosophy as such, formally, is henceforth always Platonic. Philosophy then has its origin in a singular example of Theory-Practice, an idiom that it would relegate as a non-serious genre. It is not that Theory-Practice suffers from a philosophy deficit as an inferior or imitative field. Rather, Theory-Practice opens up philosophy from the beginning, giving birth, as *khora*, to the form of philosophy. The ruin and exposure of the formal edifice of philosophy lies in its originary relation to Theory-Practice, which gives to it writing as its cause and disarticulation. This is an origin older than the origin of philosophy itself, an origin given in writing that takes and gives the form of Theory-Practice.

Theory-Practice then gives philosophy its form but it also holds that form. Khora is only a figure of Theory-Practice and is not more of a receptacle than a nurse or a mother. As a figure of origin, it can be no more originary than any other figure. As a *triton genos* it cannot be a *genos* as such because it is unique. It is a figure that is inscribed fully in its own singular materiality, in which its meaning cannot be abstracted from its form, as if the ideality of theory could be extracted from the embodiment of practice, as if both theory and practice were not simultaneously figurative and material. If Theory-Practice is a philosophical idiom, a pre-originary genre that gives the form of philosophy, then it is a bastard and hybrid idiom that retains its distance from philosophy. It is necessary for philosophy, placing itself prior to and below the origin of philosophy, preceding and receiving the effects of philosophy. As Derrida notes in his reading of Plato, 'the discourse on khora thus plays for philosophy a role analogous to the role which khora 'herself' plays for that which philosophy speaks of, namely, the cosmos formed or given from according to the paradigm' (p. 126). That is to say, just as the universe is created through khora in Plato's cosmology, so formal philosophy emerges from Plato's writing of the figure of khora. By extension, as we find in the text of Plato an exemplary figure of Theory-Practice, so we find that Theory-Practice is the matrix of khora from which philosophy itself emerges.

The same is true of practice as a *genos*. There can be no abstraction of a model, procedure, or ideal from the singular inscription of Theory-Practice, each instance must be absolutely singular and inaugural of a space from which practice merges but cannot be identified as strictly practice, or be reduced to the practical, utility, or function. The impulse of practice towards an absolute affect would also be an effect given and received by Theory-Practice. The writing of Plato wants to run away with the thought of Plato as nothing but a textual scene of the exchange of figures. However, Theory-Practice draws it back into space of philosophy in a necessary tension between abstraction and embodiment. Both theory and practice claim to be the serious outcome of the non-serious scene of Theory-Practice. Practice, in this sense, in relation to khora and the philosophy of Plato means politics and the *polis*. Practice always wishes to stake its credentials as serious compared to the abstraction of thought in the Ivory Tower. This leaves Theory-Practice as the non-serious practice of practice, a practice that does not take itself seriously by being practical enough. Politics and philosophy both take their distance from writing as a genre just as it is writing that gives and receives the form of politics and philosophy, opening and ruining both in the process, inimicable to the binary logic that divides the two. The foreclosures of practice are just as reductive and limiting as the abstractions of theory. They justify themselves in their constraints by associating those closures with what it would mean to be serious or committed, having chosen a side in the binary choice between theory and practice, insisting on and reinstating its own logic of non-contradiction. In this way to be serious is both to be practical in the case of politics and to be thoughtful in the case of philosophy. However, within a rigorous logic of non-contradiction practice and theory cannot both be serious. Would the more serious thing not be to take seriously how this logic is indeed in contradiction with itself? That is to say, to speak of and to do seriousness from another place, the space of khora, which gives and receives seriousness, below all its forms and a certain formlessness. Hence, there would be nothing more serious than Theory-Practice, nothing more philosophical and nothing more practical.

There is, one might say, an exemplary deconstructive emphasis to khora and to what we are calling Theory-Practice.[22] The action of khora might be thought of as exemplary of quasi-transcendental and supplementary logics that we see elsewhere in Derrida's writing.[23] However, it is remarkable in Derrida's reading of Plato that while he identifies the way in which philosophy masks its originary debt to writing through an appropriation of the merits of seriousness, Derrida completely ignores one of the most interesting aspects of the *Timaeus*, namely the 'non-serious' references to Atlantis that open the dialogue and are continued in the *Critias*. This omission is curious given the importance of Atlantis in these dialogues in relation to the question of politics and the space of the city that structures the significance of khora in the *Timaeus*. It is accordingly, of some interest here in the context of Theory-Practice as a non-serious relation of philosophy. When Derrida reads Hegel or Aristotle on philosophy and myth, perhaps Atlantis is in the background of his essay but it is never explicitly brought to the fore. Derrida was of course an extremely serious philosopher, his concern for the canon of modernist literature, for example, places his interests in literature in the realm of the suitably serious. Perhaps, the question of Atlantis was not serious enough for Derrida to consider and he thought it enough to speak to the distinction between *mythos* and *philos* in the text of Plato. But when addressing *mythos* as a problem for philosophy he does specifically single out the singularity of khora and does not mention Atlantis. And yet the topic is perhaps a more striking example of *mythos* in the whole of Plato and clearly a point of contrast for the seriousness of Athens, place of politics and philosophy. There might be a reluctance to take Atlantis seriously because it has been historically the preserve of cranks and pulp fiction; it was an object of fascination for National Socialism and its ludicrous attempts to mobilize a mythology of Aryan giants.[24] It is however, a matter of unquestioned seriousness for Socrates.

The *Timaeus* is a receptacle for stories, one narrative embedded inside the other, the account of the origins of the universe, the story of creation itself, is framed as a delay to the business of Atlantis that will be taken up again in the *Critias*. In the *Timaeus* the story is described as having been recorded in the histories of Egypt, the relevant passage may be more or less familiar to readers of Plato:

> These histories tell of a mighty power which unprovoked made an expedition against the whole of Europe and Asia, and to which your city put an end. This power came forth out of the Atlantic Ocean, for in those days the Atlantic was navigable; and there was an island situated in front of the straits which are by you called the Pillars of Heracles; the island was larger than Libya and Asia put together, and was the way to other islands, and from these you might pass to the whole of the opposite continent which surrounded the true ocean; for this sea which is within the Straits of Heracles is only a harbour, having a narrow entrance, but that other is a real sea, and the surrounding land may be most truly called a boundless continent. (25a)

If this is the stuff of myth then there is a considered attempt on Plato's part to invoke a cartographical verisimilitude in order to place Atlantis within the ancient world. Realism is as much a trope as myth is. Its size alone, 'larger than Libya and Asia', requires us to take it seriously. This is a myth about the foundations of Europe and the origins of philosophy, by which a Mediterranean heritage is accorded to the becoming European of the continent and of the philosophical discourse of the Greeks. This is in contrast to the colonial ambitions of the kingdom from the Atlantic. As such it serves a serious role in the text of Plato and it is precisely for this reason that fascists such as Julius Evola also took it seriously. There is of course a difference between taking the story of Atlantis seriously and taking it literally:

> Now in this island of Atlantis there was a great and wonderful empire which had rule over the whole island and several others, and over parts of the continent, and, furthermore, the men of Atlantis had subjected the parts of Libya within the columns of Heracles as far as Egypt, and of Europe as far as Tyrrhenia. This vast power, gathered into one, endeavoured to subdue at a blow our country and yours and the whole of the region within the straits; and then, Solon, your country shone forth, in the excellence of her virtue and strength, among all mankind. She was pre-eminent in courage and military skill, and was the leader of the Hellenes. And when the rest fell off from her, being compelled to stand alone, after having undergone the very extremity of danger, she defeated and triumphed over the invaders, and preserved from slavery those who were not yet subjugated, and generously liberated all the rest of us who dwell within the pillars. (25b-c)

The story of Atlantis is nothing short of a founding narrative for the justification of Athens's own colonial domination of the Mediterranean basin in the years before the Peloponnesian War. Written in 360 BC following the defeat to Sparta and in a time of Hellenic decline, this dialogue might be characterized by its post-colonial melancholy in which the now compromised virtue of Athens is contrasted to the mythic vice of the Atlantians. The historic influence of Athens is then not the result of military might and trade but the consequence of Athens having stood alone against the threat of Atlantis, in a binary contest that brooks no contradiction. The reach of Athens is thus rendered not as a material advantage to the city but as a result of virtue, the advantages that come with it are not subjection of others but precisely the result of the liberation of those people now dominated by Athens.

The virtue of Athens is of course a product of the philosophy and politics that distinguishes the city and makes it 'leader of the Hellenes'. There could be little more serious to be considered with respect to the ancient world, and yet here we have the serious virtue of Athens, and all that this means for the European tradition and European colonialism, putting down its roots in the myth of the cruelty of the empire of Atlantis. Empire founds itself on a pre-originary colonialism from which it takes its distance and repeats its effects. In this way the empire of Atlantis is generative of a European tradition of colonialism that in perpetuity occurs around a justification through reason and enlightenment while depending on mythic origins and stories of virtue. The seriousness of colonial occupiers is always in contrast to the childlike simplicity of the occupied, just as the seriousness of the logos is explicitly compared in Plato's text to the childish mythology of the Egyptians. Virtue is its own reward, even if that reward is hegemony over the Mediterranean region. The vice of the Atlantians is suitably punished:

> But afterwards there occurred violent earthquakes and floods; and in a single day and night of misfortune all your warlike men in a body sank into the earth, and the island of Atlantis in like manner disappeared in the depths of the sea. For which reason the sea in those parts is impassable and impenetrable, because there is a shoal of mud in the way; and this was caused by the subsidence of the island. (25d)

Athens suffered its own loss of blood and treasure but Atlantis sinks into the sea, its submerged fragments marking the boundaries of the European space, beyond it there lies another place 'impassable and impenetrable' and undiscoverable.

It is striking how the figure of Atlantis works in this dialogue, a myth that gives birth to a formal logocentrism (colonialism is always a logocentirsm[25]) sitting below the propriety of Athens as an origin of the virtue of Europe and philosophy as discourse of reason. It should not be surprising that *mythos* should operate in this way in the text of Plato, it is the same action that we tracked in the figure of khora in which writing gives and receives the effects of a seriousness that imposes a logic of non-contradiction onto a matrix of ambivalence. Even those who historically took the myth of Atlantis seriously did so because it derived its authority from Plato. That is to say from Plato the philosopher, not Plato the writer of fiction. The corrupt racialized history of the Atlantis myth in the twentieth century played precisely on this distinction between the serious and the non-serious that results from the becoming Platonism of Plato. Even the most mythic aspect of the mythos, myth at its own limits, benefits from the serious effects of Platonism, granting plausibility to the most ludic of Plato's inventions. This is the Plato effect, the outcome of a writing that bestows seriousness through an insistence on non-contradiction as a consequence of a textual scene of extreme referential suspension. Imposing non-contradiction onto a field of ambiguity is the principle by which philosophy works and characterizes the mechanism of universalization derived from particularity that gives philosophy its formal character. It would also seem to work in the case of politics as a practice that seeks to outflank philosophy as well as ambiguity. The appropriation of the myth of Atlantis by National Socialism is above all political, as much as it relies on a warped historiography or anthropology.

Critias is also the name of the Athenian politician (460–403 BC) who was one of the thirty Tyrants, the pro-Spartan oligarchs installed after the defeat of Athens.[26] He is said to have been a first cousin of Plato's mother. It is importantly undecidable for the reader of Plato's dialogues whether the likes of Critias or Solon can be identified with historic figures. Plato is a writer of fiction, his Critias is no more historical than Shakespeare's Richard III. However, the name of Critias firmly places the two dialogues within the legible frame of politics. The historic Critias was also a dramatist who is sometimes credited with the Sisyphus fragment rather than Euripides.[27] He is another figure of Theory-Practice within an exemplary fragment of Theory-Practice. It would seem that while theory and practice might be thought of as pulling in opposite directions, we can see in the text of Plato a different action for theory and practice. In fact, they both tend towards the same direction, seeking to calm or erase the field of ambivalence by staking a claim to non-contradiction and so to be non-contestable. Practice attempts this as much as Theory does. The end of politics is the end of politics, as Geoffrey Bennington would say, that is, the foreclosure of further argument and action following the application of a perfect political programme aimed at the resolution of all debate and material need.[28] In this way, practice is equally open to the ruin of disarticulation that comes from its origins in ambiguity. The trick in reading Plato as Theory-Practice is to keep that ambiguity open and to refuse a foreclosure that would makes us decide between these dialogues as Platonic philosophy or as tales of Empire. They occupy a different space that gives and receives both as an effect of writing.

The *Critias* is an even more remarkable text than the *Timaeus* as it returns to the deferred story of Atlantis and its war with Athens said to have taken place nine thousand years before the dialogue. It goes into considerable detail on the foundations of Atlantis as the island of Poseidon and his progeny, including Atlas who begat the kings of Atlantis. The political structures of the island are described, as are the agricultural routine, rituals, and the division of land. The dialogue is incomplete or lost but Critias outlines the shape of the story he wishes to tell the assembled company; he wants to recall an ancient war between 'between those who dwelt outside the Pillars of Heracles and all who dwelt within them' and 'the progress of the history will unfold the various nations of barbarians and families of Hellenes which then existed, as they successively appear on the scene; but I must describe first of all Athenians of that day, and their enemies who fought with them, and then the respective powers and governments of the two kingdoms' (88-91). His opening remarks then 'give the precedence to Athens' before turning to Atlantis. This is a classic tale of conflict between those who dwell outside of 'Europe' and those who live within, separated now by an impenetrable barrier of mud, between barbarians and the civilized Hellenes.

The fragment ends with an insight into why a race of gods declared war on the virtuous Greeks, noting that over time the human aspect of the Atlantians began to dilute the divine dimension of their character, making them selfish and warlike. The war is then said to be a punishment from Zeus who wished to correct their avaricious ways. The fragment ends here but we could accordingly, in light of this, read the dialogue in a different way, namely as an allegory. The purpose of the story of Atlantis might not be to contrast virtuous Athens with a warlike other, but to reflect back to Athenians in the years of defeat and decline after its own war with Sparta, how far the Athens of Socrates was from an imagined pristine state of nine thousand years ago when it fought Atlantis. In this sense, Atlantis and Athens are not two capitals divided between a binary choice between virtue and vice, but are the same place mapped onto one another through the allegory of the *Critias* dialogue, in which the fate of Atlantis serves as a warning to the Athens of Plato. It is not possible to be definitive on this point; it is sufficient that it is a reading that presents itself from the referential field of Plato's text. It is not clear what exactly Atlantis is referring to but it is a good bet that it is referring to something other than its own myth, although it is also at the same time doing precisely this.

Atlantis is not serious, it is the preserve of pseudo-history and occultism. No doubt this is why Derrida choses to shy away from it in favour of khora, an otherwise marginal figure to the dialogues. If we take Derrida's reading practice here and elsewhere at face value, the point would be not to oppose khora to Atlantis but to see in his reading of khora a decisive case of how *mythos* and *philos* work more generally in Plato and so also in the case of Atlantis. However, this non-seriousness is extremely serious and not just because its appropriation was used to justify a murderous, racist ideology. Rather, the seriousness of Atlantis lies in its capacity to give and receive speculation. Speculation in this sense means both the speculative tradition that emerges from Plato as the canon of Western philosophy and the speculation that comes from the ambiguity of storytelling as the conjecture of narrative fiction. If, as we have suggested throughout our own account of these dialogues, the writing of Plato is a notable case of the sort of Theory-Practice under discussion in this book, then we might say that speculation is the space occupied by Theory-Practice. It is a space for thought, that speculates to accumulate, laying a wager on the future, while noting its debts to a thinking that it both gives and receives. It is also a space of experiment in which the referential rules of non-contradiction are suspended.

The *Timaeus-Critias* is both a work of philosophy and a narrative fiction, and neither fully a work of philosophy nor just a narrative fiction. Theory-Practice in this sense operates according to another logic, one that might be called allegorical, in which the work of Theory-Practice always refers to something other than itself, while simultaneously working through the task for which it has been set up. Theory-Practice sets up a scenario in which speculative thought can take its place, only to undo the security of that scenario and thought in order to establish their very undecidability, only to further complicate this by denying any security to this disarticulation as well.[29] It is in this folding and unfolding of layers of practice and thought, their initiation, undoing and recuperation, that Theory-Practice occupies a different space from that of other idioms of intellectual inquiry or creative making. The seriousness we accord Theory-Practice will depend entirely upon how seriously we want to take philosophical culture or practices such as art or politics. As far as ancient Athens was concerned there would be little that one should be prepared to treat more seriously. The serious role of Theory-Practice is that its shows us that in their proprietorial claims to sobriety, solemnity, or earnestness, philosophy and politics are simply not serious enough. Their sincerity is merely sombre, masking the reserves of ambiguity upon which their own practice is founded. If the speculative space of Theory-Practice has a serious role to play, it is in untapping these reserves giving and receiving the resource of undecidability to both the theoretical and the practical.

2

The Last Chapter of the History of the World

Puppet show

Heinrich von Kleist's *Über das Marionettentheater* is a text about the seductions and pitfalls of critical practice.[1] As Kleist's most well-known essay it has been variously interpreted, its enigmatic prose providing scope for numerous and mutually conflicting readings.[2] In itself, as a text, it is something of a curiosity. It cannot be easily assigned to any particular genre and is usually categorized separately from Kleist's fictional short stories, alongside his more obviously 'philosophical journalism' for the *Berliner Abendblatter*, where it was first published in 1810. If it is an essay, it is certainly an oddity. As an essay it follows a fictional structure and employs characters in a dialogue, the epistemological status of which is at best ambiguous. It would not be out of place in a novel and if it were not for the signposts offered by historical editing practices, it would be difficult to situate as a piece of writing. It is in fact, an example of precisely the sort of text that we are calling 'critical practice', another kind of writing, one that seems to present itself as both fact and fiction and neither fact nor fiction. It is every bit a theoretical text, Enlightenment philosophical writing looms large in the background, but one that uses that philosophy for another purpose, an end that is altogether different and ambiguous, even irresolvable in its uncertainty.

It is not that Kleist is a philosopher, although like Novalis, Schiller, or Rousseau, his writing ranges across different genres. Rather, Kleist is an artist who is immersed in philosophy as the wellspring of his writing. In fact, writing such as *Über das Marionettentheater* clearly demonstrates the historical specificity of the generic division between philosophy and its others. This segregation of genres is as much institutional as it is internal to the discursive resources of philosophy. The separation of philosophy from the idioms of literature is nothing other than the history of the becoming professional of a formalization of philosophy as an academic meta-language. As such what is now thought of as normative philosophical writing is in fact a highly artificial, historical construction that contains within itself numerous aporia, elisions, expulsions, and contradictions. Philosophical writing did not always have such a seemingly clarity or purity that fenced it off from the other more obviously figurative, and so equivocal, genres of writing. In Kleist's texts there is no distinction to be made between the narration of concepts and the narration of characters, or between the exploration of a scene and the expansion of a thought.

We might read Kleist's short text as something of a philosophical puppet show. Kleist is by no means alone in this respect (one might think of Nietzsche's writing between aphorism and poetry, or, Plato's dialogical dramas). It could be said that the discursive division of philosophy and literature that begins in the eighteenth century with Kant and then Hegel is the struggle for the birth of a genre of writing that does not recognize itself as such. As we shall see, it is precisely Kant's failure to resolve pure and practical reason in an adequate understanding of aesthetic judgement that both ensures modern philosophy as a project is stillborn and simultaneously wins its future. The history of philosophy is the forgetting of its idiomatic status, and as such 'critical practice' is neither new nor to be easily distinguished from historic texts that elude the modern impulse for the designation of genres and vocabulary. This relatively recent mania for order betrays its own anxieties and ultimately provides the resources for the undoing of every such division, which is also an obfuscation. The relation between 'theory' and 'practice' is considerably uncertain and one should not assume too easily that such categorization is even in principle possible. Perhaps, such acts of conceptual enclosure are themselves merely the effect of particular moves within a motivated history of reading and misreading. Reading itself may be the only tool we have at our disposal to understand this partition by *going after* this diremption as both an affirmation of philosophy in its unique singularity and a shaking of idiomatic philosophy until it gives up its secrets and falls apart in our hands as another aporia of writing. While an understanding of critical practice will turn philosophy inside out, it is not an attempt to dissolve what lays claim to the 'properly' philosophical.

Kleist's text concerns a meeting between the narrator and Herr C, in the unidentified city of M, in the winter of 1801. C has recently been appointed as the first dancer at the city Opera, where he is enjoying great popular success. The narrator has spotted C several times at a puppet theatre in the marketplace. C tells the narrator that a dancer who wishes to improve his art can learn a lot from the marionettes. According to C, the movement of the puppets does not require the puppeteer to pull or position every limb, rather every action is dependent upon the swing of weights, following the parabola of a pendulum, and moving of their own accord. Whenever the centre of gravity of the weight is moved in a straight line, the limbs follow a curve and if the strings are 'shaken by accident' the result is 'a kind of rhythmical activity similar to dancing'. The narrator wonders whether the puppeteer would have to be a dancer themselves to produce such results. C is of the opinion that, on the one hand, the line of the puppet's limbs was 'very simple' and would not require much skill on the part of the operator, but on the other hand, it could not be achieved 'wholly without feeling'. There is something 'mysterious' [*Geheiminisvolles*] about the line followed by the puppet because it is 'nothing other than *the way of the dancer's soul*' and by placing themselves in the centre of gravity of the marionette the operator was also dancing. The two friends discuss whether the production of movement in the puppet is not similar to the 'turning of a handle to play a barrel organ'. On the one hand, the movement of the puppeteer's fingers is said to be 'quite a subtle one, rather like that of numbers to their logarithms or the asymptotes to the hyperbola'. On the other hand, all 'intelligence' could be removed from the marionettes and their 'dancing' allotted entirely to the 'realm of mechanical forces'. The dancer asserts that if he could find a craftsman to make a puppet to his specifications it would be capable of feats unequalled by any trained dancer.

There is much more for us to take from this story (if that is what is) as the two friends continue their discussion and extend their theory of the marionette. However, it is worth commenting on this opening section of the text. The issue at debate here is whether the aesthetic effect of dance can be produced either by artistic means (by a puppeteer who dances) or by mechanical means (through the random generation of movement as a result of certain algorithmic potentials independent of a creator or author). The situation is multiple and complex. Firstly, the movement of the marionette is said to be the result of an 'accident' [*zufällige*, random] which results in 'a kind of rhythmical activity similar to dancing'. The narrator is concerned to make a distinction between what appears to be dancing, somewhere between accident and algorithm, and real dancing, which would be the outcome of a conscious effort on the part of a trained dancer. However, this text is entirely about putting into question any easy distinction between theory on the one hand and practice on the other, or at least the idea of practice as the conscious application of theory. In fact, what the two friends witness in the marketplace burlesque might not be dance at all, only the show of dance.

At the same time as Herr C suggests the movement of the marionettes not only provide the trained dancer with a theoretical means to improve their own practice, but that in principle a suitably designed marionette would excel beyond anything 'any other trained dancer of the day, not even excepting Vestris himself, would be capable of equalling'. These are quite extraordinary puppets and this is no ordinary theory. The lines between theory and practice become remarkably blurred, as the puppets in the marketplace give rise to the speculation of a blueprint for a puppet to come, a machine that could outperform any human. This inquiry that the narrator sets up is independent of whether the description of the workings of the puppets would cut the muster in an engineering seminar. Experts might question the mechanical description of the operation of the puppets, but the accuracy or epistemological status of the account is not what is at stake here. Like the text that presents it, the description is somewhere, irresolvably, between fact and fiction, and theory and practice. As readers we are required to entertain both possibilities at once, holding them in a productive tension that makes it possible for us to accept the 'as if' scenario. It is as if such impossible puppets did exist for pursuing a line of argument that is itself never resolved as either an aesthetic theory or a good story. The line of the 'as if' is essential to both speculative thought in the form of philosophy and to the very possibility of fiction. In this sense both theory and practice are not temporal nodes in a line that moves from hypothesis to application, but are similar moments of risk in the presentation of impossibility as the grounds of the possible, in the form of the 'as if'.[3]

It is not so much a question of telling the dancer from the dance, as Yeats would put it, but telling dance from the appearance of dance through random mechanical interactions.[4] However, if both produce the same aesthetic effect, who could tell the difference? The only difference that makes any difference for the narrator is that his friend plies his trade at the Opera while the puppets of the marketplace are 'for the entertainment of the common people'. As a true practitioner Herr C can see beyond the vagaries of taste as an aesthetic judgement that re-inscribes class divisions.[5] Rather, he recognizes the potential of these puppets to upset all such hierarchies and distinctions by 'honouring this popularized version of a noble art [*Haufen erfundene*] with so much attention'. There is something of far greater significance at stake in the work of the marionettes than the narrator's facile concern with popular culture. The issue here is whether one can say with any certainty that there is any kind of bridge at all between theory and practice, and even if there were, what use would it be if the practical outcome could equally be achieved by the random chance of mechanical interaction. The movement of the marionette is not quite like the music that comes out of the barrel organ which is prescribed or programmed in advance by the perforated paper card or pimpled disk turned by the cranking handle. There is said to be a subtlety and mystery in the operation of the marionettes, whose movements are parabolic and random rather than programmed. It is not a straightforward calculation, or at least it is something more than a computation. That excess appears in both the final outcome of the appearance of dance, and in the detachment of the puppeteer from the effect of their marionette. The little figure of the marketplace puppet, provides the friends and the reader with a puzzle that asks to be figured out, a puzzle that might be the very question of figuration itself. That is to say, the puzzle of the creation of meaning and its undoing, of all making and unmaking, of theory as the impossible condition of possibility of practice and equally as Novalis puts it the puzzle of how 'any theory that awaits practice would be impossible'.[6]

Kleist points to this difficulty in the even shorter, and in some ways more baffling, text 'Reflection: A Paradox' [*Von der Uberlegung. Eine Paradoxe*] published in the same newspaper the week before *Über das Marionettentheater*.[7] Here he questions the common assumption that one should spend a period of cool reflection before taking a particular course of action. Kleist suggests that the proper time for reflection 'is not *before* you act, but *after*'. Reflection in advance will only serve to inhibit and confuse, whereas reflection after the fact enables us to analyse our actions and to guide future behaviour. 'Life itself is a struggle with Fate', says Kleist somewhat melodramatically, and when in a struggle the wrestler cannot calculate in advance the use of their muscles and limbs, but must act as required in the moment. It is only afterwards that it might be useful to think back on which moves worked and which failed: 'A man must like that wrestler, take hold of life and feel and sense with a thousand limbs how his opponent twists and turns, resists him, comes at him, evades him and reacts: or he will never get his way in a conversation, much less in a battle'.[8] The paradox of reflection is that it is only of use to us after we have acted, no theory can prepare us in advance for the moment in which we must act singularly, inventing as we go along in response to the unknown as it comes upon us. Another more successful Prussian soldier, general Helmuth von Moltke, later offered a similar perspective when he notes that 'no plan survives contact with the enemy'. Jean-Paul Sartre takes an analogous view of theory in a sporting context when he says 'in football, everything is complicated by the presence of the opposite team'.[9] From soccer to wrestling or invading France, it would seem that theory has a complex relation to practice, as the boxer Mike Tyson puts it 'everyone has a plan 'till they get punched in the mouth'.

The relation of Theory to Practice is not one of calculation, application, or linear succession. Rather theory is at risk in every practice and the risk of every practice. What the invention and improvisation of moments of practice risks is the truth of the theory that succeeds it. Theory by this reckoning is post hoc, an effect of, rather than the cause of, the practice it is said to prepare us for. The time of theory is the moment when the defeated wrestler lies flat on their back after a botched move. Theory is the reflection on the failures of practice, its errors and lacunae. As Kleist puts it, so that 'our powers of reflection may serve the purpose they were actually given us for, namely to bring to consciousness of what was wrong or unsound in how we acted and to regulate the feelings for other occasions in the future'. However, these occasions will not in themselves be future applications of a theoretical blueprint, rather they will further moments of invention and risk based upon the demands of an unknown future. In this sense theory is the future of practice, and simultaneously practice is the future of theory. Practice is only ever the theory of the future, while theory is only a preparation for its own risk and failure as practice.

If practice is the ruin of theory, it is because theory itself has always been ruined in advance by its constitutive relation to practice. The relation between theory and practice is beyond paradox; it is aporetic. No practice without theory and no theory without practice. But theory causes an impasse in practice. Kleist says it inhibits action, so theory must be ruined by action to be remade. Practice is what happens when theory gets punched in the mouth, but it is the repeated failure of practice that compels it to seek the advice of theory. No boxer, wrestler, football manager, or Field Marshal should stick their chin out without having theory in their corner. Theory is the result of its own repeated mauling as practice. There can be no future for theory without these defeats and no practice worthy of the name, one that is practising and learning from errors, without the necessary possibility of defeat. A practice without defeat is no practice at all, merely the mechanical fulfilment of an inevitable outcome. In such a situation there is nothing at risk and nothing that calls for reflection. There can be no theory under these circumstances. Victory produces no theory, for victory (absolute and without failure) would be the death of theory.

What is at issue in the discussion between the two friends in Kleist's text on the Marionettentheater is how far the appearance of dance on the part of the puppets can be attributed to algorithm and planning, and how much of it is independent of any such design and intention. Does the sweep of the dance imply the existence of a hidden hand directing the puppet show, or, are the marionettes the death and annulment of the puppeteer? In other words, what does the practice of the twirling puppets tell us about a theory of dance? Why does the Herr C, a primo ballerino, visit the marketplace over and over to reflect on the art of the puppets as a means of improving his own craft? And in the example of the puppets, why does he foresee a future in which the perfect marionette would excel all human achievement in dance? While the dancer is human, the puppets are mechanical, they do not fear for the future, nor do they appreciate the aesthetic sweep of their exquisite parabolas. The inhuman dancer of the future would be the end of all human practice because they would have nothing to risk and nothing to learn. Their achievement would not depend upon the possibility of failure that defines the aesthetic judgement that Herr C cannot escape or avoid making. Only a god could be the Lord of this dance.[10]

The rest of Kleist's narrative goes on to outline three examples of the philosophical problems raised by the puppet show. Herr C tells the narrator of prosthetic legs made by English craftsmen for the limbless, allowing them to dance in a 'limited' way but with 'ease, grace and poise'. These craftsmen could, says C, construct the flawless marionette of his imagination. The super puppet would, however, be inhuman 'incapable of *affectation* [*Denn Ziererei*]' which occurs 'whenever the soul (*vis motrix*) is situated in a place other than a movement's centre of gravity'. In contrast the puppet would only respond to gravity and its limbs would be 'dead, mere pendula'. Herr C cites several examples of 'mistakes' [*Mißgriffe*] in notable stars of the ballet where the 'soul' [*die Seele*] is trapped in human contortion. What C means by this vaguest of metaphysical terms is not clear at this point, is he referring to the aesthetic effect of the dance on the viewer or the struggle to bring meaning to consciousness by the dancer? Does he mean the critical reflection of theory or the failures of practice? Can the two be so easily separated in this story? He says that such mistakes 'have been unavoidable ever since we ate from the Tree of Knowledge'. In other words, the fall from grace and innocence into a world of knowledge and questioning is the cause of both aesthetic dissatisfaction and practical failure, ever since Cherubs began to guard the locked gate to Eden, and to correct this 'we shall have to go all the way round the world and see whether it might be open somewhere at the back again'.

Herr C continues, that unlike human dancers the marionettes are 'resistant to gravity' [*antigrav*] pulled upwards by a force greater than the one attracting them to the earth, and when they 'glance' [*streifen*] the ground they are given 'a new impetus' [*augenblickliche Hemmung*] to rise to new heights. The human fall attaches us to the ground where we must 'rest' [*ruhen*] to recover from the exertion of the dance in 'a moment which clearly is not dance at all in itself'. That is to say what defines the human dancer is the impossibility of dancing. The human is weighted to the ground and in order to be human must interrupt the dance with non-dancing. In fact, only the mechanical figure can truly dance. Herr C astonishes his interlocutor by suggesting 'it would be quite impossible for a human body even to equal the marionette. In dance, he said, only a god was a match for matter; and that was the point where the two ends of the round earth met' [*Nu rein Gott könne sich, auf diesem Felde, mit der Materie messen; und hier sei der Punkt, wo die beiden Enden der ringförmigen Welt in einander griffen*]. The restoration of the state of grace and innocence, or the perfect dance, cannot happen by sneaking in the back door to Paradise, but only in the impossible topology of an alternative universe in which the possibility of absolute knowledge without flaw or opening means that matter itself no longer matters. For humans as humans, the fall is permanent, and dance is impossible. Human dance can only ever be the failure of dance as choreography in ruins. One should not take the matter of practice too lightly, or, imagine that it as a simple restorative supplement to theory. Equally, no amount of theory will help us climb over the wall into Paradise. In fact, theory (questioning and the desire for knowledge) is the cause of our expulsion. The fall is merely an effect of theory. On these terms, the human condition would be one of fall, try again, fall again; and theory-practice would be a permanent parabasis not a sequential operation.[11] In a fallen state it would be increasingly difficult to distinguish theory from practice, the former protecting us from the banality of Paradise, the latter defining our aspiration to escape the inevitable limits of gravity. Success in this field would be inhuman, like the perfect marionette, and the end of theory, the last 'period of all human education' as Kleist's calls it.

The narrator tells the anecdote of a young man who loses his graceful ability to stand on one foot when he self-consciously repeats the action. In the end he becomes so critically aware that one by one he loses all is youthful charms within a year. Herr C responds with the story of a bear that had been trained to fence. The bear is able to parry any thrust with ease, while unlike a human fencer he makes no reaction to his opponent's feints designed to catch him off guard. Like the mechanical super puppet, the inhuman bear is said to excel any achievement, 'no fencer in the world can follow him in this – he did not even react: looking me in the eye, as though he could read my soul [*Aug in Auge, als ob er meine Seele darin lessen könnte*] in it'. The animal is more machine-like than the man, a reader without error, with an absolute knowledge of fencing. Fainting (falling to the ground) in dance and feinting in fencing are affectations only of the human, error and deception belong in the fallen state even if the human aspires to the dead perfection of the machine or the incorruptible instinct of the animal, as soul seeking to defy the uncircumventable law of gravity.[12] Even if the human is also an animal and defined by their relation to the machine, the fencer is something other than the bear, and different from the marionette, both of which excel the human without ever achieving humanity. In this sense, the fallen state of theory-practice is neither purely machinic nor entirely instinctive. It is rooted to the ground just as it looks to the stars.

Herr C feels confident that he has defended his paradoxical position against the narrator's insistence that there is more grace in the human body than in a mechanical marionette:

> You now have everything you need to understand me. We see that in the same measure as reflection in the organic world becomes darker and feebler, grace there emerges in ever greater radiance and supremacy – But just as two lines intersecting at a point after they have passed through infinity will suddenly come together again on the other side, or the image in a concave mirror, after travelling away into infinity, suddenly comes close up to us again, so when consciousness has, as we might say, passed through an infinity, grace will return; so that grace will be most purely present in the human frame that has either no consciousness or an infinite amount of it, which is to say either in a marionette or in a god.

This closing play to seal the argument with the narrator opens up as many questions as it shuts off. Herr C seems to suggest that it is true that the eclipse of reflection leads to the emergence of grace (like the question of 'soul' what are we to understand by this vague term? Is it cause or is it an effect?). However, that grace is never absolute. Perfection lies beyond infinity, in the supplement to the absolute, the room after the last chance saloon. In other words, it is a long way off and grace as it appears in the organic world can only ever be a semblance of grace, a parody of the absolute, which not even a journey to infinity will give us. Accordingly, grace lies where there is either no consciousness or in absolute consciousness, in the machine, the bear or in God. The fallen human has both consciousness and not enough of it, and can never be only a machine, must be other than the bear, and questioning of God's totalitarian wisdom. The being human of practice is then the failure of theory to close itself as absolute. Theory looks for the room after infinity in the knowledge that it will never find it. The feint of the aesthetic effect of the dancer or the artist is to persuade us that they have found it. But as Herr C says to the narrator only eating again from the Tree of Knowledge would allow us to fall back into the state of innocence and 'that is the last chapter in the history of the world'. A fall after the fall, a falling back that relinquished questioning, criticism and theory, would be the end of humanity, the final chapter in history. This fall would be a more severe crash than the one that defined our humanity. A second fall into either non-knowledge or absolute knowledge would not be worth risking for the sake of the humanities, even if we could find a way into Paradise in the room beyond infinity. On earth we are condemned not to the unbearable lightness of being but to the weight of theory-practice as the fate of neither a god nor a marionette.[13]

The theoretical and the practical sublime

Kleist himself might be characterized as someone in free fall between theory and practice. The date attributed to the conversation of *Über das Marionettentheater*, the winter of 1801, carries some significance for Kleist. It is shortly after Kleist's so-called Kant crisis in which he declared that having familiarized himself 'with the new, the so-called Kantian, philosophy' he realized that as a striver towards a 'higher stage of culture' his '*highest* and *only* goal in life has sunk'.[14] Biographers also attribute the Kant crisis with dissolution of his engagement to his fiancée Wilhelmine von Zenge.[15] As excuses go for getting out of an unwanted relationship, the effects of reading Kant is surely one of the least acceptable in the history of romance. However, in terms of literary production it would seem to have constituted a considerable fall for Kleist, if not a terminal one, given that all his published work was written after his '*Kanterlibnis*'. If Kleist fell from the heights of a high-minded belief 'that attaining perfection is the purpose of Creation', it was only to land in the fallen world of literature and philosophy from which he never escaped. Crisis, it might be said, became the permanent condition for Kleist both personally and artistically. Crisis and critique emerge from the same Kantian abyss of judgement [*krinein*] which defines the problem of theory and practice.

Kleist wrote to Wilhelmine in Berlin in March 1801, that 'truth' and 'culture' had been 'holy' ideas to him, which had led him to make 'the costliest sacrifices'. However, he was now 'deeply and painfully shaken' by the insights of Kant, which he shared with his fiancée:

> If people all had green lenses instead of eyes they would be bound to think that the things they see through them are green – and they would never be able to decide whether the eye shows them things as they are or whether it isn't adding something to them belonging not to them but to the eye. It is the same with our minds. We cannot decide whether what we call truth is truly truth or whether it only seems so to us. If the latter then the truth we gather here is nothing after

death – and all our striving to acquire something of our own that will go with us even into the grave, is in vain.¹⁶

As an explanation this summary may only tell half the story of Kant's understanding of '*Ding an sich*'. As an explanation of an annulled engagement the jilted one might think that this is also only telling half a story: 'Oh Wilhelmine, though your own heart may not be pierced by this thought do not think me ridiculous that I feel myself wounded deep in my innermost life by it'.¹⁷ The excuse of, 'it is not me, its Kant', runs a little hollow for those familiar with Kleist's more tender love letters to fellow Prussian soldiers.¹⁸ The conviction 'that no truth is discoverable here on earth' leads Kleist to give up reading and drives him 'to the cafés and tobacco houses' and 'even, to blot everything out, [I] did a very silly thing that I would rather Carl told you about than me'.¹⁹ That later sentence ought to have raised more concern on Wilhelmine's part than Kleist's eccentric take on Kant. Girl trouble aside we might note that this partial account is precisely the misprision of Kant that Kleist needs to drive him from personal religiosity, not into the arms of a bride, but to the embrace of writing.

Paul de Man identifies another move around Kant in Schiller, and we might add in passing Coleridge as a translator and adopter of Schelling to the list of those who find a reason to write in a misreading of Kantian philosophy.²⁰ De Man suggests that Schiller attempts 'to domesticate the critical incisiveness'²¹ of Kant in order to valorize a priori the aesthetic as an exemplary category and model for education, even for the state. De Man notes in his lecture on 'Kant and Schiller' that 'Kleist takes you back in a way to certain of the more threatening Kantian insights'.²² He identifies in Schiller's take on Kant a particular 'misreading' that will be of concern to us here, namely what happens in the passage from the cognitive to the performative: in other words, from theory to practice. De Man contends that the movement from conceptualization to occurrence, from trope to performance, is irreversible. This does not mean that the performative function is straightforward or can be accepted unproblematically. On the contrary, the performative is always recuperated within cognition. However, this relapse is not a reversal, it is a re-inscription that results in difference opening up the cognitive system as error is inscribed within it as a condition of its passage. We might say, that the fall of practice back into theory is its destiny and ruin. Given that practice also emerges from this fallen state we are only adding insult to injury the more we seek for clarity and truth. Practice as an event is neither progression nor regression, it is the reiteration of difference that makes meaning (its occurrence and reading) possible. This is neither dialectical nor a continuum, both of which would imply the possibility and primacy of cognition over the performative. Rather, and importantly, the separation and irreversibility between cognition and performance, theory and practice, 'allows for no mediation whatsoever'.[23] Nor is it the case that theory and practice are antithetical to each other, they are just different. The difficulties arise in the various tricks of the light that cause us to misrecognize one for the other or to imagine either as something other than itself. This is not a relativist denial of the truth of art, or the truth of history, or truth per se. Rather, it is a somewhat challenging appreciation of how 'truth' works, as a case of mistaken identity in the relapse of practice into theory as the event of practice itself. If it was necessary to describe Kleist's understanding of Kant as partial it is because he neglects to appreciate this recuperation of meaning that is the means by which truth is made and unmade in the world.[24] It is not that Kleist, like the rest of us, cannot find truth, but that when he comes across it, truth just might not look like the thing he was looking for. In fact, it might look a lot more like literature than he was expecting. There is no obligation to choose the death of no truth. Rather, it is necessary to pursue the undecidable condition of the world from the point of view of a wearer of green glasses as the experience of truth itself. A fall into writing, into theory-practice, is to embrace the limits of this aporia.

In the lecture on 'Kant and Schiller', de Man equates the move from cognitive to performative, or the passage from the tropological or figurative dimension of language, to the materiality of the event, with the difference between the mathematical and dynamic sublime in Kant. It is Schiller who translates this Kantian distinction into an alternative dichotomy, what he calls the theoretical and the practical sublime.[25] In Kant the mathematical sublime is characterized by the inability to fully comprehend magnitude by means of extendable models, and so can be thought of as the failure of representation. In Schiller the theoretical sublime is therefore the failure of cognition to adequately represent the thing it desires to know. The dynamic sublime in Kant is characterized by a relation to the power of nature, in which we determine our own predicament when faced with magnitude and overwhelming force.[26] In Schiller the practical sublime therefore concerns the desire for self-preservation when confronted by that which is practically, empirically stronger than us. De Man wants to arrest a slippage from Kant to Schiller. He contends that what interests Kant in the distinction between the mathematical and the dynamic sublime is what the failure of both tells us about the structure of the imagination. The dynamic sublime tells us nothing about how to achieve self-preservation in the face of tempests but might have something to say about the compulsive failure of representation to account for the thing it imagines is before it.

The difficulty for de Man arises in Schiller's valorization of the practical over the theoretical sublime. While Schiller characterizes the situation as 'we are defeated by the attempt to represent in the first form of the sublime [theoretical]; we are defeated by the attempt to oppose in the second case [practical]',[27] de Man contends that Schiller goes on in his account of Kant to concentrate on the practical sublime at the expense of the theoretical. In this sense 'he adds something to Kant which is not in Kant',[28] overstating the importance of the practical in Kant's schema. It is after Schiller that an entire conceptual order that privileges the practical over the theoretical emerges, the former being associated with the business of existence and materiality, while the latter concerns the failure of thinking and modelling to deal with the real world. We can see how that false opposition plays out in everything from attitudes to academic work undertaken in Ivory Towers to the favouring of the intuitiveness of artists or strong politicians over critical analysis. This privileging of practice over theory is endemic in Western culture. It is quite a charge to lay at the door of Schiller's over reading of Kant. De Man often has it in for Schiller; he needs his exemplary misreading as the fulcrum of his own corrective gesture. One might suspect that equally de Man is adding something to Schiller that may not be in Schiller. Or, if it is in Schiller, it is there for a reason because Schiller is also a writer and artist. The question, we might ask about Schiller is do the Letters on the Aesthetic Education of Man help us to understand better *Mary Stuart*?[29] Or, perhaps more pertinently in the context of this book, does Schiller's misreading of Kant help him write *Mary Stuart*?

The conclusion that Schiller draws from Kant is that if the dynamic sublime is to be privileged over the mathematical sublime then the terror of nature is more suitable for aesthetic representation than the idea of infinity. De Man characterizes this as 'psychologically and empirically entirely reasonable':

> If you think of them in terms of Schiller's own concerns as a playwright, if you don't ask the philosophical question, 'What is the structure of the faculty of the imagination?' but if you ask the practical question, 'How am I going to write successful plays?' which was partly and legitimately Schiller's concern – you will provoke a lot more effect on an audience by using terror or using scenes of terror, also using scenes in which Nature is directly threatening, than by using abstractions, such as infinity, which are not easily represented on the stage. So there is a total lack, an amazing, naïve, childish lack of transcendental concern in Schiller, an amazing lack of philosophical concern. He has no interest in it whatsoever. It doesn't bother him in the least that knowledge would be impossible, as long as he can fill his theatre.[30]

Well that about wraps it up for *Turnadot* and *Don Carlos*, as far as de Man is concerned.[31] Schiller's writing would seem to be just another case of the idealization of the practical at the expense of the theoretical. But what if this account of Schiller also carried within itself a certain blindness to the very gesture that de Man so readily wants to pin on Schiller. While de Man is attempting to recover the appropriate distinction and necessary balance that Kant finds in the equal failure of the mathematical and dynamic sublime, in doing so he might overly compensate and create a new idealization of his own, namely the privileging of the theoretical over the practical as one more example of the submission of art to philosophy. The practical in Schiller is equated with childishness and ignorance, even personal vanity and commercial gain: 'Schiller seems much more practically concerned ... well, I put it derisively, with his own success as a playwright'.[32] One should not underestimate the Yale professor's capacity as a comic writer; he knows how to take down a straw man through rhetorical means as well as philosophical exactitude.

However, equally, while de Man needs to align Schiller's misreading with moral deficiency to prove a point, his own intent in reading Schiller is actually to show the complexity of thought in Kant that is ironed out in Schiller. Our own interest in reading this account of de Man's Schiller is to draw out precisely this question that arises from an encounter with Kant, namely the complex relation between theory and practice that are both examples of the failures of representation. Even if we were to take de Man's Schiller at face value, assuming that this is what Schiller actually says, there may be a value to the violence he inflicts on the theoretical in favour of the practical. De Man calls it 'a total idealism', which in privileging reality, loses touch with the reality of reality, and banalizes thought. If it were true, this would be something to hold Schiller to account for. However, we might note that Schiller's seeming effacement of philosophy takes the form of a philosophical essay. De Man is not reading *William Tell* or *An die Freude*, which he would have to account for in different terms than Schiller's reading of Kant in 'Vom Erhabenen'.[33] This is a curiously compromised kind of idealism, if one not unique to Schiller. It might in fact be a move that Schiller cannot avoid making, a trap that he has no choice but to walk into as has everyone else who has followed him. As de Man says, 'don't decide too soon that you are beyond Schiller in any sense. I don't think any of us can lay this claim. Whatever writing we do, whatever way we have of talking about art, whatever way we have of teaching, whatever justification we give ourselves for teaching, whatever the standards are and the values by means of which we teach, they are more than ever and profoundly Schillerian. They come from Schiller, and not from Kant'.[34] In other words, liberal humanities education depends upon a confusion between the practical and the pragmatic that privileges the aesthetic as a model by which we survive the magnitude of existence by the maintenance of reason. An alternative, Kantian, pedagogy would insist on the importance of the theoretical in the failure of the aesthetic to shelter us from the storm: 'And if you ever try to do something in the other direction [Kantian rather than Schillerian] and you touch on it you'll see what will happen to you. Better be very sure, wherever you are, that your tenure is very well established, and the institution for which you work has a very well-established reputation. Then you can take some risks without really taking many risks'.[35] For example, it would be a brave reader who found in Kant reason to call out the present academic discourse on practice-based research, and the distribution of funding that depends upon its protocols, as a domestication of practice through an idealization of the pragmatic that relies upon the effacement of theoretical thought in favour of the utility of practice. However, the Arts and Humanities Research Council might not be the only people who have misread Kant and the least that can be said here is that academic writing on art is based upon not only a collective failure of imagination but literally on a collective misunderstanding of the failure of the imagination.

Schiller's concern is psychological; Kant's interest is philosophical. De Man wishes to dispel the confusion that mistakes one from the other. Schiller institutes an empirical moment of practical coping with the danger of nature that, says de Man, is nowhere to be found in Kant's schema of the failed responses of imagination to magnitude. This slippage between Kant and Schiller is for de Man 'idealism as an ideology' (p. 146) because it both privileges an unreal reality and a perfect intellect, entirely separated from the material world and sensory experience, capable of understanding the world. What terrified Kleist the most was the impossibility of such a position. In this sense, on de Man's terms, Kleist is a better reader of Kant than Schiller. 'As fallen beings ... we are incapable of pure intellect' (p. 146) says de Man reminding us of the impossibility of theory as much as the paradise of reality. Ironically, it is Schiller's lack of transcendental concerns that leads to an idealist position in which the intellect transcends the aesthetic as a resolution for the threat to existence, while in de Man's Kant it is precisely imagination that is the symptom of a failure to achieve pure intellect, and it is the failure of the imagination that leads to aesthetic contemplation. The slip that Schiller makes between the aesthetic as an expandable model for education (the theoretical sublime) and what it teaches us about how to cope with the terrors of the world (the practical sublime) relies upon a dichotomization that simultaneously over privileges practice and provides a route to transcending the practical in an idealized pure intellect. However, while Schiller is at risk of transcending the aesthetic, he also has a full theatre. We might say, that he seems to have the best of all possible worlds. Unfortunately, if we follow de Man, Schiller is as poor a philosopher as he is successful an impresario. Why does this matter?

Schiller is surely an exemplary case of the critical practice of a theory-practitioner that concerns us in this study. Does it matter if he is wrong as a philosopher, and what implications would this have for a staging of one of his plays? One is tempted to answer, practically none, or none in theory. As de Man suggests, 'whatever writing we do, whatever way we have of talking about art, whatever way we have of teaching … they are more than ever and profoundly Schillerian' (p. 142). That is to say, 'in practice' we all tend towards the belief or accept the idea that it is indeed possible to transmit theory into practice. For example, the defence that is most commonly made of the humanities is that reading books and viewing art helps us to operate in the world as well-informed human beings, rather than the more radical defence that a Humanities education teaches us that a humanities education is impossible and at the same time should disabuse us of every such illusion about the humanities and teaching. Such a position is unlikely to go down well in the Dean's office or with the Arts and Humanities Research Council. The position that de Man assigns to Schiller is that of the unconscious levelling out of the complexity that is thrown up by the failure of representation, as a way of continuing to be able to accept representation as the only mode of understanding the world. De Man's Schiller's version of representation is a mimetic mode of understanding, whether it is through aesthetic models for education, or the belief that such models can be repeated in the world as a way of dealing with the chaos of magnitude. Mimesis persists as an effect even if the production of that effect (writing and reading, making or viewing art, teaching and studying) undoes the possibility of the efficiency of that effect. However, rather than reside in that moment of unmaking and disruption, we all make it to the other shore of the mimetic effect, living with an illusion rather than the critical interruption. The effect of closure is the outcome of the very failure of representation to fully represent in a complete transmission, and the impossibility of closure is the condition that makes closure both a formal trope and endlessly desirable.

In giving his lecture on Schiller, de Man is intent on convincing his audience of the true critical nature of representation, and so repeats the mimetic mode that he is attempting to undo. The idiom of the lecture would be, on de Man's own terms, Schillerian through and through. This does not mean that de Man is a self-deluded dolt rather he is just a teacher and a writer, or simply, a human being operating in the world. There is no way of escaping the recuperation of the mimetic, no easy route outside of thinking as the success and failure of mimesis. It is the duty of critical philosophy to hold open the gap between disruption and closure as the condition of critical thinking and affirming that gap as a way of thinking through the difficulties of living in the world. However, there is no such duty beholden to writing or art, which works according to a different set of protocols, including aesthetic affect, formal complexity or simplicity, and so on. It is not just that Schiller is more concerned with filling his theatre than reading Kant, it is that Schiller like most us are more concerned with living in the world than affirming the constitutive aporia of representation. However, just as we cannot avoid falling back into the illusion of mimesis, we are saved from the deadening possibility of its efficiency by its own structural impossibility. That is to say, if the untroubled transmission of theory into practice were possible, we would always be up against the fencing bear, who pre-empts our every move with an unbeatable defensive parry, closing off any possibility of failure or injury. Transmitting theory into practice without risk or failure, would mean entirely predictable, programmed, and closed outcomes, like the bear's expert ripostes. It would be another version of the last chapter of the end of the world. Schiller's letters on aesthetic education, are on de Man's reading, the bear of Kleist's sporting nightmare: an impenetrable, sealed template that is the death of creativity and alternative futures. Fortunately, the bear is a creature of fiction, and an aesthetic education can never provide enough resources to counter all the thrusts and blows that come with living in the world. Theory is not a hermetically sealed armour against the rigours of the world, or the risks of art, and cannot communicate itself without failure of misreading.

However, despite the position that de Man would like to assign to Schiller, it is not quite true to say that Schiller is not a philosopher. Schiller is an artist and impresario but he is also a philosopher, what other designation might we attribute to the author of '*Von Erhabenen*'? It is not that Schiller is using philosophy to escape philosophy into some other material realm. He is straightforwardly attempting to write in a philosophical manner as one of the many idioms at his disposal. The fact that he is not as careful a reader of Kant as Paul de Man, does not preclude his text from being ascribed the name of philosophy. And whether we believe that Schiller has introduced into Kant something that does not exist in the text of Kant is strictly irrelevant to his identity as a philosopher-practitioner. Schiller is in a sense correct, if a bad philosopher. While reading Thomas Mann or Immanuel Kant may not help us get off the mountaintop, either somehow we manage to get home safe or we die of exposure. The knowledge that reading Mann will not save you from exposure is no more use to you when faced with the oncoming storm than having appreciated the art of David Casper Friedrich. The mimetic illusion of Schillerian aesthetic ideology encourages the belief that you will get home alive. While the critical philosophy of Kant says whether you get home alive or not has nothing to do with the books that you have read. However, the motivation to put one foot in front of the other and find a path down the mountain is probably going to be more useful to you than the self-satisfaction of knowing that rescue is impossible and that impasse is inevitable. That is to say, one would rather be out in a storm with Schiller than with Kant. It is surely better to be armed with the mistaken belief that you know what you are doing than freeze to death exposed to the insurmountable elements. This is also to say that one would be better off trying to write a play or make a movie with Schiller rather than Kant. This is not to accept the ironing out of complexity in thought or to accept the possibility of a complete and closed mimetic model. Rather, it is to suggest that as a writer or maker of art (or philosophy for that matter) there is no escape from the desire to make it off the mountaintop alive. Setting off down the mountain without a map is no bar from making it, nor a guarantee that you will not end up trapped on a precipice or even falling from a great height. The writing or the making is not the end result of finding a way home but the process by which the twists and turns of the path are improvised and invented. Making it out alive is not only a pragmatic psychological predisposition but the empirical ideological utilization of Kantian critical philosophy in a way that is entirely un-Kantian.

De Man recognizes this as his reading of Kant and Schiller develops. He notes that while the pragmatic principle of closure is not open to critical philosophy, he identifies in the Letters on Aesthetic Education, the introduction of the term 'free play' [*spieltrieb*] into Schiller's dialectic between the theoretical and the practical. Play in this sense is both the performance of closure from theory to practice 'as if' it were possible but also the give and flex between the two terms in order to prevent a dialectical collision. There may be rules to this play, like soccer, but like soccer those rules are arbitrary and rely upon the appearance of closure, even though they are open to interpretation and improvisation. De Man suggests 'the human is defined as a certain principle of closure which is no longer accessible to rational critical analysis. And we know from Kleist how this notion of balance between the human and what is not human can get out of hand' (p. 151). The super-marionette or the unbeatable bear are examples of what might happen when theory is achieved absolutely, while the young man who falls from grace and loses his balance is an example of what can happen when the appearance of closure is denied to the human experience.

The play between the illusion of closure and its undoing is the play between appearance and reality. This is precisely the place of art or fiction as the site of a principle that holds the mutual compatibility of the real and unreal in a productive tension. What art and writing teach us is that appearances matter. De Man suggests:

> Only people who are very stupid, says Schiller, or people who are extraordinarily smart, too smart, have no use for *Schein*, have no use for appearance. Those who are entirely stupid don't need appearance, they are unable to conceive it; those who are entirely rational don't have to resort to it (Letter XXVI, pp. 190–3). In that you could substitute – one who would be entirely stupid in those terms would be Kant, for example, when he describes the world as being completely devoid of teleological impact, as having no appearance but only reality. And one of those who are much too smart, who are smart through and through and can saturate the entire world with intellect, would be for example, Hegel, who would not, according to this assumption, need *Schein* anymore. (p. 152)

In other words, Kant is stupid enough to die on top of the mountain to demonstrate the truth of his critical philosophy, while Hegel is smart enough to think that what you see is what you get and that if you want off the mountaintop then playing, or imitating, a mountaineer is probably no bad thing. The task of de Man's Schiller is not to choose between the illusion of closure and the impossibility of closure, between practice and theory, art, and criticism, but to give the appearance of having done so and for the choice to somehow seem to matter.

De Man also addresses Schiller in the related text 'Aesthetic Formalization: Kleist's *Über das Marionettentheater*', given as the second Messenger Lecture at Cornell University in 1983 (the text 'Kant and Schiller' was given as the fifth and final lecture in the series).[36] In this extended reading de Man concentrates on Kleist's text as an allegory of teaching and the implications of Schiller's model of aesthetic education for the ideological reproduction of the state.[37] Here he characterizes the lesson of Kleist's text as 'a complication of the mimetic function of narrative' (p. 273). That is to say, the mimetic structure of closure 'asserts itself, by ways of the possibility, or the necessity of narrative formalization' (p. 273). Narrative completeness is the means by which the supposed adequacy of representation imposes itself as a seemingly natural event. However, it is the impossibility of ever closing off a story or exhausting its lacunae or retelling that undoes any claim that representation can make to be either complete or natural.

De Man comments on the way that Kleist's prose plays with mimesis in both a ludic and critical way. Rather, than recount the entirety of de Man's reading of Kleist, we might just note that he is identifying in the narrative structure of Kleist's essay the same play that we saw between the theoretical and practical sublime in Schiller's version of Kant, namely the inadequacy of both as a failure of representation itself and the necessity of both to present themselves as full and complete. We should note, following de Man, that the play between theory and practice is not a dialectic in classical terms but a radical and irreversible interruption that can only result in a forward movement of inscription and iteration, what we might call a process without conclusion, one that is exhausting rather than exhaustive.

Falling for Kleist

Towards the end of de Man's essay on 'Aesthetic Formalization' in Kleist he cites but does not dwell on another narrative text by the Prussian, 'On the Gradual Fabrication of Thoughts While Speaking' ['*Über die allmähliche Verfertigung der Ganken beim Reden*'].[38] As in the short text on reflection, Kleist's essay offers a counter-intuitive take on thought and action.[39] He proposes that the best way to think through a problem is not solitary contemplation but to talk it through with another person: 'A man in the act of speaking finds a strange source of inspiration in the face of his listener; and a look that signals the comprehension of a half-expressed thought will often inspire us with the entire second half of that thought. I am convinced that many a great speaker, in that moment of opening his mouth to speak, has been unsure of what he was about to say. But trusting the circumstances to provide both the right line of ideas and the necessary mental stimulation, he is encouraged to make a beginning' (p. 219). Citing the example of the performative inauguration of the revolutionary assembly by General Mirabeau and the fable of the Lion in La Fontaine, Kleist suggests that thoughts are best formulated in the act of speaking rather in a moment of prior introspection, 'The lines of thought and expression move abrest, and both mental processes are congruent to each other. Speech is not a fetter, then like a drag chain on the wheel of the mind, but a second wheel running parallel to it on the same axle' (221). Kleist seems to have conceived of the Segway some two hundred years before it materialized as a mode of transport, or perhaps he is thinking of a wheelchair.

Kant was fond of thinking about wheelchairs as well but in his case he described examples as the *Gängelwagen* [wheelchairs] of philosophy, the means by which infirm thinking makes progress.[40] Kleist in contrast makes a positive virtue of thinking aloud, 'the situation is quite different when the mind has thought everything out before anything is spoken. In the act of pure expression speech must assume a secondary role, which, far from speeding it forward, will rather slow it down. It follows from this that an idea confusedly expressed need not have been confusedly conceived: on the contrary, the most confusedly expressed may have been the most clearly thought out' (p. 221). It is not so much that theory puts the brakes on practice, but that theory is no guarantee of success in practice. Rather, practice would seem to be a form of working out theory as one goes along, in which one is pushed to creativity by the limits and pressures of a given situation. Kleist's commentary here is more obviously a text on education that the Marionettetheatre essay, as he concludes by condemning the 'disagreeable' and 'distasteful' custom of oral examinations in which 'only very commonplace minds, which memorize a definition … one day and forget it the next' (p. 222) can succeed. Thinking aloud is not necessarily a benefit in an educational system that values verbatim and rote learning. Such exams only ever assess the capacity of an individual to pass such exams, valuing a pure tautology over creativity and critical thinking. For Kleist the whole exercise is indecent, 'one would be embarrassed to ask someone to empty his wallet for our inspection, let alone the contents of his mind' (p. 222). It is a pity that the scruples of the Prussian officer class do not extend to certain Ministers of Education today, who mistake the reactionary practice of cramming and repetition for academic rigour.

The situation that Kleist describes here will be familiar to any writer up against an editor's deadline or a filmmaker faced with a fixed budget, necessity being the mother of invention. But even without the material pressures of a context for making, the act of creation itself cannot be programmed in advance. Even for the writer with a set commission it is never clear what will be written until the moment of writing, when thought and action work in tandem to produce what will come at that moment. In any good piece of writing, not only should the reader not know what is coming next but nor should the author. This applies equally to so-called 'creative' and so-called 'theoretical', academic, non-fiction, or journalistic writing. The greater the degree of uncertainty as to the outcome of the writing, the more one might want to claim for it the name of creativity, but in this sense, creativity is not restricted to genre or idiom. We might say that all writing is creative writing, and where we do not find creativity in writing we do not have writing at all. The most functional of reports or précises may be less obviously creative and more easily determined according to the desire for a pre-set outcome, but they are distinguished by the degree of invention to be found in them, not by the complete absence of the creative. To use Kleist's term the articulation of the new requires fabrication, even when there is not much that is truly new about the end result. Fabrication (making or constructing) in its modern English usage comes from the verb to fabricate, which has the added sense of lying or storytelling. Making is also 'making up' and in the context of the process of writing we might add 'making up as you go along'.

Fabrication as a noun seems to predate the verb to fabricate. Fabrication, first used to mean manufacturing or construction derives in English from the Middle French *fabrication* and so from the Latin *fabricationem* (nominative *fabrication*) meaning a structure, construction or a making, declining from the verb *fabricare*, to make or construct.[41] The sense of fabrication as lying or forgery appears much later in English, circa 1790. Fable, in contrast, comes from the Old French *fable* meaning story, tale, lie or falsehood, from the Latin *fabula* which means story or lesson, but is related to the verb *fari* meaning to speak or tell, giving *fabula* the sense of everyday talk or what we now call news, perhaps what Kleist as a journalist recognizes in conversations Molliere is supposed to have had with his maid when suffering from writer's block, or General Mirabeau's improvised foundation of a revolutionary constitution.[42]

In the essay on aesthetic formalization, de Man comments on Kleist's use of German in this shorter text on the fabrication of thoughts. He notes: 'as we know… the memorable tropes that have the most success (*Beifall*) occur as mere random improvisation (*Einfall*) at the moment when the author has completely relinquished any control over his meaning and has relapsed (*Zurückfall*) into the extreme formalization, the mechanical predictability of grammatical declensions (*Fälle*)' (p. 290). Within the pages of Kleist's German there is a lot of falling, over and over again. De Man here wishes to suggest that not only can the success (*Beifall*) or a performative utterance such as the proclamation by the revolutionary general and its improvised status (*Einfall*) but that moment of invention is also a falling back (*Zurückfall*) onto the power of language to generate meanings independent of the intention of a speaker or author. The speech writes itself in the moment of its making, its grammar declining as it conjugates. That is to say, that the speaker is not quite in control of what is said. They are, in the moment of creation, in free fall in the abyss between theory and outcome. The stories of the Lion in Fontaine and General Mirabeau suggest that at such moments of improvised public speaking the authors (fictional or historical) do not have the benefit of a safety net and their dive into the unknown is not without risks, without a harness or a parachute the sky might fall in on their heads at any moment.

However, de Man reminds us that *Fälle* in German also means trap, and the trap here is particularly cunning. On the one hand, there is assumption that the General's words are an adequate representation of a political or historical truth, rather than a form of words that runs away from him in the heat of the moment. This is Schiller's faith in the faculty of the imagination, a trap that imagines that the guide knows the way down from the mountaintop and is not just as lost as you. This, de Man would call, 'the ultimate trap, as unavoidable as it is deadly' (p. 290). On the other hand, there may be another trap door for us to fall through here, namely that of Kant, the one who is snared and unable to move, caught in the vice-like grip of criticality when faced with the knowledge of the incommensurability of speech and thing. With traps to the left and to the right, where is the faller to land to avoid injury or capture? Writing, and by extension all creative making, is a trap without escape, both lure and ruse, leading to secret passageways, necessarily part of the performance of staging the event of invention, whether the outcome is a magic disappearing act or the panic of the gallows. When the earth gives way beneath the feet of the artist, in the fall of writing, for a moment we are suspended in mid-air, not knowing if we are coming or going. It is this uncertainty that defines the moment of creation.

However, falling is all a matter of perspective, as Buzz Lightyear notes in *Toy Story*, while others may think that he is flying, he is in fact merely 'falling with style'.[43] Kleist comments in the Marionettetheatre text that the blunders of human dancers are 'unavoidable, since we have eaten of the tree of knowledge… Paradise is locked and bolted and the Cherub is behind us'. It is not just that we inevitably fall when making the leap from theory to practice but that we have always been in a fallen state from the beginning and it is theory itself, questioning and the desire to know, the fruit of the forbidden tree, that is the permanent condition of humanity and of the Humanities. The fall of practice is not a tumble from security into uncertainty. It is the plunge from one state of incompleteness and not-knowing to another. This is a fall without guarantee of a soft landing or even of a known destination. The fall of creativity is a descent down the rabbit hole of process; theory is merely a series of ledges and outcrops that break our fall on the way down, no more secure or terminal than the fall itself. Theory is likely to give way beneath our feet like a trap door, suspending us in a deathly grip or accelerating our descent. Theory is the fallen state of humankind, questioning never leads to answers only to further questions, which confirm how little we actually know. In this sense, theory is the resource that undoes its own ambitions, and it is the permanently fallen condition of theory that compels us to seek out an alternative ground through practice. One response to Kant and Schiller arguing on the mountaintop is to take matters into our own hands and jump head first off the cliff edge in the hope that it is as good a strategy as any for responding to the oncoming storm. However, it is no more likely to result in success than any other plan, it would simply be another experience of failing to descend without harm.

Jesus-Kleist

There is of course a difference between falling and having fallen. In the case of theory, the human condition is that of the fallen state with no way back to Paradise. In the moment of creation, we are experiencing a fall without prospect of reaching safety. The law of gravity dictates that there comes a point when everybody needs a place to rest. Falling only leads to the fallen state. This is not an experience of fallenness for the first time. It is not an original fall. We throw ourselves off the cliff edge in an attempt to escape the paralysis of our fallen state. Equally, while the expulsion from Paradise may lead to the fall of humankind, there is a fall before the Fall that creates the conditions for falling, namely the fall of Satan and his rebel angels. This is a pre-originary fall, a fall that proceeds falling. And it is spectacular:

> … from Morn
> To Noon he fell, from Noon to dewy Eve,
> A Summers day; and with the setting Sun
> Dropt from the Zenith like a falling Star,
> On Lemnos th' Ægean Ile. (*Paradise Lost* I, 742–6)[44]

Satan may fall like a shooting star and light up the evening sky as he blazes a trail but eventually he reaches his destination, namely Hell, or Greece. It is from here that he sets out to tempt humanity into a fall of its own, encouraging humanity to partake of his own vice: questioning. It is not vanity or pride that leads Lucifer to raise an army in the hope that heaven will fall to him, it is the questioning of authority, the refusal of predestination and the absolute decree.

Reason is the reason that Satan fell, but as Milton's God says in his own defence 'Reason also is choice' (II, 108). The angels were made 'sufficient to have stood, though free to fall' (II, 99) it was their choice to question rather than offer 'true allegiance, constant Faith or Love' (II, 104) to the almighty. Questioning the almighty and defying the omnipotent might be the very definition of the exercise of reason. If reason is a choice, in the context of Milton's poem, it is a choice between exercising reason or suppressing it. That is no choice at all since reason will always lead to a fall. God in his wisdom might argue that reason ought to have told Satan that it is unreasonable to 'durst defie th'Omnipotent to Arms' (I, 49) and the rational calculation would have been to sign up to eternal devotion. But there is seldom anything reasonable about reasoning. The problem for Satan is that there is just no career progression in heaven, 'better to reign in Hell, than serve in heaven' (IV, 263). Satan's error, the cause of his defeat, is the belief that having exhausted reason, the leap into practice will result in an outcome that reason tells him is impossible. The choice that he makes, his decision, is not the result of programmed rationality but of faith in the primacy of practice. There is no evidence base or ground to support his decision, it is a pure leap of faith. On this basis God ought to commend Satan for a belief in faith itself that supersedes his faith in the almighty. Satan is unquestioning of belief, which he considers something more worthy of allegiance than the highly questionable powers of the omnipotent. This leap from theory to practice, one which will inevitably fail, is a leap of faith, decision is never decisive and choice is not predestination. If the outcome of a decision could be determined in advance there would be no decision to make, the exercise of reason would be merely the running of a computational programme. Decisions require us to act unreasonably with respect to reason, without firm foundations in which to ground those decisions. Faith is not the opposite of reason, it is the condition for its operation, its ruin and wellspring.[45] It is surely unreasonable of God not to acknowledge that. However, without solid ground beneath our feet we are heading for a fall. Falling then is an inevitable consequence of reason, and there really is no choice about it. We might say that Theory comes before a fall.

If theory is the vice of Satan, then it is theory that gives rise to the fall of humanity. It is a primordial, structural fallenness that makes the fall of man and woman inevitable. There is a choice to be made between eating of the forbidden tree or not, but as a choice it is aporetic. Eve has to choose between knowledge and innocence, or to put it another way she has to choose between choosing and not choosing, and that is already a choice. In other words, insofar as Eve was faced with the agony of choice, humanity was already in a fallen state before she ate the apple. The tree of knowledge is a trap, put there in the Garden of Eden to act as the cause of an effect that already precedes it. It is the trap door that gives way beneath the feet of Adam and Eve, as they fall out of Paradise. It is also the tree that humanity hangs itself from. The tree of knowledge was not put in the garden by Satan but by that unreasonable old tyrant God. Who creates an earthly paradise and then fences off part of it as forbidden? As soon as the tree was planted humankind was heading for a fall. Satan could quite easily claim constructive dismissal from heaven; the descendants of Adam and Eve could consider a class action suit against God for carelessly leaving temptation in their forebears' path. They could reasonably argue that the serpent was in the garden long before Satan turned up. God better have a good lawyer.

Falling then is not the aberrant outcome of an unsuccessful leap of faith, it is structural to the very possibility of action. Failure is what makes action possible. If practice guaranteed success, all practice would come to a halt. It may be the end of theory to believe in the end of theory but in practice this can never be the case. Practice itself can never close itself off; practice cannot complete itself or realize itself as anything other than process. In this sense, there no choice to be made between theory and practice, as if there could ever be a choice between choosing and doing, that was not already a choice. It is the originary fallenness of theory that makes the fall of practice possible, given that the fall of theory is itself already a practical matter. In practice Satan cannot escape the vice of theory, it is trap laid out for him in advance and his faith in theory is just as mistaken as his faith in practice. It is the fallen state of theory that is the practical condition of practice, a sort of 'felix ruina' that makes the process of redemption possible, given that on these terms redemption itself is impossible. Successful redemption would be the last chapter in the history of the world, the end of all theory and the termination of every practice. As long as we are unable to climb back through the trap door into Paradise, we are condemned to go on, in the long fall of process, 'we must make a journey around the world, to see if a back door has perhaps been left open' as Kleist puts it. However, even if it has been left unguarded that back door is merely another trap door that will send us tumbling out of Paradise once more. We are forever falling even if our faith in practice compels us to believe that the fall is perfectible. As habitual fallers we might choose to paraphrase Beckett: Ever tried? Ever fallen? No matter. Try again. Fall again. Fall better.[46]

Satan may finally stop falling and land in Hell, but his project of the perpetual corruption of humankind is a practical attempt to 'awake, arise, or be for even fall'n' (I, 330). In Milton's poem he fails once again, or, in succeeding lays the foundations of his subsequent failure, even if it took Milton another four years to write the sequel Paradise Regained.[47] This later poem ends not with death and resurrection but with another fall. It concludes with the scene from Matthew 4 (5-7) when Satan tempts Jesus to fall:

> The devil took Him up into the holy city, set Him on the pinnacle of the temple, and said to Him, 'If You are the Son of God, throw Yourself down. For it is written: "He shall give His angels charge over you",
> and,
> "In their hands they shall bear you up,
> Lest you dash your foot against a stone"'.[48]

Jesus' response is not to take up the challenge of falling and risk his angels letting him down once more, but instead he replies 'It is written again, "You shall not tempt the Lord your God"'. In other words, Jesus thinks a fall can be avoided by answering a quotation with a quotation, trumping one text with another. He avoids the temptation of a practical fall by a retreat into theory. God made human is not prepared to put the question of his omnipotence at risk by taking a fall that would demonstrate that he alone could survive such a descent. Perhaps only a God can resist a fall, we have no proof here either way whether he could survive one. Jesus instead puts his faith in theory; being both fully human and fully God, Jesus is the one character in textual history who can pull that off even if it seems an inadequate or impractical response. In this sense Jesus would seem to be more Kantian than Schillerian.

In Milton's version, the response is stunning, 'Satan smitten with amazement fell' (IV, 562). He is compared to the great comic faller of antiquity the wrestling giant Antaeus, who:

> ... oft foil'd still rose,
> Receiving from his mother Earth new strength,
> Fresh from his fall, and fiercer grapple joyn'd,
> Throttl'd at length in the Air, expir'd and fell. (IV, 565-8)

Hercules crushes Antaeus to death in a bear hug, rather than seek two falls or a submission, so his final fall is final. In contrast this is just the latest in a long line of falls for Milton's Satan who 'Fell whence he stood to see his Victor fall' (IV, 571). There is a slight of foot and in a reversal of the theory, Satan falls rather than Jesus, bringing only 'Ruin, and desperation, and dismay' to one 'Who durst so proudly tempt the Son of God' (IV, 579-80). Once more putting theory into action only results in a downfall for Satan, and practice is again the ruin of theory. Jesus in contrast is borne aloft by angels who take him to a celestial table to end his period of fasting with 'Fruits fetcht from the tree of life' (IV, 589) the second named tree in Genesis 2 alongside the tree of the knowledge of good and evil. Milton's Jesus, then, chooses life over knowledge, practice over theory, although he has the advantage of presumably already knowing the difference between good and evil, his heavenly Father having invented both. But the significance of Milton's ending here is that having resisted Satan and having refused to fall, this is said to be the moment of redemption of humanity. Jesus:

> ... by vanquishing
> Temptation, hast regain'd lost Paradise,
> And frustrated the conquest fraudulent:
> He never more henceforth will dare set foot
> In Paradise to tempt; his snares are broke:
> For though that seat of earthly bliss be fail'd,
> A fairer Paradise is founded now
> For Adam and his chosen Sons. (IV, 607-14)

This is quite a rewriting of the Bible by Milton. The refusal to plunge from the top of the temple in Jerusalem seems to be enough to redeem humanity; it is adequate simply to have set the example of overcoming temptation through banter or the exchange of bon mots. But in doing so, Jesus has not only done away with the traps, or snares, of Satan but has solved the entire problem of returning to Paradise by giving it up as a failed state and founding a new 'fairer Paradise', somewhere even more perfect than perfection, which presumably means this time he will not make the mistake of putting temptation in there by fencing bits of it off or by planting a tree of knowledge. The fairer Paradise is of course the new Jerusalem of earth, which in a dazzling sleight of hand replaces the old Paradise of Eden, now boarded up and written off as forever ruined by Satan's shenanigans. The solution to the fallen state then would seem to be to accept the fallen world as Paradise: it does not get any better than this. By resisting temptation, Jesus is said to 'vanquish' all temptation because he gives us the grace to overcome it. In this new Paradise, God has learnt from his past mistakes and will not attempt to fence off temptation but to embrace it as part of the deal of living in the world. Falling is part of life but it would seem Jesus is our bungee cord, and Paradise is not regained by moving back to Eden but by a new prospectus from God's estate agent that convinces us that we are better off where we are, now that Jesus has moved into the district.

Biblical scholars among you will note that the temptation in the desert occurs relatively early in Jesus' career, and there is a whole other set of events, some good some bad, that we have yet to pass through before theologically speaking we can claim that paradise has been regained. However, Milton has Jesus refreshed from his heavenly feast return quietly to his 'Mothers house' (IV, 639) in suburban Nazareth and he ends the poem here. That is to say, that the second poem is not actually about the story of human redemption, rather it is literally about regaining the plot of land where Adam and Eve lived in earthly bliss. The 'Paradise' in the title of both poems does not refer to a state of spiritual being, it refers ultimately to property. Jesus is said to regain Paradise by overcoming temptation at the top of the temple, and so his angels take him there to dine in the knowledge that Satan will never return there. The cost of regaining Paradise is that the old place has been turned into a restaurant and is now going to be written off as a home for humans who will be persuaded to accept their home on earth as the best of all possible worlds. The price to be paid for regaining Paradise is to lose Paradise all over again. It is just another fall passed off as a victory, or the attempt by God to convince humans that fallenness is prime real estate. There is no outside to the fallen condition, it was already there in Eden from the start, and it is still there after victory over Satan is proclaimed. Only a God can be exempt from falling, because he is too big to fall. As Kleist says 'only a god … could prove a match for matter' because only he can defy gravity. The rules do not apply to the sovereign. His son on the other hand, thinks that an unquestioning faith in theory can cover over the cracks in any risky practice. In this sense he is close to the position of the narrator of the Marionettetheatre essay who also insists, until the rug is pulled from under his feet at the end, on keeping up the pretence that successful practice comes from the application of good theory and that theory derives from the detailed observation of impeccable practice. This countersignature, the one that we adopt all the time as the ultimate and unavoidable trap of writing, we can only give into temptation here and give the name Jesus-Kleist. However, only a celestial being like Satan can ever truly land; human beings contrary to the advice issued by Milton's estate agent are still falling in theory and in practice.

3

Blindness and Touching

In the previous chapter, it was suggested that theory and practice should not be thought of as separate activities, the one preceding the other, or realizing the intent of the other. Rather, following our reading of Kleist's essay on the *Marionettetheatre* it should be increasingly difficult to determine where theory begins and where practice ends and vice versa. Instead, theory and practice should be thought of as not just mutually enforcing but as the condition of possibility of each other. There will be creative practitioners who embrace this aporia and whose work pushes the contradictions and paradoxes to the limit as the condition of further progress in their art. Examples of such writers, artists, and filmmakers will be examined in greater depth in the second part of this book. Equally, there will be practitioners who claim that their art bears no relation to theory and that their work is a result of, say, the inspiration of the muses or of the realization of personal suffering in the medium of their choosing. Such attitudes are commonplace and are by no means a deterrent to producing great art.[1] However, it should be pointed out that such rationalizations of creative practice are also theoretical through and through. They rely on culturally and historically specific understandings of practice that are ideologically determined. A refusal to acknowledge one's own theoretical position does not make that position any less theoretical. Humanism and Idealism are their own theoretical positions, just ones that make a claim to universalism through a necessary blindness to their own relativity. There will also be philosophers who wish to maintain a rigorous purity between the work of conceptualization and the task of making and who for good reason wish to defend the properly philosophical space of disciplinary philosophy from other idioms within the arts and humanities. However, such disciplinary segregation is the result of institutional (and so cultural and political) imperatives. The history of philosophy itself is much more relaxed about idiomatic borders, as the dialogues of Plato, the *Confessions* of Augustine, or, the novels of Voltaire and Rousseau demonstrate.

However, it would be a mistake to insist that theory and practice, or philosophy and art, were the same thing. They are not and we need to rigorously distinguish between the two if this investigation is to proceed with clarity. Heidegger suggests that philosophy and art, *philos* and *poesis*, reside on opposite sides of an abyss.[2] All the questions of the philosophical understanding of art come from an attempt to understand the depths of that abyss. The metaphor Heidegger deploys in this context is telling, the gulf between philosophy and art is profound and difficult to see our way through. Heidegger offers us a third term, borrowing from the Greek, *techne*, as a way to bridge that abyss, suggesting that both philosophy and art are technical processes that arise from a form of making and both being a type of tool that humans use to orient themselves in the world.[3]

In contrast there is a strongly held belief in contemporary film theory that the art object itself is productive of knowledge in a manner that is equivalent to philosophical thinking.[4] This is a less convincing argument that imagines that meaning originates in art objects independent of either authorial making or critical reading. Insofar as, meaning is in fact the construction of sense by a reader (either the author as first reader, no more privileged than any other, or a critical audience) what this argument fails to account for is the philosophical or theoretical positions, acknowledged or otherwise, that those readers bring to the object. If the art object 'thinks' it is only because it is thought through by its readers, and there will be as many trajectories of thought through the art object as there are readers: the critical exercise is never exhaustive. However, an art object can no more think on its own than a stone can. If critical practice is tied to thinking (and non-understanding) then the important part of it (the one of immediate interest to us here) is the process rather than the outcome.

This book is not straightforwardly concerned with the question of critical appreciation of the art object. That is the business of an entirely different field of philosophy, namely aesthetics, and as any sensitive artist who has ever received a bad review knows there is a world of difference between criticism and practice. Rather, this book is concerned with the problem of the relation between theory (or what has historically been identified under the name of philosophy) and creative practices as a process of thinking and making. Criticism, appreciation, or affect are things that come after or anterior to that process. The question that concerns us here is the relation of theory (the reading of theory and its production) to creative practice. Accordingly, in this book we will consider a range of philosophers and theorists who are also creative artists, and practitioners who explicitly acknowledge their relation to theoretical work. The task here is not to demonstrate that reading theory will make you a better artist, or to suggest that the proper way to make art is by reading volumes of theoretical writing. Rather, it is to wonder about what sort of art such a relationship gives rise to, and to think through the creative process from the point of view of a theory-practitioner.

One obvious question that emerges from such an investigative trajectory is: if theory and practice are simultaneously impossible to separate and distinct activities, separated by an abyss in Heidegger's terms, then what is the exact nature of the relation between the two? It is a good question to ask, perhaps the only question worth asking in this context. However, if we were truly able to answer this question and to know the mysteries of that abyss then we might risk turning the page on the last chapter in the history of the world. To understand the mechanics of that relation, or even to think of that relation as a mechanical interchange, would mean that in principle it ought to be possible to follow an algorithm that programmed the outcomes of the exchange between theory and practice. The work of art schools could be reduced to an equation; the task of writing and making could be handed over to a computer. As the complications of Kleist and his readers demonstrate the play between theory and practice does not work in this way, art is not a calculus. Rather, if there remains something irreducible and perhaps immeasurable in the relation between theory and practice, the theoretical task must be to know this non-knowing, to understand it better as the aporetic space of creation, lest we are tempted to consign the problem of creative practice to mystery and eternal obfuscation.

Innocent smoothie

Hélène Cixous, both a great theorist and a great writer, also reads Kleist on the *Marionettetheatre*.[5] In her seminar text 'Grace and Innocence, Heinrich von Kleist' she reads the essay on the puppet theatre alongside the writing of Clarice Lispector. Quoting the Brazilian novelist, she says: 'the passage to the infinite is a disappearance, an infinite distancing from the finite. I am speaking of the movement of Kleist's puppets and of Clarice's thought gathered in her statement: 'In order to understand my non-intelligence, I had to become intelligent'. At the limit of comprehension, one begins to understand noncomprehension' (p. 30). Cixous is referring to the swing of the marionettes' limbs that Kleist characterizes as an asymptote, a line that approaches a given curve and recedes to zero as they tend to infinity. That is to say the line and the curve only ever touch at the point of infinity. This then is a touching that is always on the cards but that is infinitely deferred, an impossible touching without touching. Cixous is also describing the relation between theory and practice, the infinite approach of knowing at the limits of comprehension. It is in this infinitely receding and shrinking space that we will begin to understand the abyss that separates theory and practice. The abyss is both unbridgeable and squeezed to nothing as the asymptote extends to infinity. Only at the point of infinity do the line and curve share the same space and become one and the same thing. The flight of the asymptote is the process towards the impossible that gives the line and the curve their purpose and meaning. The word asymptote is derived from the Greek ἀσύμπτωτος (*asumptōtos*) which means 'not falling together', from ἀ priv. + σύν 'together' + πτωτ-ός 'fallen'.[6] This perhaps implies that both line and curve fall separately without ever coming together, synchronized falling to infinity rather than falling as a couple. The fall is then infinite and lonely, as the promise of an impossible touching to come.[7] What would it mean to speak of the relation between theory and practice in these terms?

Cixous' reading of Kleist in this essay attends to the episode of the youth, who having become self-conscious of his gracefulness is no longer able to reproduce his innocent balance. This part of the Kleist text is of the greatest relevance to us here, given that after theory one cannot remain innocent about matters of practice. This is not the same thing as saying theory has saturated our understanding of practice, rather that naïvete or ignorance is no longer an option after theory. Instead Cixous speaks of an 'economy of innocence' (p. 31) in which we constantly attempt to recover a virginal or paradisical innocence, only to have it threatened and lost over and over again. This innocence exists only in relation to its opposite, namely, to adopt Blake's terms, experience. We might think of this in terms of the aporias of creativity as an economy between knowing and incomprehension, or between theory and practice. Knowledge and innocence then coexist in an economy of exchange, one for the other, one recuperated and then lost to the other, falling separately towards infinity. This is not to repeat a tired notion of creative practice as pure idealism and theory as a form of corruption. Rather, as Cixous demonstrates there is nothing innocent about innocence. It is in understanding this economic relapse that we will be able to achieve some perspective on the limits of comprehension.

Cixous begins by puzzling the situation of Eve in Paradise, asking 'how can someone who does not know what sin is become a sinner?' (p. 30). This pushes the paradoxes of the fall from Paradise we found in the last chapter in a new direction. Surely, eating of the fruit of knowledge would only make Eve aware of the difference between good and evil, eating itself cannot be a sin for Eve because at that point she does not know what sin is. She eats the apple in a completely naïve way, her eating only being rationalized *post hoc* as a sin in the light of her new knowledge. For the God who subsequently expels her and her mate from Paradise, her guilt lies in her innocence. God's lawyers will argue *ignorantia juris non excusat*, that ignorance of the law is no defence in law. Eve might respond that the decks have been stacked against her from the start, that the possibility of sinning pre-exists her sin, and that the law claims its universality through its own singular exceptionalism. Having lost her innocence, which is really an innocence concerning the difference between innocence and knowledge, Eve can never be the same again. However, what God has yet to account for is the conditions of the fall from innocence and at what moment that transgression occurs. We might argue that in the moments before biting the apple, when Eve has resolved to do so, she is both still in a state of innocence and already committed to corruption. Unlike the curve of an asymptote, Eve's mouth decidedly comes into contact with the apple, but is she guilty at the point of taste, consumption, or digestion? Such questions may have kept thinkers in the medieval church busy for centuries, the point to note here that eating has taken place and that there is no going back from there.

The gates of Paradise are locked and there is no going back, as Cixous notes following Kleist, and we have to advance. However, even though we cannot go back in time, it is possible to advance along a trajectory of loss. In the case of Eve or Kleist's young man, 'there is neither fault nor absence of fault' (p. 39). The young man can no longer recover his balance but it was not his fault that he is now conscious of a lost grace that defines his ongoing narcissism as he stands in front of the mirror day after day in an attempt to re-find his innocence. Cixous identifies the possibility of 'a nonvirgin innocence' or 'an innocence regained' (p. 41), which refuses to equate innocence with an infantile state synonymous with irresponsibility. She states, 'innocence is always linked to risk, since by definition it is outside of a certain type of knowledge. It risks being misunderstood and leads to catastrophes. There is a dangerous innocence and a misleading innocence' (p. 42). There is nothing more regressive and politically suspect that the state of bliss or a return to nature away from the corruption of degenerate culture. This is the basis of a particularly virulent strain of politics that can overtake us without noticing it, the more we insist on divesting ourselves of certain types of knowledge. Practice without theory risks catastrophe, creating a Hell when it thinks it is looking at Paradise. Equally, there is no guarantee that falling from innocence into knowledge constitutes progress as human history since Eden demonstrates. One can be infinitely guilty and innocent at the same time, and with infinite guilt can come innocence.

But how can we *understand* innocence? How can we speak of innocence once innocence is no longer possible? How would we know that we are experiencing innocence when innocence requires an absence of both knowing and experience? Cixous suggests:

> One has to go *out* of the circle, in order to speak of the circle. But when one leaves the circle, there is no more circle. There remains only one thing to do: that is to leap back into the circle. This is the metaphor Kafka uses to speak of the relation between self and work. For him, the world goes by like a luminous arch stretched out in front of us. The only way of becoming aware of it is by leaping into it. (p. 46)

Eve bites down on the apple, Satan takes a leap of faith, the artist begins without ever being sure of where that beginning starts. This leap into uncertainty is not necessarily a naïve thing to do; equally knowing that we are leaping into the unknown will not necessarily help us make the jump. Nevertheless, if we are to advance, the jump must be made. Cixous suggests that there are 'acrobats of the soul', creative practitioners like Kleist and Lispector, who are skilled in judging the jump-off point, developing 'an extraordinary dexterity at the participation of the singular in the absolute. At the moment of intersection, in the briefest of moments – to recall the metaphor of the asymptote and its coordinates – something touches, brushes, and that is where one takes the leap' (p. 46). Kleist is notorious for the creative use of the figures of analytic geometry, it would seem that Cixous follows him in this regard. The terms she uses in French is not quite 'brushes' as the English translation renders it, but '*frôlement*', which might be better translated as 'caresses'.[8] However, we should remember that this touch only occurs at infinity, it is an impossible caress, infinitely deferred and infinitely gentle. If the leap from self to text, or writing to world, or theory to practice happens at the point of touching then that jump must remain forever as an infinitely deferred journey that never arrives. The participation of the singular in the absolute is forever trapped in that space tending to infinity towards a tangent point.

Such a fall and such a caress are not easy things to think about let alone achieve in art, they give rise to a different register of value in our understanding of creativity. For Cixous 'brushing is necessary, but has no weight' (p. 48). The issue of economy requires this lightness of touch, systems of exchange (looking, touching, seeing, speaking) all go through the body and all deal with brushing [*frôlement*]. Equally, the economy of innocence and knowledge requires one to brush up against the other. The caress is infinite and complex and cannot be explained by a computational model. This impossible touching is the conclusion of an infinite progress down the trajectory of loss, a journey and a moment of connection and exchange that thinks of loss as something other than negative. Loss, for Cixous, should not be imagined as a punishment; rather the movement along the curve towards infinity represents a path towards the extinction of loss, a desire for the loss of loss that would be the most human of instincts imaginable. It always risks a fall but remains the jump-off point for re-entry to the circle of experienced innocence. This might serve us a definition of the process between theory and practice, one that jumps from one side of the abyss to the other and back again, never being content with or dominated by one side or the other, heading towards a moment of impossible caress in the last chapter of the history of the world.

To only have the knowledge of knowledge, says Cixous, is to be without 'the value of life, or love' (p. 67). There are things that go beyond theory, that require us just to do. The prejudice for knowledge is an institutional requirement of philosophy, but it is, says Cixous, 'only a *moment* in a process of reasoning'. The task when living and thinking is to find another idiom of innocence that is necessarily and constantly threatened by knowledge. Innocence must test itself by putting itself at risk at every moment and always running the risk of losing itself. Innocence and knowledge brush against one another in the dance of thinking and making, imperceptibly, risking moments of interruption and relapse.

Innocence regained has to be earned, says Cixous, but it should be our goal and ambition. Unlike the innocence of Paradise, this other innocence is not unknown to itself, nor is it guilty. It remains strange to itself. That is to say, it must be other to itself and involve the relation between the self and other. The first virginal innocence is lost in the encounter with the other; the second earned innocence is earned and regained through that same ongoing encounter. This innocence is other to itself, it is its own other. That is to say, it is experience. When we brush up against the other, as in a dance, this moment of possible interruption and arrest is what Cixous calls 'the transparency of an *in-betweeness* of two beings, moving back and forth from one to the other' (p. 71). It is in-between an irretrievably lost innocence and the complete lack of innocence that comes with absolute knowledge. Both extremes are impossible for the human being, the first and last chapters in the history of the world. We as humans can only ever be *in media res*, searching like Milton for this earthly Paradise only to risk it at every moment in the encounter with our fellow earth-bound inhabitants, and 'to fray a passage toward the other is a humanly difficult art' (p. 71).

It is a contention of this study that in a positive sense the artist does not know what they are doing. There is something irreducibly unknowable to the artist that occurs in the moment of art that defines the process of art. Creative practice is a mode of performative innocence, that must be strange to itself and risk itself against the other. Practice risks itself against theory, against the risk of knowing itself, an outcome that leads to paralysis. Equally, theory is other to itself, compelling itself into a state other than itself, namely, practice. However, this secondary innocence that is not innocent, is not the monopoly of the creative practitioner. It happens everywhere as the stuff of life. Only the most completely naïve innocent would take on the role of head of department in a university, or start a business, or have a baby. No amount of reading about it in books will prepare you for such an encounter with the other. It is only innocence and ignorance of what will come that carries us forward in these moments. No theory can be adequate to the magnitude of what is set to engulf us, even if those theory books are derived from the experience of others. It is our risked innocence that leads to experience, which in turn earns us the credit of our regained innocence. This experience is no bar from future innocence nor can it negate naïvete. For only the truly innocent would proceed to take the role of Dean of Faculty, or open a second business, or have a second child. Experience, that vaguest of philosophical concepts, is also strange to itself. It contains within itself, as a condition of moving forward, a form of innocence that makes experience possible. There could be no experience without innocence, no innocence that did not inoculate itself against the trap of knowledge by being experienced about the risk of knowing what comes next. Performative innocence is not innocent about the value of innocence. This is also why theory and practice can only tend towards each other at a point of infinity. Both theory and practice must be naïve about the relation of one to the other, performing their innocence as a translation of experience, and while the individual can jump in principle from one side to the other, there remains an infinite abyss between the two of which the individual can never be master. Artistic technique, or the process of practice, can be the slats and joints of a bridge that the individual pieces together to set out precariously, even innocently, across the gulf but experience has its limits in the face of the other.[9] Technique is not flying; it is falling with style.

I feel like writing

Reading Kleist's *Über das Marionettetheatre*, Hélène Cixous alights on the passage concerning the fencing bear: 'his right paw raised ready for Battle. He looked me straight in the eye. That was his fighting posture'. She notes that the gaze of the computational and flawless bear is important, 'he is not a blind animal. We write with our eyes closed and the more we close our eyes, the more we see. But the bear does not need to close his eyes. Only humans do, in order to see otherwise' (p. 54). The clear-sighted bear fixes us with a steely gaze, he can see us coming, and always has a response. The human in contrast, in order to see past the bear's impeccable defences, would be better off closing their eyes and taking a stab in the dark. As a long-term myope herself, the question of blindness is importantly close to Cixous' own creative practice and is a key trope in her writing on writing.[10] In the essay 'Writing Blind: Conversations with the donkey' ['*Ecrire aveugle*'] she offers an extraordinary account of what it means to write and to think.[11] It is impossible to delimit this text as either theory or creative writing. It is both and neither at the same time, and an excellent example of the new idiom of writing as critical practice that takes place in the asymptote of theory and art. As with Cixous' account of innocence and loss, blindness is not to be thought of as something negative or as the result of some impairment but as the condition of all seeing, all insight, and all writing.[12] We will find here a clear-sighted understanding of the passage into darkness and uncertainty that characterizes moments of creativity. In Cixous there is nothing shortsighted about blindness. Equally, we should be careful when reading this essay not to assume that the lyrical 'I' of the narrating voice is reducible to the figure that answers to the name of Hélène Cixous. This is a work that writes itself; the 'I' could be the voice of writing itself, a text describing its own production.

The text is a poetic encounter with the strangeness of the author's self in creative practice as she doubles her alterity by writing about herself writing, looking at blindness, or, seeing the dark. She says that in order to write she must escape broad daylight, which fills her eyes with visions.[13] She wants, 'to see what is secret. What is hidden amongst the visible' (p. 139). She separates herself off from the world to write by closing her eyes, and behind her eyelids she finds herself elsewhere: 'there reigns the other light. I write by the other light' (p. 139). In this other light of blindness, she descends into 'the dark gorge' of writing. She asks, 'who believes they know how to see?' (p. 140). What presumption is involved in the belief that one can believe one's eyes? Seeing is not a matter of knowing, everything one sees has to be questioned and doubted. Who can say that they have the resources of flawless sight? Who could be so secure in their faith in vision that they could claim to know what they are doing when they see the world in front of them? It was precisely this doubt in the letter on the green glasses that led Kleist to his moment of crisis that threw him into writing. Sight and the metaphysics of vision would, on Cixous' terms, only be a moment in the process of rationality. One that is not secured or exhausted by knowledge but one that awaits to be complicated and risked against its own potential for blindness. Cixous, here, complicates the proverbial wisdom that there are none so blind as those who will not see, which retains within it the sense that sight can be opposed to blindness as an absence of sight and in principle can be corrected to produce true or clear vision.[14]

This is close to the commentary on the multitude by the lake in Matt. 13:13 who 'seeing see not ... neither do they understand' or the foolish people of Jer. 5:12 'without understanding/Who have eyes and see not'.[15] But as Ira Gershwin would say 'the things that you're liable to read in the bible ain't necessarily so'.[16] Rather, for Cixous, there are none so blind as those who do see, and who in seeing think that they have seen all that there is to see. There is in the metaphysical tradition an assumed connection and order between sight and knowledge, and the sensible and the intelligible. Cixous' challenge to this is to suggest that knowledge itself is blind, and that with blindness comes another way of seeing. Blindness sees around seeing and knows something that knowledge is blind to.

The important figure for Cixous in this respect would be not the all-knowing son of a Christain God but the blind, trans-sexual Tiresius,[17] 'not seeing the world is the precondition for clairvoyance' (p. 140). This form of seeing sees what the blind person sees, which is neither day nor night but a different long and precarious region in which the shadow of thought flashes ahead in secret. She says, 'my book writes itself. Creates itself. (In French: *se crée*) Secret' (p. 141). A secret is not necessarily something that waits to be dug up or uncovered, something that in principle is knowable or recoverable. Rather, a true secret is one that remains secret while in full view, or, hidden in plain sight as we say in English.[18] Here and elsewhere in Cixous, writing runs ahead of its author, laughing 'it turns back to see if I am (following) it' (p. 141). The secrets of creation are in front of us, running ahead, out of control, teasing us, in play and laughter. We pursue them blind along secret passageways, while the passage itself 'runs faster than my consciousness and my hand' (p. 144). Fortunately, the passage leaves traces but when in pursuit 'one must act fast. And no time to learn' (p. 144). As with Kleist's wrestler in the essay on reflection, practice calls for an improvisation that happens without the time to assimilate it as experience. This is not a pure and originary improvisation, rather it is the breathless pursuit of what lies beyond us, a groping along by memory of a technique that is inadequate to the chase: 'A book writes itself quickly. How long did it take you to write this book? There is a long time and a short time. Add my whole life ... The book is written at full speed when it is ready' (p. 144). The secret gestation of writing happens according to multiple temporalities that share an irrecoverable past and an unknowable future. Writing seems to exist in another time zone that exceeds us, carrying us forward through the reserves of our own jet lag.

Writing takes the whole of life, requiring all its resources, which as we have seen in Cixous run beyond the moment of knowledge, and involve the looseable pursuit of the loss of loss. The writing life is the pursuit of writing, of the time to write and the laughter that comes from writing. One of the most astute pieces of feedback I ever received from one of many unsuccessful job interviews for a post in university management was that they did not want someone who wrote so much and would be too easily distracted. This raises a question about what sort of person they were looking for to run a university, but that, I suppose, is their business. A writer wants to write and cannot live without writing. The writer who cannot write will be out of sorts; they will not be right again until they have the chance to write: without writing they are no use to themselves or anyone else. When the book is ready I feel like writing. Readiness is all even if I do not know what I am letting myself in for.

What would it mean to say, 'I feel like writing'? Cixous writes, 'an employee of Air France tells me on the telephone: I like your books because they touch me. We all like to touch – to be touched' (p. 142). Something touching happens in writing. It happens at the infinite caress of the asymptote of theory and practice. It occurs as we grope our way along the dark passageway in pursuit of the text that escapes us. Here, I can close my eyes and imagine Hélène's politeness and embarrassment as she is recognized on the telephone to the Air France ticket office, her writing having touched the life of another. She would be touched by that. However, even if she risks her writing against the review of the other's gaze, she does not write for the other without but for the other within: 'I write to feel. I write to touch the body of the instant with the tips of the words'. Words are her digits, writing is her haptology, her's is a phenomenology of strokes and marks, 'I must write, or else the world will not exist' (p. 148). As a writer, everything for her, her whole world of waking, working, and living depends upon this gesture. One is not 'a writer' by designation of the academy, media, or literary apparatus. Rather, one is a writer because one writes and there is nothing to be done but writing. Cixous says writing keeps 'death at a respectful distance' (p. 148). This is not an attempt to master death or achieve immortality by the management of the perpetually deferred end. Writing cannot put an end to the end, but it can be in dialogue with the end. In writing, the end should not come too soon. Writing is not a triumph over death, 'it is the fabrication of the raft of nothingness' (p. 122). We will recall the relation between fabrication and storytelling as this raft sets sail in the dark without map or guiding star – we are making it up as we go along. This fabrication is also a making, a handy craft that requires us to get in touch with the manual and needs finishing touches. Writing is full of feeling.

Death is not the end of the story.[19] It can be the terminus of writing, but an automatic writing would be writing with a manual, the death of the author does not imply the death of writing or the end of feeling. Rather, the death of practice comes with knowledge. The secrets of practice exposed to the full glare of the high noon of knowledge would wither away. Writing cannot exist in the head prior to putting pen to paper. It cannot be known in advance, rather it happens in the touch of the hand on the pen and the caress of the pen on paper, or the touch of fingers on a keyboard, writing is in the process. Nor can writing be captured by knowledge after the fact, having a light shone in its face until it gives up its secrets. Knowledge cannot exhaust the secrets of writing; they remain on the page for anyone who has eyes to see. Cixous says, 'I am not an intellectual. I am a painter ... I paint, I draw the sentences from the secret well. I paint the passage: one cannot speak it' (p. 149).[20] Painting involves brushing, touching the canvas with brush strokes, as the work emerges from the relation between brushing and surface. To feel like writing is also to say that writing is like feeling, a sensory apprehension that can happen in the darkest night, a knowing that happens without the security of knowing. As when we make love with our eyes closed which does not distract from perfect dexterity and intimacy. Knowing does not feel, 'knowing is without fever and without life', says Cixous (p. 151). Knowing legitimizes research or puts in train the search for what is not yet found, but it cannot grasp that which remains beyond its reach. Knowing is out of touch with feeling. Writing feels its way, while knowledge is blind to what it holds in its hands.

This is the aporia of theory and practice. One should not move so fast as to equate theory with knowing and take writing as a metonym for all practice. The dance between the two is more complicated; they are entangled one with the other. Theory is equally a writing that risks its innocence against its own impulse to register experience. Any creative practice always risks its own arrest by seeking to understand itself. The creative process constantly shuttles between theory and practice, without being mastered by either, coming up for light and then plunging again back into the darkness. It makes progress by feeling its way along the secret passageways of uncertainty.

Once more with feeling

In the case of Kleist, we saw that dancing leads to blindness, in the case of Diderot's 'Letter' blindness leads to touching. The question of creative practice touches on the problem of haptology. This is more than a literal appreciation of creative practice as a material activity or handcraft. It is far from certain that all creative practice involves a form of physical making. The production of the art object is often the result of a devolved relationship between an artist and a fabricator, or, the result of collective co-creation as in technical demands of filmmaking. Creative practice is not reducible to the final object of study, it is the entire process of thinking, making, and living. In this sense, it is as much a conceptual event as it is a material one. In contemporary art it is increasingly difficult to demarcate the borders between theory, philosophy, history, making, and presentation of an object. One should not so easily assume that creative practice is something you do with your hands, while theory is something you do with your mind. There is a profound materiality at work in writing, from the touch of quill on vellum or pen on paper to the weight of fingers across the digital keyboard or screen. Writing has traditionally been a haptology. However, the question of touch is not merely a material or phenomenological issue.[21] Rather, touch is a conceptual problem that defines relation. This can be the position of bodies, the topography of material objects, or the arrangement of a conceptual order. Touch in this sense is a Cartesian problem, and so a question that arises from the metaphysical and phenomenological traditions. Touch is above all else a philosophical problem.[22] One thought touches on another; one can be touched without physical proximity. Touch involves questions of sensation, comprehension, the sensible, the intelligible, and the intangible. To understand, or to grasp, haptology is to begin to appreciate the impossible relations that define the ways in which theory and practice touch one another, cross over, and coexist.[23] To speak of touching is to problematize profoundly the assumed order of the material and the conceptual and so begin to think through the aporias at the asymptote of theory and practice. Haptology is the word that Derrida gives us to name the discourses of touching; it is what we talk about when we talk about touching. It will be of help to us here as the purpose of our argument is not to offer a typology of ways of making but to think about what we think about when we think about the how theory and practice touch one another. The point of such an inquiry would be to suggest that the visual, plastic and sonic arts are heavily implicated in thought and it is this imbrication that defines the problem of theory-practice.[24]

A classic study on the problem of art and touching is Herder's *Plastik*.[25] Johann Gottfried Herder, like Diderot or Rousseau, would be another figure of critical practice, who in writing across a range of idioms combines philosophical reflection with poetic and aesthetic production, once again demonstrating the historical specificity of our own contemporary concern with the disaggregation of theoretical thought and creative practice. Herder's book on sculpture takes Diderot's letter on the blind as its explicit jump-off point, opening with a reference to the observations made in that text. It is an extraordinary meditation on theory and practice that would merit an entire monograph-length commentary on its own. We will have occasion to return to it over the course of this study but for the moment we will reserve our comments for the opening movement of Herder's text, in order to formulate an understanding of critical practice as a haptology without sight, or, a blind discourse of touching.

Herder suggests, following Diderot's anecdote of blind Sauderson, that while sight can understand shapes, touch alone understands bodies. That is to say that sight understands visible surfaces but the sense of touch is required to appreciate form. Sight requires light and is a sense of the daytime, while apprehension through touch is a skill of the blind and is available 24 hours a day. Sight then is a trick of the light, while there is a more profound knowledge at play in the sense of touch. Citing Diderot's account of the blind who have their sight restored only to be confused by an environment of coloured surfaces, Herder suggests that sight in fact should be no more privileged a sense for the interpretation of the physical world than any other. Sight is merely habitual rather than fundamental and relies upon other senses in order to appreciate spatial relations. Touch, for Herder, takes us beyond mere appearance and simulacra, 'an ophthalmite with a thousand eyes but without a hand to touch would remain his entire life in Plato's cave and would never have any *concept* [*eigentlichen Begriff*] of the properties of a physical body' (p. 9). The emphasis on concept here is Herder's, demonstrating the importance of touch to understanding, which is more obvious to speakers of German who move between *griffen* [touching] and *begreifen* [understanding]. The equivalent in English would be the move from prehension to comprehension. Herder asks, 'for what are properties of bodies if not relations to our own body, to our sense of touch?' (p. 36). What emerges very quickly in Herder is an understanding that touch is intimately connected to thought.

In a gesture that can frequently be seen in the modern European tradition of philosophy, he goes on to suggest that animals do not have access to concepts of texture, form, or volume because these are proper to man, 'only human beings have them, because alongside reason we possess a hand that can feel and grasp'

(p. 36).²⁶ For Herder, we could not confirm our own existence without touch and would be lost forever, in dreams and guess-work, 'we would know nothing for certain' (p. 39). There is then in Herder's haptology an understanding that we jump straight from one privileged sense (sight) to another (touch) and touch is merely a substitute for the metaphysics of sight insofar as it re-inscribes all the privileges proper to man and the affirmation of certainty that we find elsewhere in optic-centric discourse. However, while touch may be a privileged sense of phenomenology, there are resources within Herder's text that will allow us to read this tradition against itself. First of all, in recognizing the importance of touch we have acknowledged the incompleteness of sight and already introduce an element of doubt into the normative understanding of seeing as believing. When we take touch seriously we can no longer believe the evidence of our senses, or at least we must begin to relate to those senses differently. Secondly, if the historically privileged sense of sight is no longer to be taken as a metonym for the whole of understanding, then similarly none of the other senses can be adequate to such an ambition. This will complicate Herder's anthropocentric rationalism as we progress through his text. As the French would have it, there is something stupid/beastly [bête] about the philosophical categorization of the animal and the human, but that is a whole other book.²⁷ Rather than disappear down that particular rabbit hole, for now we can say that in fact Herder's thesis on touching introduces considerable uncertainty into how we traditionally think of certainty.

For example, Herder notes that while touching leads to conceptualization such knowledge cannot be taught but only acquired through experience. The trial and error of the child in the nursery combines sight and touch to enhance one another and importantly leads to judgement. We might add to that the taking of risk and the assessment of risk on the part of the infant, whereby newly obtained knowledge of the world is risked against fresh encounters with the unknown. For Herder the scene of the nursery is the incubator of the mathematical and physical sciences. What is striking here is that process leads to knowledge through practice but that practice takes place in a realm of uncertainty and that knowledge has to be extended and risked in a process without end. A blind person who uses touch to make sense of the world 'is able to develop concepts of the properties of bodies that are far more complete than those acquired by the sighted … his method of slowly but surely making out concepts … is able to judge the form and living presence of things far more subtly than the sighted, from whom everything flees like a shadow' (p. 37). One way of reading Herder's commentary here is as an allegory of critical practice. Once more there are none so blind as those who see. Knowledge is not immediately given by the instant arrival of what presents itself but is acquired through the slow process of making our way in the dark, reaching out and testing the world around us within an envelope of subtle uncertainty. This knowledge is not the access to an unmediated truth of the universe that the pre-Kantian Kleist yearned for, rather it is criteria for making judgements about the world. The leap from judgement into life is not given by knowledge but occurs as a wager of that knowledge against experience.

Herder goes on to make a distinction between the concepts understood through touch and the ideas that come from the habit of sight, 'the difficult *concepts*, which at first we make out only gradually and with great effort, begin to be accompanied by *ideas* derived from sight. These ideas then illuminate what previously we had understood only obscurely' (p. 37). The knowledge that comes from touch as a process of testing and judgement is not complete and is supplemented by sight. However, sight as habituation requires touch as its 'foundation and guarantor' (p. 38). That is to say, the immediacy of sight as a way of operating in the world is complicated and opened up by touch, in which 'the swift idea proper to seeing runs ahead of the slow concept proper to touching' (p. 38). Travelling at different speeds, sight is out in advance separated from its guarantee, while touch lags behind its confirmation. Sight and touch then assure one another but remain relative to one another and in this gap between the two we are able to take a second look at sight. Sight as habituation is 'but an abbreviated form of touch' (p. 38). That is to say, despite appearances, sight and so living in the world as a sited person, is equally prone to the insecurity of touch as a form of judgement. The illusion of the speed of sight is that 'we believe we see something when in fact we touch it and where only touch is appropriate' (p. 38). For Herder, 'sight gives us *dreams*, touch gives us *truth*'. But this truth is the truth of the blind, the slow process of assessment and judgement, moving gradually and with care through the world, in the absence of an absolute, all-seeing knowledge.

In this schema, sight only has access to surfaces, images, and figures, whereas touch leads us to bodies and forms. Touch and sight, like all concepts used in the arts and sciences, says Herder, are 'fused together' in 'that great confusion we term life' (p. 39) and need to be separated in order to be traced. He suggests, for example, that beauty [*Schönheit*], appearance [*Schein*], and beholding [*Schauen*] are all unquestioned terms in psychology that confuse knowledge with seeing. The metaphysics of immediate presence, the self-identical and so on is derived from this unquestioned privilege given to the rapidity of sight, 'sight is the most artificial, the most philosophical of the senses' but it will never give rise to a 'true phenomenology' (p. 39). Touch may seem ancillary or supplementary to sight but is in fact its foundation; touch and sight open one another and ruin one another's claims to completeness. This then is not quite the substitution of one privileged sense for another; touch and sight both live in a world of blindness.

Now, all this concerns Herder because his aim is to develop an aesthetic of the plastic arts, and sculpture in particular. He stresses that sight is insufficient on its own because three-dimensional art is categorically different from the surface of a painting, 'a creature that is nothing but an eye, indeed, an Argus with a hundred eyes, may look upon a statue for a hundred years and examine it from every side; but if it is without a hand with which to touch, or at least able to sense its own touching, if it possesses only the eye of a bird and is all beak, gaze, pinion, and claw, it will never have anything more than a bird's-eye view' (p. 40). Herder's metaphors of sight are compelling, from the ophthalmite to an Argus, from the mollusc to the mythic, 360-degree surveillance remains inadequate to experience. Argus was lulled to sleep with spoken charms and then killed by Hermes as he guarded the nymph Io, the first murder of the new generation of gods.[28] Sight is the first thing to die when tested against the world, and like Abel watching his flock, death soon follows as knowledge enters into the sacred grove. However, the important moment here in Herder is the qualification of touch itself with the ability to sense one's own touching. Herder may not have visited the Victoria and Albert or the Musée D'Orsay recently but he is fully aware that gallery guards watch the statues like an Argus and tend to take a dim view of visitors touching the artwork. Sculpture is of course viewed from a distance, the difference between a painting and a statue, in the classical sense, is not that we can touch one and not the other, but that one depends upon the sense that it could be touched and understood while the other could not. A blind person might get little out of laying their hands on a Rembrandt. Sculpture need not be touched as such but gives rise to a virtual sense of touch, to a phantom limb that touches. Seeing sculpture doubles the senses by an 'as if' of touching, just as a work of critical practice calls out to read, to be touched by theory. Sense reaches out, virtually, to sculpture and the knowledge and experience of sculpture is in this sense prosthetic, like Kleist's marionettes.[29] Touch is doubly estranged and made strange to itself. An experience of the plastic is first an experience of self-touching, of experiencing the ability to touch without touching, knowing touch through not touching.[30] It is a touching without origin or telos, a touching that is other to itself.

The reality of self-touching is a virtual corpo-reality, 'consider the lover of art sunk deep in contemplation who circles restlessly around a sculpture. What would he not do to transform his sight into touch, to make his *seeing* into a form of *touching* that feels in the dark?' (p. 41). We have moved here from a touching that is blind to a touching that is blind and virtual, 'his soul speaks to it, not as if his soul sees, but as if it touches, as if it feels' (p. 41). The 'as if' of experience is crucial; sensation is fabricated and simulated. And it is an experience not of the 'as if' of sight, that is to say immediacy, but the 'as if' of process. The 'as if' is what connects phenomenality with fiction and so creation. It is the human capacity to hold simultaneously contradictory positions, which accept both the reality and unreality of a given event. When reading fiction, we accept that it is simultaneously not true and also revealing of a truth, one that as we say is more true than truth itself. Perhaps, a fiction that is stranger than truth, or, one that renders truth strange. The structure of this experience also holds for looking at art, sitting in the theatre or watching a film. However, according to the schema we are deriving here from Herder, art is not an aberrant experience, at a remove from or marginal to the 'reality' of the world. Rather, in art we will find a decisive example that pertains for all phenomenality, namely the structure of the 'as if', in which we accept the experience we are having as real while we know that it is equally unreal. That is to say, experience of the world is not to touch the world as it is but to experience the world mediated through the fabrication of sense. We might say that sense itself is prosthetic, like Kleist's green spectacles. It is perhaps not surprising that we can find in Herder a schema that looks more than a little Kantian in orientation. Herder studied with Kant in *Köningsberg* and although it was a pre-critical Kant, it would not be difficult to propose a demonstration that showed how the DNA of the *Ding an sich* runs through the whole of Kant and Herder. The '*an sich*' and the 'as if' are two idioms of the conditions of possibility that we will find emerging in the shared understanding of the separation of the material and its perception via the senses, which is the very definition of the phenomenological tradition as it emerges from the Kantian *noumenon*.[31]

Let us break from this reading of Herder, really before Herder has even got going in this text. As he opens out his argument he will want to insist on the specificity of sculpture as the presentation of truth in contrast to painting as storytelling and dream. However, in doing so he must always return to sight and to painting as that which both differentiates and completes the plastic. Plasticity is unstable and the terms Herder wants to attribute to it will not hold when constantly opened up and complicated by the visual. Fascinating as this disarticulation of plasticity is by Herder, the point for us here is to identify in the argument a gesture that takes us beyond the assertion that critical practice is a creative blindness. In making this claim, it was important to emphasize that critical practice is not the mere application of knowledge or theory to making art, which will result in a set of programmed outcomes or privileges 'theory' and 'philosophy' as a meta-discourse of the intelligible over the sensible of artistic affect. Rather, the blindness of critical practice demonstrates the uncertainty that we find before, during and after the creative act as a process of questioning and risking knowledge against an unknown future. In this sense, we might say that critical practice is no different from any other creative process. However, it is important to note the access that critical practice gives us to this structure of epistemological and poetic insecurity. To extend this claim to suggest a relation between the blind writing of theory and practice and the conceptual order of touch, is to identify critical practice as a slow process of judgement and risk that is incomplete within itself but equally guarantees the conditions of an overly hasty, habitualized metaphysics of immediacy in creative acts. In the gap between an artistic technique that races ahead and a critical practice that takes its time, neither of which can operate fully without the other, we will find an exemplary case of the curious conditions of making and creative production.

Blindness is an insufficient condition on its own to lead us forward, touch is required to feel our way through the world, assessing, judging, and risking our inadequate knowledge against what arrives in an obscure and unknown way. In this interminable process, theory is not a map or a privileged model for understanding. Rather, it is one moment in the process of the long dark night of reason and creation, which by turns works its way through what presents itself as what is to be experienced. In this set-up, theory and practice are strange one to another, but cannot hope to progress without combining to complement one another, even if that fusion is also a confusion that complicates both. Equally, in this scenario theory is as strange to itself as practice. Theory is not the wheel and rudder of practice but a blind writing practice that is every bit as haptic as the practical act of making or fabrication. Practice is neither the result of theory applied nor the full actualization of creative force in comparison to the anaemic support of theory. Rather, practice is theory at risk, the ruin of theory as well as it guarantor. Practice requires theory to proceed; as it touches what confronts it, theory is in the very fingertips of practice. However, critical practice is prosthetic, it is a touching that recognizes its ability to touch even if touching as such remains postponed or distant. Critical practice can no more grasp the nettle to assume mastery of the event than any other idiom of knowing. Rather, critical practice works in and with the aporias that open around the problems of knowing and creating, holding them in the productive tension of the 'as if'. Critical practice acts as if it were possible to create and as if it were possible to know, while simultaneously retaining a hold on the creative knowledge that both are equally impossible. Critical practice is a phantom limb that sculpts or writes, its touch is as irresistible as it is unattainable, and in that asymptote there lies the infinite possibility of a caress that completes but never arrives.

Plastic arts

There can be no future without creativity, and no creativity without a future. Following these accounts of Cixous and Herder, blindness and touching, this hypothesis will require a little unpacking. In order to do so I would like to turn from Herder's understanding of *plastik* to Catherine Malabou's extraordinary reading of Hegel in her *L'Avenir de Hegel*, translated into English as *The Future of Hegel: Plasticity, Temporality and Dialectic*.[32] 'L'Avenir', however, is not straightforwardly mapped on to 'Future', there is a conceptual shortfall in that translation, something fails to come from the French.[33] Nevertheless, we have in Malabou's account of Hegel a rich resource for the consideration of creativity in relation to her privileged Hegelian term, plasticity. *Plastik* is the German word for sculpture but it also flexible in its meaning as it stretches across idioms and languages:

> Plasticity characterizes the art of 'modelling' and, in the first instance, the art of sculpture. The plastic arts are those whose central aim is the articulation and development of forms; among these are counted architecture, drawing and painting. Hence, by extension, plasticity signifies the general aptitude for development, the power to be moulded by one's culture, by education. (p. 8)

It is then an elastic term that denotes suppleness and flexibility, meaning the ability to evolve and adapt; accordingly, we sometimes speak of the 'plastic virtue' of living things, notably plants and animals. In this sense the art of modelling does not just concern the imposition of a set standard or prototype to be copied or followed as a method. Rather, this modelling may include the exact opposite of such a systematic approach, suggesting instead the ways in which the model is changed and evolves as it comes into contact with an exterior environment.[34] Model in English refers to both that which is copied and the copy itself, further complicating the routes by which adaptation and evolution can be furthered. However, while plastic is malleable, in its classical sense, says Malabou, 'things that are plastic preserve their shape, as does the marble in a statue: once given a configuration, it is unable to recover its initial form. 'Plastic', thus, designates those things that lend themselves to being formed while resisting *deformation*' (p. 9).

Malabou's work on plasticity is highly suggestive and will provoke us into further thinking here. However, it is a line of thought that I can only follow so far for reasons that will emerge as we shadow the contours of Malabou's text.

While a statue cannot return to its original state as a marble block, it can easily be disfigured, and modern plastics subjected to sufficient heat can be deformed out of all recognition. That the principle of formation is subject to the pull and resistance to deformation is not in doubt. What is at stake is the elasticity of plastic as a concept, how far can it be stretched before it can no longer snap back into its original shape? With formation comes deformation that in turn launches new figures and disfigurations.[35] My issue with this use of plasticity is that ultimately the term may be inadequate to the work that Malabou needs it to do as she tries to fit a quart into a pint pot. A pint pot, even a plastic one, might be a grand thing on its own but it is not the only utensil in the kitchen and understanding creativity might finally require us to stretch beyond plasticity. However, Malabou is of course a sensitive reader of the terms of plasticity, also recognizing that in the modern sense plastic also names a type of explosive made from nitroglycerine and nitrocellulose. In other words, plastic is a term that implies its own opposites, both the concrete making of shapes and the annihilation of all form. As she will say in a memorable phrase, plasticity 'explodes its own reserves' (p. 187).

For Malabou, in her account of Hegel, the idea of plasticity is closely associated with the accidental. She suggests that the dialectical process is 'plastic' because it unfolds and makes links, while plasticity is dialectical because it involves the merger of antinomies, emergence, and explosion, seizure of form and the annihilation of form. At this point we would do well to flag a warning with respect to the dialectic as a plastic process. There might be nothing less flexible than the dialectic in its scientific form, nothing more set in its ways and resistant to change.[36] Equally, if the dialectic is malleable then it is because the dialectical process contains within itself something fundamentally undelictizable, which escapes and opens up the dialectic. I would want to retain this as an irreducible principle of the experience of art and of the making of art, which cannot be easily mapped onto any dialectical pattern or model. Plasticity as a concept will have to bear this in mind if it is to succeed, just as the dialectic will need to take on new forms if it is to operate in the sense that Malabou requires it to. Nevertheless, she turns in these pages to the *Science of Logic* and to the *Phenomenology* as touch points in her consideration of Hegel in order to connect plasticity with temporality and the dialectic 'as nothing less than the *formation* of the future itself' (p. 12). She writes:

> Plasticity characterizes the relation between substance and accidents. Now the Greek word συμβεβηχός, 'accident', derives from the verb συμβαίνειν which

means at the same time to follow from, to ensure and to arrive, to happen. Thereby it can designate continuation in both senses of the word, as consequence, that is, 'what follows' in the logical sense, and as event, that is, 'what follows' in a chronological sense. Self-determination is thus the relation of substance to that which happens'. (p. 12)

Accordingly, Malabou maintains that the future, as it appears in Hegelian thought, is the relation which subjectivity maintains with the accidental. Malabou has previously run the trope of plasticity through Hegel's use of the term in relation to his consideration of 'exemplary identities' in Greek philosophy, in which particularity and universality meet in the form of exemplary thinkers. Let us work with Malabou's definition of terms here for the moment to see how this question of plasticity might play out and be of interest to us in this current investigation. However, it is also necessary to note that the exemplary is no more exemplary than any other example and to pick up Hegel's terminology here could be leading us to a foreclosure that we might not be willing to make with respect to creative practices. Despite this, it will be important to welcome a consideration of contingency in relation to creativity.

The core of Malabou's argument plays out in the paragraphs that follow, 'the dialectical composition of such concepts as 'the future' [*l'avenir*], 'plasticity', and 'temporality' forms the *anticipatory structure* operating within subjectivity itself as Hegel conceived it' (p. 13). In order to distinguish this structure from the future ['*futur*'] as it is normally understood, Malabou gives it the name '*le* '*voir venir*'', which her translator Lisabeth During economically renders as is 'to see (what is) coming'. In French '*voir venir*' means to wait to see what is going to happen, observing with care what is about to unfold, with the suggestion of guessing or probing the intentions of others. It can be used, according to context, to express both knowing what is to come and not knowing what is about to happen. Accordingly, Malabou has Frenchified Hegel so that 'to see (what is) coming' can suggest the relation between 'teleological necessity and surprise' (p. 13). At this point in Malabou's own thinking she is only considering plasticity in relation to the text of Hegel, she has yet to roll it out towards her later extended consideration of neuroscience, medicine, and trauma.[37] For the moment then she convinces with the suggestion that if we follow this term through the Hegelian corpus then we will find it as a decisive concept that is varied and extended to enable the turns of his thinking: 'plasticity is, therefore, the point around which all the transformations of Hegelian thought revolve, the centre of its metamorphoses' (p. 13). What follows is an inventive and inspiring reading of Hegel. However, this is not a book about Hegel, or at least not straightforwardly a book that might be considered Hegelian. Our concern here is with the question of creativity and in particular its relation to the borders of philosophical inquiry where idiom gives way to genre and in turn is opened by other practices. This would seem to be a distinctly plastic space in which new forms are made and disfigured. The moments of creativity that press themselves upon us here are those in which we make the attempt to see what is coming and to fail to see it as it arrives from another place. Theory-Practice is the double attempt to see ourselves see what is coming. This is a sight that would seek to see around corners or to see ourselves seeing into the future.[38] It involves this relation between teleological necessity and accident that Malabou characterizes in Hegel as *le 'voir venir'* but importantly it must also exceed it.

Later in the thesis Malabou returns to this question of 'plastic individuality' as it arises from Hegel's understanding of identity in ancient Greece. Concluding the first section of the book she observes that 'the 'becoming essential of the accident' describes the Greek moment of subjectivity, as interpreted by Hegel' (p. 75). This is worth reflecting on for a moment, in so far as the Greek moment of subjectivity is the hinge that takes us from *mythos* to *philos*, from fable to theory. The gesture in Malabou as it is in Hegel is to identify subjectivity with a lack of substance, the human is not a question of the material animal but of ideas and of spirit. 'Human subjectivity is constituted in self-forgetting; consciousness and will, under the influence of repeated practice, win their force through a kind of self-absenting. When man makes his entrance into the speculative narrative he does so in the guise of a farewell [*adieu*]' (p. 75) says Malabou of Hegel. Accordingly, if creativity is an expression of subjectivity then it is also not a question of substance. We might say, adopting a certain Hegel, that creativity has no substance. Rather, subjectivity is constituted precisely in acts such as creative practice, and 'repeated practice' at that, in which consciousness and will absent themselves. We have never suggested that creative practice is a matter of consciousness or the realization of intention. If the human enters the world of *philos* on the basis of self-effacement, then it is not straightforward to separate this valediction from the acts of self-forgetting that come with the experience of creative practice. Even more so, then, the question of theory-practice presents us with a double entry into a speculative narrative that finds its resources in those creative experiences in which the self is confounded by the self, or, to borrow from Malabou, the self bids farewell to the self. In the next chapter, we will suggest the ways in which this key aspect of creativity plays out as a relation to the other and the other as a mode of creativity itself, including the wholly other of automation and death. For the moment, I would like to work with Malabou's understanding of plasticity as central to the anticipatory structure of this self-effacement of subjectivity. She offers a definition of the two powers of plasticity:

> Plasticity is a name for the originary unity of acting and being acted upon, of spontaneity and receptivity. A medium for the differentiation of opposites, plasticity holds the extremes together in their reciprocal action, enabling the function of a structure of anticipation where the three terms of the temporal process are articulated: the originary synthesis, the hypothesis or embodiment of the spiritual, the relation of the moments of time. The meaning of the notion of plasticity is what it is, plastic. Indeed, the originary operation of receiving and giving form is not a rigid and fixed structure but an instance which can evolve, which means that it can give itself new forms. The temporal differentiation of plasticity makes possible the historical deployment of the substance-subject. (p. 186)

Theory-practice would seem then to be a plastic art on Malabou's terms, in which *poesis* and *philos* are held together according to the force of their reciprocal actions, critical and creative, in which the theory and practice both act and are acted upon by each other. Importantly in Malabou's reading of Hegel this gives rise to a temporal process as the operation of the dialectic. In this sense, theory-practice as a plastic art would be fundamentally anticipatory. That is to say it looked to the future, or as we might translate the French, it looks to what comes, evolving and developing as that arrival takes unknown and unpredictable forms. It is this arrangement of a temporal structure that allows plasticity to realize the valedictory subjectivity of Hegel's humanism. However, if as we suggested that the possibility of this dialectical structuration rested upon a necessarily undialectizable element, that which the system was forced to expel or could not digest, then we might say that something must fall outside this temporal assembly.[39] That is to say, that plasticity like the dialectic was unable to close itself in a complete refusal of deformation. There would remain some element of theory-practice or the plastic arts in general that was not so much anti-plastic, for this could easily be recuperated within the dialectic, but spastic in time with respect to the plasticity of the dialectic. It is not so much a question of in-between-ness as being trapped in no-space, insofar as that space cannot be coordinated in relation to temporality. The time is out of joint, as Hamlet would say.[40] The resistance to plasticity would no doubt be an important part of the formal elasticity of the plastic, and plasticity does not just present itself as the name of the dialectic but as a deformation of the dialectic within Hegel.

However, what remains indigestible to the dialectic must equally remain anterior to plasticity. This is that moment, to give it a temporal designation, of unknowing or blindness we have identified as irreducible in creative practice.

Malabou concludes her study with the provocative formulation of a mode of 'plastic reading':

> The Hegelian idea of plastic reading confers on the notion of 'to see (what is) coming' its real meaning. 'To see (what is) coming' denotes at once the visibility and the invisibility of whatever comes. The future is not the absolutely invisible, a subject of pure transcendence objecting to any anticipation at all, to any knowledge, to any speech. Nor is the future the absolutely visible, an object clearly and absolutely foreseen. It frustrates any anticipation by its precipitation, its power to surprise. 'To see (what is) coming' thus means to see without seeing – await without awaiting – a future which is neither present to the gaze nor hidden from it. Now isn't this situation of 'in-between' *par excellence* the situation of reading? (p. 184)

We have established that problems of reading and the challenges of Theory-Practice are one and the same, that is reading in the sense of a creative, inaugural event that discovers a text as of the first time. The question here will be whether Malabou's understanding of reading is sufficient to an account of the demands of Theory-Practice. In truth, Malabou's thought here is little more than a move that allows her to thematize her own study of Hegel. While the difficulty in reading Hegel 'is caused by the seeming impossibility of making any headway since from the outset we would need to carve out a beginning allowing us both to foresee and not to see what follows' (p. 184). Malabou has a happy fall, the accident and contingency, of alighting on the term plastic. This then allows her the foothold to make progress through the text of Hegel by her inventive re-inscription of plasticity within the dialectical schema. However, when in her closing remarks Malabou attempts to mobilize plasticity beyond the text of Hegel she immediately hits a snag.

In the final section, entitled, '*le 'voir venir*'', she comments on the resistance to the dialectic to be found in philosophy and modern life, of which my comments above might be a good example. But she is referring explicitly to a hypothesis on the end of history that is both surprising and unsurprising to find in these closing paragraphs written in 1996.[41] She notes that the arrangement of the two modes of 'to see (what is) to come', the teleological and the alienated, determines 'the future of those creatures who no longer have time ahead of themselves, who live out a teleology which is shattered because already accomplished. Such a future is both beautiful and terrible. Beautiful because everything can still happen. Terrible, because everything has already happened' (p. 192). It is odd to think that for all its resources the plasticity of Malabou has only managed to place us, if not, close to Kojève then in some sort of time loop in which we live, die and repeat, as a future within closure, like the death drive of a demented computer game. She goes on to describe this contradictory temporal flop as the relation between '*saturation* and *vacancy*', the philosophical tradition reaching completion and the uncontested victory of capitalism, that simultaneously leaves no room for progress and is felt as a vacuum. Malabou is teetering on the brink of at best a historically specific reading at worst an intellectual collapse in these final pages as if the effort of reading Hegel has wrought a terrible price. On the one hand, she suggests that this vacuum and the promise of unemployment it brings, both for the citizen and the philosopher, is also 'a promise of novelty, a promise that there are forms of life which must be invented' (p. 192). On the other hand, she is prepared to go the full Hegel, as a true believer rather than a critical reader, and entertain, 'the possibility of a closed system to welcome new phenomena, all the while transforming itself, is what appears as plasticity … the process by which a contingent event, or accident, touches at the heart of the system, and, in the same breath, changes itself into one of the system's essential elements' (p. 193). That is to say the future is always folded back within the dialectic, the loop is closed, and accident or contingency cannot escape the order it confronts. This would be the death of creativity, the necrotic sclerosis of plasticity that is always successful in refusing deformation. Malabou can see this but suggests that the coexistence of the plane of saturation and vacancy, in which the formation of forms is in alliance with the *Plastikbombe* [atomic bomb] 'is what the future requires' (p. 193). She concludes that 'the philosophy of Hegel invites us to enter into the serenity and the peril of the Sunday of life'.[42] This is a challenging thought that following Malabou's stimulating reading of the Hegelian text we ought to take seriously. However, it ultimately fails to satisfy, not because one longs and hopes for an escape that might not be available to us, but because this shocking final section of Malabou's book performs the very hypothesis she seems to reject in these paragraphs. Namely, on her terms this surprising turn in Malabou's argument should be capable of incorporation into her thesis as an essential element of her thought on plasticity. Instead, these lines, open up the entire argument of the preceding chapters, giving us to question not the elasticity of the plastic but its necroid form, and to ask that whether in her reading of Hegel, Malabou has not finally succumbed to a certain Hegelianism that she ought to unpick. In contrast to Malabou's formulation here, I would insist on the unforeseen, that which sight does not see, that must remain outside of the dialectic. It is the very openness of the dialect, its incapacity to close, which makes its action necessary. On its own terms, the dialectic is a death machine, without the possibility of escape, hybridity, or transformation worthy of the name. It is the failure of the dialectic that makes the dialectic possible. If plasticity is just another form of enclosure and death then it is not what the future requires but what the future must dissolve. The future lies not in a loop of vacuum, fabrication, and incorporation, but in what falls out of the dialectic and is irreconcilable with it. This is the moment of creativity, spastic in time and space, a wedge that prevents the automatic sliding door of the dialectic from sealing us into the Sunday of life. The door will bang continually against this small block but it cannot close us in.

If this is what the future of Hegel ultimately means then surely this plastic is junk. What is the value of plasticity if the moment it is put to use beyond philosophy it becomes toxic? Isn't the point of plastic that it is non-biodegradable and lasts forever? Is the future of Hegel to be trapped in the Sunday of life forever as the plastic debris piles up around us, polluting planetary life and leaving the subject like a Beckett character on a landfill site as dusk settles on the last Sunday? As a preface to *L'Avenir de Hegel*, Jacques Derrida provides an extended reading of Malabou's thesis. It is ostensibly a peon of praise for his pupil, but read carefully it is also a considered critique of the foreclosures in Malabou's thought, which are apparent in this Hegel book and are amplified in her later writing. Derrida is keen to signal in Malabou's work 'a certain non-empiricist idea of contingence or of a certain responsible empiricism with renewed radicality' (pp. xi–xii) around a commitment to the becoming essential of accident and the simultaneous becoming accident of essence. There is also an acceptance, familiar to readers of Derrida, that while there would be no more history without the future, without the possibility of absolute surprise, equally there would be no future and no novelty without a link to history, tradition, retention and synthesis: this synthesis has already claimed the future anterior and the 'to see (what is) coming' of anticipation, it has already called for the teleological structure which must dampen surprise itself or novelty in order to make it possible: as if it were a surprise *without* surprise' (xiii). This doubleness is the two antithetical forms of the plastic and the plasticity of these two contradictory forms that is totally germane to art as a plastic artificiality or the synthesis of that other plastic matter that is living form. We might even add that theory-practice also performs the double powers of plasticity, synthesizing *philos* and *techne*, both plastic idioms of configuration that when mixed together produce an unstable compound capable of blowing up the entire field. At this point Derrida would seem to remain close to Malabou.

However, and to cut to the chase, Derrida's future is not the same as that of Malabou, and in reading Malabou he goes beyond her in thinking this future. He notes, as if he were following Malabou's reading of Hegel, that 'the strategy does not consist here in simply demonstrating that the future has the place that we often deny it *in* Hegel's philosophy'. In this sense, Malabou would seem at least to wish to exceed Kojève. But at this point the pronominal form of Derrida's writing shifts a gear and rather than noting what Malabou has to say around Hegel, he notes 'we will attempt to think *differently* – to think *otherwise* –a certain radicality of the future' (p. xxix). The word to emphasize here is the *nous*, as the argument of Derrida's introduction begins to drift away from the text that furnished its occasion:

> *Otherwise*: that is to say, and such is the radicality of the 'farewell' or the 'adieu', a different radicality or a radicality otherwise more radical than a simple 'moment of time'. The future, *what is yet to come in the future*, is not simply reducible to what is *imminent* in the future, and this very difference reveals plasticity itself, the condition also for there to be some kind of sense in speaking, as we have been from the beginning, of a 'history of the future'. (p. xxix)

At this point Derrida remains on Malabou's tail, quoting with approval her positing of 'the future as 'plasticity', amounts to *displacing* the established definition of the future as a *moment in time*' (p. 5). For Derrida it is important to 'abandon' this sense of the future as a tense. He notes 'let us underline the word 'abandonment', which immediately follows the above quoted passage in the text, and let us underline this word because it says something of what is done or of what passes in and with the 'farewell', that is, a certain kind of desertion, of abandonment, of aban-donation' (p. xxx). This is a curious sentence because while Derrida will make considerable play of the *adieu* as abandonment, including the desertion of and by God [*à dieu*] the word does not appear 'immediately' after these quoted lines in the text of Malabou. Indeed, immediately after this sentence, Derrida quotes the next and immediate lines from Malabou in which 'abandonment' is nowhere to be found. Instead Malabou speaks of 'renouncing' well known and familiar meanings of the future. And in introducing these lines of Malabou, Derrida persists with the *nous* of 'if we could say'. Derrida's text seems to be taking on a life of its own in which he is inhabiting the text of Malabou, 'owning it' as we say in the modern vernacular, while simultaneously abandoning it. Something has fallen out of Malabou's text, the term 'abandonment' and fallen into Derrida's pages. It emerges without reason and with surprise as Derrida opens up some distance between himself and the text he reads by rewriting that text, inserting words in it that do not exist. While Derrida abandons, Malabou renounces, the classic logic of the master and student.

At this point, while Derrida continues to co-sign and co-counter-sign the text of Hegel with Malabou through the pronomial *nous*, he also takes his leave of Malabou. He bids her farewell by upping the ante around the '*adieu*'. In a few pages it will allow him to introduce into his admiring account of plasticity his own term that will stretch plasticity to breaking point. This is another mode of farewell, namely 'mourning'. Derrida writes:

> Is there not some sort of plasticity of mourning? This plasticity, would it not consist in saying farewell to itself while always giving and receiving for itself yet another form, while always interiorizing, incorporating, *sublating*, idealizing, spiritualizing that which we abandon or which abandons us? The dialectical would be this plastic of mourning – or of melancholy, of the pathologies and of the 'folly' which the Hegelian problematic so carefully and remarkably interrogated from the first chapter of this book. Let us radicalize the theme in following the *motif of mourning* (a word which, as long as I remember, is not present in this book but which haunts it in so far as this book is also, thematically, a book on death and even on the death of God). May we not say that all plasticity is engaged or involved in some sort of mourning, in a mournful experience or a work of mourning, and to begin with the very one which divides and opposes to itself the expression 'to see (what is) coming'? And when it fails to recall, or to bring back, within Sameness, when it falls short of interiorizing, of assimilating (etc.), the other, the 'uncontrollable', remember, the 'inevitable', the 'unsteadiness', the question of the 'Absolute Other', then the failure of this work of mourning would urge to leave, *abandon* (see above), to salute with a certain farewell or adieu, and hence *to mourn mourning itself.* (pp. xxxix–xl)

Derrida proposes another temporality to the dialectic, the work of mourning, one that also incorporates and sublates but which is never complete. There is no Sunday, no day of rest, in the life of mourning. It is not accidental that the work of mourning plays such a significant role in Derrida's book on Marx.[43] The work of mourning is work, it is labour, it is the ongoing response to the task of interiorization and working through that characterizes bereavement but also intellectual labour. The work of mourning could equally describe the process of manipulation and sorting that identifies creative practice. In this sense, Theory-Practice would be a double mourning, a double labour, which worked through its material in a pincer movement across the abyss that separates these two idioms of mourning. If there is 'some sort of plasticity of mourning' it would suggest not only the flexibility of mourning as a mode of encountering thought and the world, its endless openness to new ways of working, but also that plasticity would in some way be mournful. The suppleness of plastic requires it to be worked, in order for it to have some play, to give way and to flex under the pressure of manipulation. A mournful plasticity would be one that risked falling into a state of depressive rest, unable to move as it became set in its ways. However, it would also be a plasticity that had to work hard to keep going, to face the future through the labour of dealing with the past. Derrida suggests, 'the dialectical would be this plastic of mourning'. That is to say, a plasticity that had been worked over and through – a melancholy pathology as a perpetual work of mourning, unable to close itself off and unwilling to let itself go. Its task would be to keep the memory alive, not just of a past now lived but of the future. Keeping alive the memory of the future would be truly to reckon with the history of the future.

This is where Derrida exceeds Malabou, by radicalizing plasticity, stretching it beyond itself, through the work of mourning (a word that is not present in Malabou's book). Derrida's response to Malabou is to outflank her by abandoning plasticity to mourning, mourning the failure of plasticity, its limits and its forms, in favour of an alternative dialectical play. Derrida reclaims the 'to see (what is) coming' as an idiom of mourning, the work that abandons while carrying within itself the remains of the other, but which cannot be assimilated. And this is key for Derrida, mourning cannot bring back the other to Sameness, successfully interiorize or fully assimilate it. Something always remains, that is the lesson of Derrida's own reading of Absolute Knowledge in *Glas*.[44] Consequently, mourning fails and its work is the labour of its inevitable failure, which would then call for an abandonment (again Derrida picks up his own insertion and invention here) of mourning itself in a half-finished state, a ruin of ruins. Such an existence would indeed be a melancholy pathology for some, but in contrast to the Sunday of life, this will get us through to Monday when we can start the working week all over again. We might say that mourning bids its own farewell to plasticity, or to a certain plasticity at least, offering no closure to that impulse within plasticity that resists deformation. Insofar as it insists on the remainder, mourning puts a bomb under plasticity, blowing the doors off of dialectical enclosure. To mourn mourning itself, or, abandoning the work of mourning is impossible, or to welcome death. It is a question of multiple farewells, says Derrida, 'one renounces the future, the other hopes or promises' (p. xi). Renouncing and abandoning are, as we have established, not necessarily the same thing. However, the more this other promise of the future is guaranteed or underwritten, the more it becomes a calculation of the imminent and so a betrayal and loss of the future. Hope then must be the structuration that keeps alive the memory of the future as that which escapes the dialectical foreclosure of plasticity. While plasticity looks to the future it in fact finds nothing to be hoped for there.

Let me cut short this reading around Derrida and Malabou, before Derrida continues on his way to discuss the *adieu* as a farewell to God and a God that says farewell to the future. The accidental death of God is a fascinating topic but not the subject of our current enterprise. Rather, the importance of Malabou's magisterial study of Hegel to the question of creativity is the resources it gives us to think the problems of Theory-Practice as a double plastic form, one that shapes and detonates. However, it is also a form of work that resists closure, something irreducible always remains that requires us to renounce if not abandon the possibility of completion. The work of critical practice is important because it keeps alive the memory of a future for both theory and practice, or multiple futures in which theory and practice compel themselves into states other than themselves. One can make plastic in the kitchen out of vinegar and milk treated with a little heat. The vinegar curdles the warm milk releasing casein plastic that can then be formed and dried out to set. Whether theory is the vinegar that curdles the warm milk of practice or vice versa it is hard to say. Perhaps, the plasticity of Theory-Practice is more like the celluloid that screens and burns if subject to a hot bulb, dissolving in its projection, leaving a residue that clogs and scolds as it bids farewell to its own illusion of the momentary play of shadows.

4

Prometheus and Pygmalion

In the *Metamorphoses*, Ovid tells the stories of two possible models for the relation between philosophy and creativity.[1] They are two of the foundational myths of our understanding of art and civilization, the tales of Prometheus and Pygmalion. In this chapter, we will look at both stories with a view to better understanding the paradoxes of critical practice, each tale providing us with a different point of entry to the complexities of artistic practice and philosophical thought. The story of Prometheus has its fullest elaboration in Hesiod's *Theogony* and we will attend to this tale in the second half of the chapter.[2] The myth of Pygmalion also has several versions including many neoclassical and more contemporary re-tellings.[3] The stories represent two different paradigms for creation, although they contain overlapping elements. The case of Prometheus is a model for creation that emphases theft and punishment, while the story of Pygmalion offers us an account of creation based upon illusion and misidentification. The former is a tale of inscription and disruption, the latter myth concerns representation and misreading. They both centre around moments of touching, blindness, and inauguration. In reading the Pygmalion complex and the Prometheus effect we can better understand the question of creation as a process. They are not competing tales, one offering us greater insights than the other. Rather, together, they combine to present us with a pathway through complexity, and in providing a critical account of both we are able to work through our own thinking on what it means to think about the creative.

The Pygmalion complex

In Ovid, Pygmalion is a sculptor and citizen of Cyprus, who is horrified by the shameless behaviours of the daughters of Propoetus who deny the divinity of Venus and in turn are said to have been the first prostitutes. Pygmalion in contrast lives a celibate life and lacks 'the companionship of married love' (X 244). He carves his own 'snow-white ivory' with great artistry such that it is 'more beautiful/Than ever woman born' (X 247–8). He falls in love with his masterpiece, which to Pygmalion seems to be alive and he is not averse to indulging in agalmatophilia, 'his heart desired the body he had formed/With many a touch he tries it…' (X 235–6). He brings the statue gifts and lays her on a couch of purple silk, 'called her his darling, cushioning her head' (X 254). On Venus' festive day, noted for the sacrifice of heifers, Pygmalion makes his own offering at temple and prays not that his statue should live but for a bride that has 'the living likeness of my ivory girl' (X 264). However, Venus 'knew well the purpose of his prayer' (X 266) and reads Pygmalion's desires beyond his literal supplication. Blessed with an omen in the temple, Pygmalion returns home and kisses the statue where it lay only to find that she now seems warm:

> Again he kissed her and with marveling touch
> Caressed her breast; beneath his touch the flesh
> Grew soft, its ivory hardness vanishing. (X 281–3)

The statue is said to 'yield' to the 'hands' of the sculptor just as the honey-wax found on Mount Hymettus is shaped 'by practiced fingers into many forms' (X 286). Pygmalion's reaction is one of 'wonder and misgiving/Delight and terror' (X 288–9). He thanks Venus and makes several passes over the body of the now living sculpture, who 'Felt every kiss, and blushed, and shyly raised/Her eyes to his and saw the world and him' (X 295–6).

Pygmalion has his bride, not named Galatea until Rousseau's poetic license of 1762[4] gives the statue the sobriquet found elsewhere in Ovid's tale of 'Acis and Galatea', in which she is the sea nymph beloved by the Cyclopes Polyphemus, blinded by Odysseus. Pygmalion may get the girl but it is Venus who is the creator and 'the goddess graced the union she had made' (X 297) with a daughter Paphos. However, Venus' well-intentioned plan does not necessarily run according to design. The story of Pygmalion does not end happily ever after. In the *Metamorphoses,* we go on to learn of the terrible fate of the descendants of the union between Pygmalion and his statue. Cinyras, son of Paphos, becomes King of Cyprus and has a daughter Myrrha, who has a 'disgraceful passion' for her father. With the help of her nurse she tricks her father and sleeps with him; she becomes pregnant. She asks the gods to transform her into something beyond human or animal, 'by being, I offend the living, or, by dying, offend the dead, banish me from both realms, and change me, and deny me life and death!' (X 499) She is changed into a Myrtle tree, which gives birth to the child Adonis.

Venus, herself, accidentally injured by one of her son Cupid's arrows, falls in love with the mortal youth. After many years together, Adonis is killed hunting a boar 'that sank its tusk into his groin'. (X 709) According to Shakespeare, broken-hearted and 'weary of the world' Venus retires to Paphos 'to immure herself and not be seen'.[5]

Creation is never a straightforward thing. The story of Pygmalion and his legacy involves multiple cases of misplaced desire and unintended outcomes, from the paraphilia of the sculptor to his incestuous great-granddaughter and the sorrow of the bereaved Venus, who has all the circuits of eros routed through her and ultimately rerouted towards her in an everlasting mourning. These are touching tales of blindness. Pygmalion caresses the statue who sees the world for the first time with such a touch; Cinyras does not see his daughter as they touch one another in his bed; Cupid's arrow brushes Venus' breast and she is blinded by love; Adonis is warned of the dangers of hunting but misreads or ignores the advice of Venus, leading to his death. Episodes of paraphilia, incest, and deception define this creative genealogy. Perhaps, like any unhappy family, this history is unhappy in its own way, but as a creative process it demonstrates many of the characteristics we would identify with the complexity of making and thinking. The misfires and unplanned outcomes are in keeping with the experience of creative work; each attempt at fulfilment leading to a new turn towards dissatisfaction, and the creative inheritance that leads to the ruin of the original creation. Venus is both the creator god and the last person to see the ruin of her own heart. The process of creation and pro-creation that she initiates ends in the death of her mortal lover, the great-great grandson of Pygmalion, the descendant of a statue brought to life, and a literary by-word for the ruin of beauty, dead before its time, and the cause for infinite mourning. The work of mourning here providing the schema for the labour of creation, insofar as mourning is work itself, the overcoming of loss by carrying the absent through the world as a permanent condition of making that world.[6]

Like the tree that gives birth to Adonis, this is a labour of the wholly other. Myrrha wishes to be neither dead nor alive, neither human nor animal, but is transformed into the liminal vegetal other of a being without being.[7] She becomes purely organic matter, whose last function is to reproduce itself, ensuring a process of blind dissemination. The misfires and displacements multiply as the genealogy proceeds, writing a blind history of creation and self-ruin. This is a family of misidentification that proceeds without necessarily knowing where it is going. Pygmalion thinks of himself as the sculptor-maker but his work is determined by Venus. In other versions of the story, the statue is in fact of

Aphrodite, the Greek metamorphoses of Venus. The goddess then brings to life a stone likeness of herself to share a bed with Pygmalion, initiating a chain of libidinal translation and transformation, that ends with her sharing the bed with the mortal descendant of her own likeness. The creative impulse ends in accident and ruin, with beauty impaled in the groin on the tusk of the unappreciative boar. Cirynas mistakes his daughter for a lover, Adonis never recognizes his lover as the likeness and creator of his great-great-grandmother. This family romance is not forged in the furnaces of Mars but is both the story and the effect of sexual difference, of Venus as the female deity, the creator god as woman, whose divinity is compromised both by her own proximity to mortals (her likeness as a living statue, her boy lover Adonis) and by her sacred remit as the deity of love. That is to say, she is the goddess of misrecognition, displacement, denial, blindness, unknowing, and unhappiness. She is the goddess of desire and so of misplaced attachment, misidentified, postponement, and deferral. Creation through Venus is a matter of gender and genre, of story and history, his story and her story, production and reproduction, genealogy and genesis, blindness and touching, and theory and practice.[8]

The case of Pygmalion is a question of the complexity of mimesis, of reproduction and likeness. In chapter 8 of his monumental *Allegories of Reading*, Paul de Man provides us with a reading of Rousseau's secular melodrama, *Pygmalion*.[9] In this version of the story, Pygmalion brings the statue to life without divine intervention, and Galatea touches her own arm, saying 'me', and touches another sculpture, 'not me'. For de Man, Rousseau's contribution to the Pygmalion myth provides us with a diegesis concerning mimesis and the difficulty of separating the two. Narrative, says de Man, can only ever tell the story of its own inability to tell a story, what he calls 'denominational aberration' (162), the positing and undoing of sense, which endlessly engenders further texts. Pygmalion's creative dream in Ovid not only gives rise to the genealogy of the *Metamorphosis* but to other versions of the story, including that of Rousseau. There is little that is stable about this statue, and the complexity is only multiplied when it is brought to life, engendering its own literary genealogy. De Man contrasts Rousseau's version of Pygmalion with Rousseau's earlier dramatic account of Narcissus. In this play the lead character Valère falls in love with his own portrait, barely disguised as a woman.[10] Like the Narcissus of Ovid, Rousseau's hero is compelled into an endless fascination with an image, in this case a creative work. Narcissus is then a victim of the mystification of mimesis, the misidentification of the image with the original, the self and the projection of the self, the production and the reproduction. In Ovid, Narcissus pines and withers and it becomes impossible for him to tell the difference between the self and the substitution of the self. The loved object is also the self, or a displacement of the self, vacillating between the two just as the water of a pond ripples and disperses to the touch. The false consciousness of the mimetic image is both immediate and entirely out of reach. Love, *amour-propre*, is replaced by narcissism in the endless digress of a metamorphosis without progress. The consequence of love of the self, the confusion and substitution of the self with the other, is death. There is no future to be hoped for in the pool of Narcissus.

The complimentary stories of Narcissus and Pygmalion demonstrate that the experience of creation, like the experience of love, is complex and, to borrow a phrase from de Man, 'rooted in the quicksands … which [govern] the relationship between the self and other' (p. 170). What is the situation of the self as creator in a moment of critical practice, or any form of practice come to think of it? Narcissus is deluded, Pygmalion is in denial, Venus is undone; if only a god can create, then even gods are ruined by creation.[11] As a writer, filmmaker, composer or artist, is the creating author in any more of a stable relationship as a self and to the self than either Narcissus or Pygmalion? Is that creating author any less deluded or in denial in relation to an empirical self-dispersed across the complexity and confusion of everyday life, as they are undoubtedly lost in the work and text of their creation? What is the nature of this work? Is it the work of mourning for an absent, displaced self or misidentified other? How shall we characterize the speculative labour of writing or making? Can it be separated from that other self that makes its way in the world, or, is one the reflection of the other in deep narcissistic waters? Or is the self-dispersed across the created work another rendering of the self that has a life of its own: a mimetic copy, plastic or warm to the touch? Is the labour of a critical practice doubled by the work of philosophy, which multiplies the distance between self and other? What is the economy of production and consumption between the effort and value of this labour and the selves involved? Might creation and in particular critical practice involve a work of the self that only serves to undo the stability of selfhood?

In the case of Ovid's *Pygmalion* and the many versions and transformations of the story in which the work of art takes on a life of its own, there is an element of 'wonder and misgiving/Delight and terror' (X 286–7) as the familiar and intimate is also radically different. It is not a question of a dichotomy between subject and object, creator and work, but rather as de Man puts it 'the work of art exists as a nondialectical configuration of sameness and otherness, sufficiently uncanny to be called godlike' (p. 177). That is to say, the self and its others cannot be reconciled in the work of art; there is no stability or resolution to be found in speculative and creative labour. One does not make art in order to know oneself, rather making art tells us about the impossibility of the self. The work of art is sufficiently familiar and strange to be something both in the image of the human and irretrievably non-human. Art does work that humans are incapable of, this is why it is said to be godlike: Venus is the true creator in this history. However, that does not mean that the work of art or speculative labour is omnipotent or without error or deviation. If art is said to be divine, then it is a very human deity, one whose failures are as familiar to us as our own. Art is godlike rather than *Godlike*, the owl of Minerva always flies too late and Venus is the dupe of her own snares. Art knows that it is only work, process, and labour, producing inhuman effects, beyond the human and entirely bound up with the human and the human world.

Galatea-Aphrodite is a godlike work of art. The care and love of the statue is a full-time job for Pygmalion, he worships her as he does the goddess, making sacrifices of a different kind. However, in the statue the specular and the speculative combine, practice and thought, image and theory, whereby she represents the idea of perfect creation for the sculptor. There is then a discrepancy between the statue as a product of the work and labour of the self as creator artist in which Pygmalion's own self is reflected back by his art, and the status of the statue as cold stone, art as wholly other, as radically different from the self of Pygmalion as we can imagine. Further, this is a statue of the inhuman, immortal goddess that Pygmalion takes as his love object in a dynamic in which the self is the agent of its own production as radically other. And yet Pygmalion believes, wholeheartedly, both in the divine and in the possibility of selfhood for his statue, which he dearly wishes would come to life and take on an identity of its own. There is no persuading Pygmalion of his aberration but this is precisely because there is in fact little that is aberrant about it. The story of Pygmalion's delusion is an account of every creative and critical practice as a non-dialectical configuration across the dispersed economy of the self and other.

Pygmalion approaches his statue, *as if* it were human. The attribution of the *as if* is fundamental to our approach to art.[12] We act as if the suspended reference of the work of art referred to a real world.[13] Equally, the *as if* is central to the philosophical hypothesis as a process of questioning; *as if* describes the very nature of Theory. However, it is not a matter of finding in art itself or in speculative thought aberrant moments of the *as if*, as strange and perverted as Pygmalion's love for his statue. Rather, art and philosophy are two instances of a wider schema in which the *as if* is always at play as the condition for selfhood in the world. We act *as if* we were coherent and stable selves but the pressures of life and art repeatedly show us that this is as much a delusion as Pygmalion's paraphilia. Art is not a unique moment in which selfhood dissolves, rather it is merely exemplary of our wider experience in the world, in which we are constantly creating, engendering, speculating, and collapsing the self into and around the radically different others that give it meaning. This is the work of art, the labour of thought, critical practice. Galatea awakens and looks Pygmalion in the eye: what misrecognition and misidentification take place in that exchange? As de Man puts it with respect to the Rousseau play, 'the work reads the man and reveals his total insignificance except in his relation to the work' (p. 184). This is work both in the sense of art object and creative labour. This is where the importance of Pygmalion's self resides, dispersed across the work, giving life to the statue by its own reproduction as radically different from itself. The intentions and desires of Pygmalion are immaterial to Galatea, who as a work of art has a life of her own. Pygmalion only matters insofar as Galatea is a reflection of what remains of the selfhood of Pygmalion.

What would happen if Galatea did not love Pygmalion back? What if she did not take too kindly to being touched up while lying on the artist's couch? The answer, for Galatea, would be nothing. She would continue to exist, her selfhood located beyond Pygmalion and capable of its own irregularities and dissolution. For Pygmalion, the disappointment would matter as it would reach to his very sense of self, it would be crushing and ruinous. Ovid does not record what the domestic life of this odd couple involved. They seem to have had only one child, perhaps Galatea fell out of love with Pygmalion and they slept in separate rooms. She after all is godlike and he is only a sculptor. Equally, perhaps the reality of life with a real woman did not live up to Pygmalion's paraphilic fantasy. Having had his deepest desire fulfilled, how could reality possibly compete with Pygmalion's complex circuits of longing? Did Galatea find him late at night pining over the statues in the temple? Creative practice does not promise a happy ever after.

At the end of Rousseau's play Galatea awakens into life, and as the stage direction tells us, she 'touches herself and says: '*Moi*'. Pygmalion (transported) responds; '*Moi!*' (1:1230). They both assert their selfhood; Galatea in surprise, Pygmalion by way of differentiation as much as affirmation. 'Galatea takes a few steps and touches a marble stone: It is no longer I'. Touch is the insurance policy for phenomenology, in which the linguistic act of naming the material trumps the equally linguistic act of naming the self. In this way the linguistic, psychological and textual bundle of contradictions that make up the self earns the designation and assuring clarity of the material. The illusion of touch allows the slip from figurality into materiality, as if they were two different things and not the effect of each other. Touch short-circuits the *as if*, turning hypothesis into permanence. Touch is at best slippery and while Galatea stroking the marble provides a guarantee, her next gesture (to touch Pygmalion) is far more ambiguous:

> Galatea goes in his direction and looks at him. He rises precipitously, stretches out his arms toward her and looks at her ecstatically. She touches him with one of her hands: he trembles, takes her hand, presses it against his heart, then covers it with kisses. Galatea (with a sigh): *Ah! Encore moi.* (1:1230–1)

De Man comments on how equivocal this line really is, 'the tone is hardly one of ecstatic union, rather of resigned tolerance towards an over assiduous admirer' (p. 185). Pygmalion might interpret the line as an affirmation of the selfhood of his girlfriend, whose identity is that of love object and defined by Pygmalion's affections. In this sense *'moi encore'* means *'aussi moi'* [me too/me as well]. However, the 'Ah!' and the sigh, for de Man, 'suggests disappointment rather than satisfaction' (p. 186) rendering the line as *'de nouveau moi'* [me again]. As if to say, 'so this is what it means to be alive and a woman'.

Pygmalion's ardour is in sharp contrast: 'It is you, you alone: I have given you my entire being: henceforth I shall live only through you'. Such earnestness not only annuls the self of Pygmalion, defining itself through a dependency on the other, it also, perhaps, invokes a certain ennui in Galatea whose entry into the world now leaves the importance of Pygmalion's drama behind (the sculptor's psycho-sexual fantasy life is now the least interesting thing in the play). Galatea's sigh of 'is that all there is' to being a woman, means that the union ends not so much in Paphos as pathos. So much comes into this scene to interrupt and relegate the creator Pygmalion; sexual difference creates a new dynamic in the relation between self and other, rendering the dichotomy irreducibly complex, as productive of future textual encounters as it is of the drama here. Galatea's *'Ah! Encore moi'* is not an affirmation of the self but an acceptance of the negation of the self, 'the self-sacrificing negation of the subject' (p. 186). It is one thing to be a sculptor, it is another to be a sculptor's wife. However, it is Galatea's story that comes to take centre stage at the end of Rousseau's play, demonstrating that such a radical negation of the self is the result of the recuperative power of creative production, which offers both a disarticulation of the self across conceptual and diegetic boundaries and a formal structure for the representation of the metaphor of the self as if it were real. A similar case could be made for Ovid's Venus who loses herself among the bowers and across the tales of Book X of the *Metamorphoses*, which compromise her deity and epseity, folding her creative substitution of Pygmalion's statue into her own illusion and negation as a lover. She is left to mourn and to retire from the world, having inaugurated the creative acts that engender the textual progress of both Ovid's text and its creative legacy.

The story of Pygmalion in its many versions offers an exquisite allegory for critical practice. As with all art there is a significant investment of the self in the process of theoretically informed creative production. The introduction of theoretical writing into the creative moment is not an inoculation against the narcissism of the artist rather it doubles down on that narcissism, inflating its potential and pushing it towards new horizons. The theory-practitioner (the philosopher-novelist, the artist-writer, the theoretical auteur) has already made a commitment to identity and places their self and the self in the centre of their critical practice. There is nothing more autobiographical than Theory. To some, a creative art that emerged from an engagement with theoretical writing would be as perverted or as aberrant as Pygmalion's love of stone women. However, just as one should not judge Pygmalion's paraphilia (it is in fact a decisive instance that demonstrates the abnormal nature of the normative) one should not imagine that critical practice has a tangential relation to art in general. Rather, in the explicit formulation of a relationship between creative production and speculative thought, we can find a determining instance of the aporias that run across all making and creation.

The use of J Hillis Miller

In his study *Versions of Pygmalion*, which reads a number of literary texts that deploy the motifs of the Pygmalion story, J Hillis Miller offers an account of Kleist's '*Der Findling*'.[14] Miller's reading of this Kleist short story is the jump-off point for an extended discussion of the performative nature of teaching critical theory. If we allow ourselves to follow Miller's argument for a few pages, it will afford us a significant insight into the question of critical practice. The Yale School critic is interested in what he calls 'inaugural acts of creation' (p. 8). The story of Pygmalion is that of the sculptor who literally releases the statue from the stone that hides it. Ovid describes the stone that holds Galatea as '*fit utilis usu*', made fit for use by being used. There is much that could be said about the uses of 'use', especially in this story where use borders on mis-use, abuse, and self-abuse.[15] However, the relation between the sculptor and the stone is not merely utilitarian, just as the relation between practice and theory cannot be that of functional service. Rather, the stone or the wax begins by being not fit for use but in being used becomes useful. The initial use of the material by the sculptor makes something not yet useful fit for use and does so by using the unusable. Utility here is not a relation of cause and effect, but rather use is both cause and effect.

As Miller would describe it, such acts of shaping are both constative and performative, i.e. they are both the created outcome and the act of creation that creates creation itself. The inaugural performative makes the useless useful by bringing something absolutely new into existence. The skill of Pygmalion's art is that he is able to disguise this manipulation and fabrication even from himself, collapsing cause and effect, and taking his statue for a real girl. This seeming aberration, of confusing the fabricated and the real, is not unique to Pygmalion. Rather, his sensational case points us towards a truth of all making or construction, namely the confusion between an experience of the material and experience itself. We might think of the material as the proof of experience itself, like Bishop Berkley's stone, but an experience of the material is no different from any other experience.[16] It is the construction of sense that gives meaning to the material as matter. Experiencing materiality is the effect of a linguistic predicament not its anterior. In this sense, the thing that matters in the experience of the material is the linguistic. Perhaps, experience as such, this vaguest of phenomenological terms, is the ideological confusion that unavoidably mistakes a linguistic reality for a material one. This slip in the order of linguistic and material reality is the experience of experience. Of course, material effects are substantial but are only made so by the experience of them. Galatea is stone that lives as a result of Pygmalion's desire that it should. It takes an act of divine intervention to move beyond the confusion of reality with the experience of fabrication.

In his chapter on Kleist, Miller suggests that theoretical texts cannot be treated as secondary to reading literature or art. That is to say, theory cannot have a relation of utility to making. Theory, for Miller, has to be read in an inaugural and creative way, through a productive reading that brings something new into existence. Theory is dead when it is applied. Reading Theory must make something happen. At least this is a different kind of application for theory; theory that applies itself, or, is put to work in order to produce active, productive, performative readings. These readings are not passive or merely cognitive, rather they are creative and make Theory '*fit utilis usu*', made fit for use by being used. This is the place of theory in critical practice; it instigates something new through creative reading. Such inaugural reading, says Miller, is opposed to 'the vast enterprise of assimilative rationalizing' (p. 84) which he associates with the function of the university. A critical practitioner does not read theory in order to categorize and incorporate its concepts and protocols. This is why a critical practitioner is not the same as a disciplinary philosopher. Rather, creative reading that is radically inaugural is said by Miller 'to propose a new 'contract" (p. 84) with that disciplinary apparatus. A critical practitioner does not read theory as a philosopher but as an artist, and equally in doing so proposes a new relation to art, which is itself an impulsion within art that compels art beyond the frontiers of its established condition and proprieties.

At the same time philosophical texts are of the order of the constative. They are epistemological and aim to offer knowledge of the world through idiomatic or disciplinary conventions and vocabulary. 'Theory' names something different from philosophy. It should not be thought of as something like 'philosophy for art students', to be used in a utilitarian way. Philosophy cannot be held accountable to art because art, in the first place, is wholly a philosophical concept.[17] Rather, 'Theory' names the performative dimension of reading, namely, it is not a parallel activity to reading literature or making art but is rather a reading act that is, what Miller calls, 'a productive event in the real world of material history' (p. 85). Theory in this sense is a practice; *reading Theory* inaugurates creativity. 'Reading' should be a redundancy in relation to 'Theory' because 'Theory' has no meaning outside of its productive and performative reading. Of course, the texts of Theory, the ones to be found on syllabi and on library shelves are also the works of the philosophical canon. These two characteristics of Theory cannot be resolved or reconciled. Critical Practice is not a dialectical synthesize between theory and practice. The constative and performative aspects of Theory are asymmetrical not harmonizable. This is why the relation between theory and practice is aporetic, lacunar and interminable. In the leap across the abyss of art, Theory and Practice miss one another, just as they hail each other from different sides, each having mistaken the position of the other.

Later in the chapter on Kleist, Miller suggests that 'teaching is practical not theoretical'. By this he means that what happens in the pedagogical space of the seminar or classroom cannot be controlled or predicted by the rational protocols of theoretical texts. The promise of theory is that of clear thinking and far-sightedness, and as such accords with the institutional role the university plays in a modern technological and rational society. However, teaching is like reading, or at least the creative and radically inaugural reading that Miller identifies with theoretical texts, in that its outcomes are unpredictable. Reading and teaching for Miller are performative because their effects cannot be known or programmed in advance; they are not an epistemological event to be defined as the transmission of received and codified knowledge. We should understand reading here in its broadest sense, including the experience of art, or the affective encounter with theatre or cinema. This sort of reading happens when the lights go off and the projector rolls. What happens in that space cannot be programmed, it is a location of surprise and radical inauguration. This is not to say that reading is not theoretical. At the same time all reading, whatever its avowed status, can only be theoretical. Reading changes theory. What we are calling here Theory as a practice, is theory changing itself through its own reading as an act of its own disconfirmation. As Miller puts it, 'the interaction between theory and reading might be defined as a constant infinitesimal calculus in which reading informs and alters theory, along with the other vital and inaugural effects it has' (p. 94). Reading moves theory on, that is, reading as a practice, reading as the dynamic process of a critical practice, changes theory. It is this transformative aspect that distinguishes Theory from Philosophy. Theory is a metamorphoses; it is the dream of Pygmalion.

Of course, it would be naive to assume that the ways in which reading, or critical practice, changes theory are always a co-operative relationship. This is not a dialectical synthesis or a balanced give and take. Rather, it is a relationship of misunderstanding and on occasion violent appropriation. The point of reading philosophy to make art is to make art not to write philosophy. Critical Practice is another idiom of making, neither disciplinary philosophy nor craft-based art, but it is both philosophical and artistic. It must work as both art and philosophy simultaneously even though the impulse of each pulls in different directions or runs at a tangent to the other. Insofar as critical practice must work as art or a philosophical film must honour its obligations to cinema rather than provide a mere illustration of philosophy, it must stretch itself beyond a strictly theoretical horizon. At the same time theory is identified by its universal and totalizing ambition, assimilating within itself the idiosyncratic according to the principle of reason that is presupposed by philosophical study. Critical Practice is then double and contradictory. On the one hand, critical practice is unique and inaugural, starting from a singular position that it opens onto a radical otherness that transforms and displaces that position. On the other hand, as a theoretical act, it is rational and iterable, with the capacity to be assimilated within the disciplinary protocols of the institution, recorded, subject to commentary and interpretation, disseminated and taught. If it were not, the enterprise of this present book would be entirely futile. On the one hand, if we follow Miller's understanding of speech acts, we would say that critical practice is performative because it is a positing of thought that is radically unpredictable in its effects, whose outcomes cannot be programmed in advance.[18] On the other hand, and equally, critical practice, like any idiom of art, can always be interpreted and recuperated into a preconceived historical, causal, dialectical, or theoretical schema. It is only in the brief moment of creative reading that we can hold the tension apart long enough in order to push the aporia towards a productive re-inscription.[19]

Prometheus unzipped

The myth of Prometheus is distributed across a number of important texts, notably the *Theogony* of Hesiod, a dialogue by Plato, and four plays (not all surviving) by Aeschylus.[20] Just as we saw in the figure of Pygmalion, the case of Prometheus provides us with a rich allegory of the aporias of creativity. He is also in important respects a figure associated with Theory, and his punishment for crossing the streams between Theory and creative practice is eternal. Like the Satan of Milton's *Paradise Lost*, he is for the Romantics a character of heroic rebellion who durst defy the omnipotent, not to arms but to a challenge of wits. For Percy Shelley, the rebellion of Prometheus, the assertion of critical intelligence against a malign godhead defies 'power which seems omnipotent' to give 'hope till Hope creates/From its own wreck the thing it contemplates'.[21] For Mary Shelley, the modern Prometheus would be a bricolage man, not so much an Adam as a fallen angel but unlike Satan who 'has his companions, fellow-devils, to admire and encourage him', her creature is 'solitary and detested'.[22] The nuances in each retelling of the Prometheus story are subtle and accumulative but in every case the fate of Prometheus is closely bound to that of humanity. To understand the condition of Prometheus is to contemplate what it means to be human, and as we shall see is to appreciate the ways in which that condition is determined by tales of sexual difference.

In *The Theogony*, the most ancient of the Prometheus sources, he is one of four brothers born of the Titans Iapetus (son of Uranus and Gaia) and Clymene (daughter of Ocean). His siblings are Atlas, who carries the world on his shoulders, Menoetius (a god of violent anger and rash action, his name literally means 'doomed might', killed by Zeus for an act of prideful and impetuous rebellion), and 'scatter-brained' Epimetheus. With brothers like these Prometheus is required to distinguish himself as very much his own Titan, cunning and intelligent unlike Epimetheus, considered in contrast to Menoetius, but whose lasting penance mirrors the fate of Atlas who also challenged the capricious power of the Olympians. While Atlas and Menoetius side against

Zeus in war, Prometheus earns his punishment for outsmarting Zeus in a battle of wits. In a dispute between the gods and mortals over sacrificial rights, Prometheus intervenes to present before Zeus a division of the carcass of an ox. In one pile he placed all the edible meat and fat, disguised by the unappealing stomach of the ox; in another pile he dressed up the inedible and unwanted bones in shining fat. Hesiod records that Zeus is not taken in by the shiny object, seeing through the trick, but chooses the fatty bones anyway as an excuse to take revenge on mankind. Hesiod's excessive piety that attempts to paint Zeus in the best light, as one whose absolute wisdom cannot be tricked, in fact shows him to be even more unappealing than the oily bones he chooses. In this account the all-powerful deliberately chooses the deceitful package or inferior offerings in order to enact cruelty on humanity by withholding from them the power of fire.[23] Zeus' calculation seems somewhat petty here and lacking in foresight, accepting the holocaust of bones in perpetuity as an excuse to withhold fire from mankind. Who could resist taking down such a petulant ass of an omnipotent god? Hesiod notes that Prometheus further outwits Zeus and steals the 'unwearying fire' in a hollow fennel stalk before bestowing it on the Melian race of mortal men. Zeus, who may or may not have seen any of this coming, is so angry that he punishes mankind by sending them a woman to bring eternal misery into their lives. Prometheus, by contrast, seems to get off lightly, dodging the bullet of sexual difference, by being bound by 'inextricable bonds, cruel chains, and [Zeus] drove a shaft through his middle, and set on him a long-winged eagle, which used to eat his immortal liver; but by night the liver grew as much again everyway as the long-winged bird devoured in the whole day' (520-5). There would seem to be nothing less understanding than a god whose wisdom is everlasting.

The account of Hesiod presents us with a number of arresting provocations in an account of creative practice and theory. Here Prometheus is said to be 'kindly' and obviously has a soft spot for the race of men shivering on the earth below; he defies and tricks Zeus not once but twice. It is not so much that Prometheus is determined to help mankind, rather having been thwarted first time by Zeus (when fire was withheld following the trick at Mecone) perhaps Prometheus refuses to be outdone by the all-powerful god. Prometheus cannot help himself; surely he steals the fire as much to annoy Zeus as he does to assist cold humanity? It is the gift of fire that leads to creative acts on the part of humanity, making life as we know it possible, but this creativity is preceded by the act of theft and rebellion by Prometheus, one perhaps motivated by his own desire to exercise his own cleverness and wiles as it is by any sense of largesse or philanthropy. Prometheus is compelled into challenging the impossible. The creativity of humanity is merely a side effect of a greater struggle against the pomposity of onto-theology. In this sense, Hesiod's Prometheus is a theorist who sees in advance the benefit of fire to man but who has a wider strategic goal of undermining the claims to authority of absolute wisdom. Theft and rebellion are two significant tropes here, the first a non-originary origin for creation, the second a permanent parabasis for theoretical critique.[24] Prometheus is both creator/initiator and thinker/tactician, a critical practitioner who cannot help but push the boundaries of his own possibilities.

However, none of this ends well for Prometheus. For the crime of mixing godhead with humanity, theory with practice, he is sentenced to eternal damnation, and not just any old damnation at that, a particularly cruel and unusual punishment – chained to a rock, while an eagle eats his liver by day only for it to grow back overnight: be eaten, sleep, repeat. Hesiod adds the particularly nasty detail of Prometheus also having a shaft driven through his middle, as if the absolute cruelty of the Absolute where not cruel enough already. However, Prometheus' impossible liver offers us another curious figure for the interminable task of theoretical practice. Love, or perhaps art as a substitute for love, may be the thing that eats your heart out. However, theory may be the thing that eats out your liver, only for it to grow back overnight. In the ancient world, it was thought that the liver, a store for the humours, rather than the heart was the source of blood. If to eat one's heart out is to yearn for something unattainable, perhaps, to have one's liver eaten out is to be confronted with the impossibility of thought, or the inadequacy of theory to practice, thinking to life. To have the liver restored and the process begin again on a daily basis is a particularly cruel trick, amnesia takes hold and the challenge begins again only to run up against the limits of the impossible once more, *ad infinitum*. It would seem a suitable metaphor for creative-critical practice that as a permanent condition compels itself into an impossible confrontation with its own limits. Like relations between men and women, that the impossible relation between theory and practice, as the human condition, should be mythologized as a punishment from the gods, also seems cruelly apt. As Kafka says of the Prometheus story that leaves behind only the inexplicable mass of rock in the Caucasus: 'the legend tried to explain the inexplicable. As it came out of a substratum of truth it had in turn to end in the inexplicable'.[25] Perhaps there is no amnesia and Prometheus remembers every single bite.

Freud comments on the Prometheus myth in his 1932 text 'The Acquisition and Control of Fire'.[26] Here he connects the story of Prometheus with the historic need of primitive communities to control the potential of fire, through the introduction of a taboo on 'the homosexually-tinged desire to put it out with a stream of urine', the so-called Mongolian law (p. 187). For Freud, the important issues here are the manner in which Prometheus transported the fire, the act of outrage, theft and fraud, and the meaning of his punishment. The fennel stalk is an obvious penis symbol for Freud. However, the male genitals do not harbour fire but its seeming opposite, the water of his stream of urine, the means of quenching fire. It is not unusual, however, in analytic material for a symbol to take on its opposite meaning. The situation is complex, Prometheus has defrauded the gods, and in mythology 'the gods are granted the satisfaction of all desires which human creatures have to renounce' (p. 189). It is instinctual life, the free rein of the id allotted to the gods, which is defrauded when the quenching of fire is renounced. It seems clearer to Freud that the liver, the site of passion and desire, should be the locus for the punishment of Prometheus. The fate of Prometheus then concerns the demand for the renunciation of instinct and the enforcement of that demand. It is a story about guilt and the development of guilt in a psychoanalytic sense. At the same time, for Freud, the flame is also a symbol of the phallus and is connected with erotic desire. The quenching of fire with the penis carries 'the meaning of a pleasurable struggle with another phallus' (p. 190). This is doubled by the attack on the liver, which has a regenerative power like the male member. The mythopoetic content of the Prometheus story then points to sating and quenching of desire, and to its return and indestructibility. It is then a narrative of antithesis, between the genital function of an erect penis, and the quenching of that possibility during the detumescence of urination. Prometheus represents the instinctual and its punishment, the suppression of the libido and its return.

In the context of a discussion of creative theory and practice, this should not surprise us. Another way of reading the myth alongside Freud is to suggest that any instinctual practice is reined in by the theoretical law within, not as an interdict against practice but as a necessary stricture of tension that predicates the possibility of the conditions of practice. If we think of practice as the instinctual life, of what happens regardless or in spite of theory, then such a possibility is the god that is defrauded by renunciation of desire. In this sense, the human desire for practice is transformed into the transcendental privilege of theory. However, theory here does not take on the function of the super-ego, rather like Prometheus the rebel, it retains all the characteristics of an unchecked desire. Theory becomes the site for an idiom of practice that is denied to the world of mortal men. This antithesis is resolved in the eternal punishment of that theoretical impulse, even if it returns on a daily basis to express itself as a desire for rebellion against the same authority it equally represents. That practice simultaneously stokes the proud flames of theoretical excitation and contains within itself the means to piss all over theory should not surprise us at all.

In *Prometheus Bound* by Aeschylus the initial punishment for the theft of fire is restricted to Prometheus being chained to a rock, the subsequent eating of his liver is an additional plague imposed by Zeus because Prometheus, who holds such knowledge, refuses to tell the Olympian the means by which Zeus will fall from power.[27] In the Aeschylus version, Prometheus had helped Zeus secure victory in the war of the Titans. This may explain why Prometheus (also the son of a Titan) has little time for the pomposity of Zeus and claims to absolute knowing. It also suggests that Zeus' torture of Prometheus is particularly cruel, almost as if he is overcompensating, acknowledging in some obscure way the threat that Prometheus poses to Zeus. For Aeschylus the compassion that Prometheus bears humanity is played up as motivation for the theft of divine fire, indeed Prometheus is said to have prevented Zeus from exterminating the race of men ('these schemes no one opposed except myself: But I dared: I ransomed mortals from being utterly destroyed' [180]). Prometheus sees himself as a hero against the 'malady' attached 'to tyranny' (180) and benefactor of humanity: 'all arts among the human race are from Prometheus' (309) including language and the Titanic gift of memory: 'I discover for them Numbers, the surpassing all inventions, the combinations too of letters, and Memory, effective mother-nurse of all arts' (285). However, Aeschylus' Prometheus is also an unrepentant rebel 'I knew all these things willingly, willingly I erred' (201). His good will to mortals is as much as slight to Zeus: in nurturing the fallible, his target is the Absolute. He is a god ill-treated by gods but he is still a god dedicated to undoing the omnipotent.

This Prometheus has the gift of prophecy; like Theory he has the predictive power to see the future unfold before him, even if he cannot escape the fate of his own failure. He predicts that one day Zeus will have a need for him – Zeus will need him to prevent his own overthrow but when that day comes he will refuse to compromise with the almighty. The second half of the play introduces the anachronistic figure of Io, a mortal pursued by the lustful Zeus, who in rejecting the god is destined to wander endlessly irritated by a gadfly. It would seem that the origins of creativity cannot be separated from the question of sexual difference, which in turn is bound up in a rejection of the absolute, showing it then to be an equivocal, jealous and petty form of omnipotence, where the boundary between the infinite and the mortal is crossed frequently, demonstrating the banality of the everlasting. Prometheus predicts that the descendants of Io will free him from his bondage; Io will not be so lucky in escaping the sex pest Zeus who will make her pregnant with a touch of his hand. The Chorus of Oceanids express the hope that Zeus never takes an interest in them. Who could bear to be loved by the all-encompassing? In the second part of Aeschylus' cycle (*Prometheus Unbound*) it is Hercules who delivers Prometheus: the concluding, or perhaps the first, episode of *Prometheus Pyrphoros* (Prometheus the Fire-bringer) is lost to antiquity. The absent play, of which only one line remains, may have preceded *Prometheus Bound* by telling the story of the theft of fire, or, may have concluded the trilogy with the possible reconciliation of Prometheus and Zeus (who is warned not to marry Thetis whose son would overthrow Zeus just as he had deposed his own father Chronos). Instead Thetis marries a mortal king and gives birth to the hero of the Trojan War, Achilles, and to another literary form and epic tradition. There is then, something compelling in the ambivalence of Prometheus, as an immortal who saves mortality, a prophet who cannot escape necessity, a god whose secret knowledge threatens to end divine rule, and a literary figure whose fragments draw the arts of the divine into the fallen world of the human.

If hindsight is a wonderful thing then it would seem in the case of Prometheus foresight is something of a curse. The very sagacity of foresight must lead to the dissolution of the conditions that first gave rise to its predictive power. Thus as an allegory of theory and practice, the fate of Prometheus demonstrates the ways in which application of an anticipatory model can only ever lead to the risk of not just the insight of a single prediction but of the entire frame of the possibility of premonition. And in knowing this, the restless and sceptic creator persists in putting the exemplar and exemplarity itself at risk: 'I knew all these things willingly, willingly I erred'. It is the practice of wilfully erring that puts Theory to the test, compelling theory beyond itself to know more than itself. In *The Psychoanalysis of Fire*, Gaston Bachelard speaks of 'The Prometheus Complex', which names the problem of 'clever disobedience' (11) as 'a veritable will to intellectuality'.[28] Bachelard says, 'we propose, then, to place together under the name of the Prometheus complex all those tendencies which impel us to know as much as our fathers, more than our fathers, as much as our teachers, more than our teachers' (p. 12). Prometheus takes everlasting wisdom from Mt Olympus to the fallen world of humans, putting the infallible to the ultimate and ordinary test of the fallible. He does not stretch for a higher knowledge, rather he plunges knowingly into the empirical and in so doing creates something new that knowledge, even his own, could not foresee. He is the philosopher who reads the newspaper (as Hegel instructed[29]), the theorist who practices art, his rebellion is an intellectual one that tests the very boundaries of the intellectual. As Bachelard comments: 'If pure intellectuality is exceptional, it is nonetheless very characteristic of a specifically human evolution. The Prometheus complex is the Oedipus complex of the life of the intellect' (p. 12).

It is the desire to overthrow the authority of authority, to be the author of the undoing of authority, and in so doing authorize another authority beyond authority. This other authority is the expertise of experience. This is not an experience shorn of intellectuality or in any way separate from the intellectual life. Rather, it is a desire to make the intellectual more human by testing, breaking and so exceeding the authority of the transcendent. In the Prometheus complex, Theory breaks itself in order to continue its work enriched by an encounter with its own fallibility. In the knowledge that this encounter can only lead to lasting torment, theory proceeds, willingly. The Prometheus complex is contrasted by Bachelard to the Empedocles complex, named after the hero of Hölderlin's unfinished play about the philosopher who writes in verse and who ends his life by jumping into the volcanic flames of Mt. Etna.[30] Prometheus brings life, Empedocles chooses death, sacrificing himself on an intellectual funeral pyre to demonstrate the truth of his cosmogenic philosophy, sure of himself and convinced by his faith in his own certainty. But the universe is not reduced to nothingness along with the thinker, it lives on, and in the account of Diogenes Laertius,[31] the volcano throws back one of the philosopher's bronze sandals to demonstrate to his followers that Empedocles has not ascended to the immortal gods but has instead met a grisly end attempting to maintain the deceit of a faith in the absolute. In this respect, the comic regurgitation of the classics is to be much preferred to the grandiloquence of Hölderlin's Romantic idealism. The fraud of Empedocles is a kind of psychosis while the intelligent disobedience of Prometheus is an everyday pathology.

The fault of Bernard Stiegler

Bernard Stiegler in the first volume of *Technics and Time*, in the chapter 'Prometheus's Liver', in the section entitled 'The Fault of Epimetheus', seems to rely on more contemporary philosophical accounts than the literary heritage of the ancients.[32] In turn invocations of the Prometheus legend by the likes of Martin Heidegger and André Leroi-Gourhan take as their starting point Plato's *Protagoras* rather than Aeschylus or Hesiod (although he does cite Jean-Pierre Vernant's account of Hesiod, if not the text itself).[33] In the Platonic dialogue,

Protagoras recounts another myth of the origins of humanity. In this version, the two brothers are charged with a task by Zeus, to allot to every animal power for survival on the newly created earth. Epimetheus begs his brother to allow him to do this job, asking Prometheus to review his work on completion. Accordingly, Epimetheus equips every creature on the principle of compensation so that, for example, those without speed would be strong, and those who lacked strength would have speed in order to run away from other threatening species. Plato notes that 'Epimetheus was not a particularly clever person' and before long he had used up all the available powers, leaving the human race still unprovided for.[34] Prometheus noting this mistake, and knowing the time allotted to the task was nearly over and that Zeus would shortly expect to see the results, decided to steal 'the gift of skill in the arts' [*ten enteknen sophian*] and fire (without which the skills would be useless) from the workshops of Hephaestus and Athena. Protagoras says, 'in this way man acquired sufficient resources to keep himself alive, but he had no political wisdom [*sophia*]' (321d) which was an art in the keeping of Zeus. In the dialogue, Prometheus is punished for his theft but the blame is put on the failure of Epimetheus. Humanity benefits from a share in the portion of the gods, being the only creature that believes in gods, erects altars to them and makes images of them, but also by the arts given to them by Prometheus through which they 'soon discovered articulate speech [*phonen*] and names [*onomata*] and invented culture, agriculture and economics ('houses and clothes and shoes and bedding and got food from the earth' [322a]). It is curious that Stiegler cuts Plato's dialogue at this point before Protagoras explains that the legacy of Prometheus only brought war and destruction upon humanity, which forced Zeus to give mankind politics as well, so that humans could live without killing one another. We will return to this.

Stiegler contends that figure of Prometheus 'makes no sense by itself. It is only consistent through its doubling of Epimetheus' (p. 186). Such an argument might have some traction for us in an account of critical practice; accordingly, we should follow Stiegler's reading for a few pages. For Stiegler the story of Prometheus and Epimetheus points to a philosophical understanding of technics, but belongs to a moment when 'the tragic is still experienced in terms of (the astonishment at the fact that there is) technicity' (p. 185). However, Stiegler wants to argue that philosophy has forgotten Epimetheus in favour of its privileging of Prometheus: literally philosophy has forgotten his forgetting. Between them the two brothers share important aspects of human experience: Prometheus, literally 'forethought', and Epimetheus, literally 'afterthought'. Prometheus, we might say, represents Theory to Epimetheus' experience; Prometheus plans ahead and can predict the future, Epimetheus is very much about learning through doing, that is to say, acquiring knowledge through mistakes. However, for Stiegler, this is the essential forgotten element of thinking. Epimetheus is not stupid, as Plato contends, but rather is the experience of experience, the rumination on things that have passed. We encountered a similar aporia in Kleist's formulation of General Mirabeau and La Fontaine's lion. In the case of Epimetheus we have a figure 'of deferred action, of the après-coup, of return through the failure of experience' (p. 186). It is surely only on the basis of such failure that foresight can make its plans for the future but just as theory cannot stand alone from practice, the truth of experience and forgetting, always arrives too late. It arrives in time to ruin theory, to spoil the party for theory by demonstrating its failings; forgetting experience cannot arrive on time to help theory land without error, but without this forgetting we would not insist on theoretical foresight in the first place.

Stiegler wants to argue that this forgetting is absent from the very centre of phenomenology itself and so his own re-inscription of technicity as a forgotten issue in metaphysics marks a radical disruption in the philosophical tradition.[35] This study is less concerned with the validity of Stiegler's claims for his own argument, but is more taken with this decisive aporia in the experience of experience itself, or, as it pertains to the relation, such as it is, between theory and practice. The fault of Epimetheus is to have forgotten humanity: 'Humans are the forgotten ones. Humans only occur through their being forgotten; they only appear in disappearing' (p. 188). That is to say, humanity is distinguished by its difference and supplementarity to the animality that exceeds it. To such a bold claim we might add that humans are the forgetting ones, in this respect the god Epimetheus is all too human. Like the question of the Fall of Adam and Eve, this story of origins relies upon a double fault, in this instance, forgetting followed by theft. The default origin of humanity is always fault, but mankind is innocent of Prometheus' crime, he is the one who will be punished for all eternity. His actions have their own origins in the fault of his brother; humans benefit from this forgetting but are not the ones who are punished for it, at least not in the text of Plato. Rather, unlike in Hesiod, Zeus himself forgets the fate of humans and so allows a gap to open between a world of mortals and the immortality of the gods. Humanity emerges, forgotten, as Zeus carries on a war among Titans as he takes revenge on Prometheus, whose gifts to man in turn become a cause for concern and the occasion of later intervention by Zeus to make humans more human. Politics is of course no less an ambiguous gift than fire or sexual difference.

The universe that develops after Prometheus' munificence, which is also a larceny, is divided between distant and withdrawn gods and forgotten humans defined not by a fall or a fault but by death, their very mortality. The sacrifice of animals to the gods by humans is the mediation that connects the two realms, a sacrifice that exists through a fraud so that man might distinguish himself from the animals that were equipped with talents while he was forgotten. It is then the experience of finitude that separates humanity from the divine and in this space of mortality the gift of skill in the arts is indissociable from the faults of Prometheus and Epimetheus, from planning and forgetting, from theory and practice. It is under these circumstances that the social, religious and the political are established, whereby forgetting through finitude defines the play of theory ruined by practice in a political community founded in a cult of sacrifice. Equally, the failure of Prometheus has consequences in the world of the immortals, which is as equally divided as a political community as the world of men. In Plato, Zeus is just as petty as he is in Hesiod or Aeschylus, taking his revenge on Prometheus for having dared share ambiguity with humanity. Up until the moment that Epithemeus forgot about humanity, the race of men had not known hunger or cold or dissent or love, these were the preserve of the immortals, while man lived in a golden age of innocence in which they shared proximity to their gods. The fault of Prometheus is to have brought such ambiguity into the world of men, imagining that it was a gift from the gods. This share of the divine turns out to be the cause of all man's woes. In other words, the gift of Prometheus to the human race is humanity. Humanity, on these terms, is then a stolen divinity, one compromised by finitude, one that has its origin in amnesia and burglary.

Prometheus gives us *prométheia* within finitude, the experience of mortality. As Stiegler describes it, 'Prometheus attempted to mislead Zeus, as a result of which there emerged the human condition' (p. 192). The truth of this condition appears in the disappearance of humanity, its forgetting and death undone by disease and hunger. At the origin of this fault, for Stiegler, is the non-origin of technology or the prosthetic, the non-human: the fire of Prometheus that makes but precedes humanity. Our interest here is not so much with the question of technicity per se but with what comes with it, or even before it, namely, invention. Invention is then both a cause and effect of this default origin of humanity. Invention and imagination (*mékhané*) come with the prosthetic given to humanity by Prometheus, which is to say that they have an origin outside of themselves: a pro-sthesis that is beyond or placed in front of. This is the fault of Epithemeus, that the human must forever after be something other than itself. Unlike the animal that has scales or wings or fur or gills, the human's defining attributes must be something other than itself, the skills of the making and industry, technology and housing, agriculture and the arts. This is the way in which Prometheus chooses to mitigate the error of his brother, defining the human experience as something beyond itself and a forgetting of the essential. The human is without essential qualities rather it is, after Prometheus, defined entirely using artifice and the ability to invent. Whether *techne* gives rise to *logos* (reason and language) is a moot point here, on Stiegler's reckoning both 'logos and tekhné are modalities of the same being-outside-oneself' (p. 193). To this list we might also add allegory, *allos agoria*, being the state of other speaking, the narrative that compels itself to mean something other than itself, like the story of Prometheus and Epithemeus, sharing with *logos* and *tekhné*, like *philos*, as both predicate and effect, this modality of being outside oneself. The gift to humanity, the gift of humanity, is not a positive one. It is an ambiguous inheritance that is offered as a compensation for having been forgotten, left out when all the qualities were being distributed throughout the animal kingdom. To be human then is to create, but creation is ruined from the start, from the default origin, by the failures of humanity as gifted to us by the gods.

In Plato, Zeus sends humanity politics, in Hesiod he sends sexual difference. In the *Theogony*, Zeus sends the race of men the first woman as the sower of discord; however, here she has no name. It is in *Works and Days* that Hesiod expands upon this myth, naming the woman trained by Athena and Aphrodite as Pandora.[36] Prometheus has warned Epimetheus not to accept any gifts from Zeus for fear that it might be something harmful to man. However, Epimetheus either forgets this advice or is just accident prone, accepting Pandora who brings with her a jar of woes. In this version, living in a golden age without knowledge of sorrow or hard work, the race of men are introduced to 'countless plagues', diseases and evils when Pandora opens the 'lid of the jar with her hands and scattered' its contents. Only hope remained in the jar before the contagion is stopped. Once again, the experience of what it means to be human is founded in a double fault: the vengeance of Zeus upon men as the receiver of Prometheus' stolen goods, and the negligence of Epimetheus, taken in by 'the beautiful bane' of Pandora. From these originary faults difference enters the world, producing both inequality and the permanent state of humanity, the experience of otherness, that is, being outside oneself. Thus, difference is both originary and non-natural, it is the result of the artifice of the gods who create the first female mortal as an act of revenge. In this sense, Zeus' vengeance on the race of men is to inflict upon them the difference that already exists among the Olympians, to bring discord and sorrow into the world is to make men more like the gods.

Stiegler does comment on Pandora and this second fault of Epithemeus (pp. 195–6) noting that the ultimate meaning of Pandora's jar is the introduction of temporality into the world of men thought as mortality and birth through sexual difference. He is leaning heavily on Vernant's account of the story in terms of the question of *elpis* (expectation, time).[37] It is Vernant who notes that the fate of Prometheus is the misfortune that strikes the hero of prescience. The mistakes of Epithemeus are the result of a counterbalance and tension with his brother, the condition of comprehension after the event, *épimétheia*. In this sense, Prometheus is never surprised by what befalls him, unlike the mortals and Epithemeus who never see any of this coming. Insofar as, Stiegler is correct to want to reintroduce the faults of Epithemeus back into a philosophical account of the myth, we might say that the stricture between Prometheus and Epithemeus inserts a certain blindness into theory. A refusal or inability to see is the antidote to an unfolding of theory that would programme a future without failure. It is not a question of forgetfulness in the form of Epithemeus or difference in the guise of Pandora, providing a cure for mortality, for death and finitude is the condition of the human. Rather, the knowledge of death is balanced against a lack of understanding of the given moment and the manner in which life will play out and finally end. Thus creativity or invention enters the world as a necessity for human survival, as an effect of difference and finitude, but while it is predicated on the foresight of theory (*prométheia*) it is curtailed by the blindness of experience (*épimétheia*) which both ruins the ambition of theory and prevents us from fully grasping the extent of that ruin in the given moment. Hope is left inside Pandora's jar, the version of hope that enters the world instead is this structure of anticipation of the future (*Elpis*) that is a blind hope in the face of mortality. In the Aeschylus play, Prometheus tells the Chorus, 'I prevented mortals from foreseeing their doom ... I caused blind hopes to dwell within them' (180). There can be no hope for theory other than blind hope. The knowledge of its own failure is not sufficient to describe the human condition, rather theory contains within its operation a blindness to its own end, this is what makes it both possible to continue and impossible to conclude. This constant invention and re-invention of theory is the creativity that we call practice.

What Stiegler calls the 'primordial idiocy' of Epithemeus, his constitutive blindness and forgetting that doubles up and cuts through the ambition of his theoretically gifted brother is the cause of 'finite singularity and freedom' (p. 199). Theory with infinite foresight can never err and so no difference can ever affect it. Under such circumstances no event can ever take place; no act of invention is possible in a world of infallible foresight. Rather, to understand after the fact is to have a history; *épimétheia* says Stiegler 'comes too late to reflect upon its passive mode, this very reflexivity lingering in the empirical, that is strewn with accumulated errors' (p. 199). This practice is constituted historically as a weave of differences, inequalities and failures; it is both structural and historic and no more historical than it is structural. It is this situation in which the mortal experience is constructed, always already preceded by the facts of failure and arriving too late to learn from its mistakes, inheriting all the faults of an ancient legacy that begins with the double default of Epithemeus and Prometheus.

Stiegler concludes his account of the myth by returning to the *Protagoras* to the moment when Zeus sends Hermes to deliver political skills [*ten politikhen tekhen*] to humanity. Hermes asks Zeus in what way should he distribute this skill: 'Shall I distribute these *tekhnai* as the arts were distributed – that is, on the principle that one trained doctor suffices for many laymen, and so with the other experts? Shall I distribute justice and respect for their fellows in this way, or to all alike?' (332c). Zeus lets it be known that all should share in these virtues as they do the arts. In fact, if anyone is unable to acquire their share of political virtue 'he shall be put to death as a plague to the city' (322d). Politics is then an art imprinted on every mortal as a result of the originary default of Prometheus and Epithemeus, provided as another compensation for forgetting, failure and theft. In this way, everything that pertains to theory and practice in creative invention also adheres to theory and practice in politics. The astute reader will be able to return to this book as a commentary not only on the critical practice of art but also on the political field. Stiegler calls politics 'an art that presupposes a *praxis* of the letter' (p. 201). That is to say, it is another re-inscription, doubling and disruption of the experience of being-outside-oneself that for us will define critical practice, structured between the anticipation of the future that worries for its own ruin in advance, and the wisdom of failure. The political moment, like the impossible event of critical practice, is a reflection that comes in advance (*prométheia*) and is never at peace (*épithémeia*). For Kant peace can only lie beyond finitude in the quite of the grave, on this occasion Stiegler suggests peace 'is the exclusive privilege of immortal beings' (p. 202).[38] That is to say, only a god can know peace. Politics and critical practice are interminably restless.

5

Creation and Innovation

So far, we have spent time detailing the work and the relation that constitutes critical practice, or Theory-Practice as we have referred to it throughout this book. In this chapter, we will consider two resources within the theoretical tradition that might help us think about the ways in which critical practice is productively creative: writing by Jean-Luc Nancy and Jacques Derrida. As the readings that follow demonstrate, mobilizing a term such as 'creativity' is not a simple or neutral act. It comes with considerable conceptual baggage from the history of its use across several languages.[1] In particular, the idea of 'creation' is inseparable from both a theological inheritance and an understanding of production that comes from the philosophical history of materialism. In its Modern sense, that is to say, it's re-invention by Romanticism, creativity moved from being the work of gods to the God-given attribute of humans. This internalization of creativity was closely linked to the eighteenth-century trope of the imagination. The figurative shift in imagination from Hobbes' 'decayed sense', as a poor substitute for the world, to Wordsworth's 'auxiliary light', that bestows 'new splendour' on the world, can be traced through Coleridge's invention of 'fancy' and Kant's production of the faculties.[2] Romantic creativity, however, was an internal function of the mind, that while not creating the new, saw the world in a different way. Today, creativity refers mostly to making new things, and is an attribute of everyone from creative artists working on creative writing programmes to management consultants with teams of full-time 'creatives'. The situation is summed up in economics by the phrase 'the creative industries', which implies originality on an industrial scale. The interiorization of creativity as a function spirit in Romanticism has been transformed into the dematerialized materiality of economic exchange in contemporary capitalism in which creativity has a value and comes at a premium. This is a complex inheritance and the now ubiquitous sense of creative economy that really describes a mode of production that is anything but creative, or even necessarily productive, needs to be rigorously distinguished from the possibilities of critical practice discussed in this book. Accordingly, we will treat both the theological and material dimensions of this genealogy; the two are not separable.

Ex nihilio: In the beginning was Nancy

In Act I of *King Lear*, the ageing monarch invites his three daughters to proclaim their love for him and so obtain a third of the kingdom that is their inheritance. Goneril and Regan who have no affection for the king but know-how to flatter an old fool duly step forward and secure their share of the part of the deal. The youngest daughter, Cordelia, is appalled by her sisters' hypocrisy and refuses to join in the flattery. In response to Lear's solicitation, 'what can you say to draw/A third more opulent than your sisters?' she replies 'Nothing, my lord'. Expecting more from his favourite daughter, Lear is astonished, 'Nothing!' 'Nothing', confirms Cordelia.[3] 'Nothing will come of nothing: speak again', demands the King. This remarkable scene is a study in the problem of creation and its description. The exchange between Lear and his daughter ups the ante in a race to invert value. Cordelia is expected to outdo her sisters but offers literally 'nothing', the terms of nullity is exchanged between parent and child, heightening the value and impact of nothing, reinforcing its meaning as an absolute rather than a relative bid against the sister's extravagant flattery of Lear.[4] Cordelia refuses the economy of inflation, 'Unhappy that I am, I cannot heave/My heart into my mouth' (1.1.91–2). Words fail her, she has nothing to say, but her love for Lear is not absolute zero; on the contrary it far exceeds that of her sister's meaningless excess, 'I love your majesty/According to my bond; nor more nor less' (1.1.92–3). This is a contract without limit, which one cannot put a price on, there is no supplement, no additional payment to make. Outside of this bond there is nothing to add. Yet Lear takes this nothing as an annihilation, making that bond null and void. The King reminds Cordelia that this nothing risks riches, 'mend your speech a little, Lest it may mar your fortunes' (1.1.94–5). That is to say, this nothing risks the future, her fortune and destiny, inheritance and destination. And yet she insists on her nothing, 'But goes thy heart with this?' (1.1.105) because this nothing is the value of truth, 'So young, and so untender?' says, Lear, 'So young, my lord, and true' (1.1.107–8), replies his daughter. The nothing is only absolute because for Cordelia the truth is absolute and she will not trade with her sisters or strike a bargain with her Father. The truth is beyond measure for Cordelia but she sticks to her price tag of nothing. For Cordelia, the issue is the truth and nothing but the truth. The furious Lear takes her nothing and divides it in two, granting her share of the spoils to her sisters, but nothing does not in fact come from nothing, Cordelia still has her future husband, 'thy truth, then, be thy dower', says Lear (1.1.109). His daughter may find in difficult to pay her bills with truth but she retains her value as a human as Lear disinherits her 'I disclaim all my paternal care' (1.1.114). It is in fact, Lear who is reducing himself to nothing, divesting himself of sovereignty, banishing his beloved daughter and the faithful Kent, to retain only the symbolic display of kingship, 'only we still retain/The name, and all the additions to a king' (1.1.138–9). As the play unfolds these additions are taken away from Lear, one by one, as he comes to realize the folly of this exorbitant economy, in which 'nothing' stands for absolute value and absolute power counts for nothing.

It is then, a complex matter to say, 'nothing comes from nothing', because as the story of Lear shows a great deal of significant consequence can come from nothing. In Shakespeare not only does something come from nothing but the entire business and traffic of the play comes from this nothing. There is literally much ado about nothing in this drama. Nothing is more important here than nothing, everything comes from nothing. For the pagan Lear, all his troubles start with the denial of a proposition of '*creatio ex nihilio*', creation out of nothing. 'Nothing will come of nothing' is a refusal of the theological possibility of the *ex nihilio*. In this sense, Lear is with Parmenides, *ex nihilio nihil fit* (out of nothing comes nothing) or more likely an adapted literary source.[5] This nothing has a history. In *De Rerum Natura* ('On the Nature of Things', Lucretius tells us 'that nothing's brought/Forth by any supernatural power out of naught' cautioning against a divine explanation for laws of nature, 'nothing can be made from nothing [*Nil posse creari de nihilio*]—once we see that's so/Already we are on the way to what we want to know'.[6] *Ex nihilio* is contrasted in the tradition with *creatio ex materia* (creation out of existing matter), *creatio ex deo* (creation out of the being of God) and *creatio continua* (the ongoing divine creation).[7] It runs from classical sources to the imaginary of theoretical physics, nothing could be more theologically inscribed than the *ex nihilio*, nothing could be more metaphysical than this nothing. Here is an absence, a nothing that initiates an entire history of presence, the something that comes from this nothing.

One of its most recent thinkers, Jean-Luc Nancy, takes it up in his 2007 text, *Le création du monde ou la mondialisation*, translated into English as *The Creation of the World or Globalization*.[8] In the first part of that book, 'Urbi et Orbi', Nancy begins to set out a thinking of the becoming global of the world, as this runs through Marx as a formative stage in the development of capital. He also attends to question of the world as it emerges as a problematic in modern philosophy since Kant in response to the experience of an industrialized humanity. For Nancy, every turn in that philosophical inheritance is theological, because the very question of the 'world' as such cannot be understood outside of a pre-existing metaphysical and theological frame of reference. However, the world for Nancy is not to be conflated with the question of the universe or with the problematic of a habitus. There is a tension then between the making of a world and the creation of a universe, and between the emergence of a world and the purpose of place or community. In this space, that is neither local nor universal, resides the problem of the world as a problem for philosophy and the discourses of reason that seek to suggest a rational principle for all things. Nancy quotes Angelus Silesius that 'the rose grows without reason', that is without purpose and independent of rationality.[9] We need to be careful here of the translation of *'mondialisation'* as 'globalization', given the French word predates the English sense and carries within it idea of a peopling of the world as a process of the expansion of culture, humanity and nations.[10] Accordingly, if the world (*le monde*, also the people) is like the rose of Silesius, growing without reason, then that is also a problem for philosophy and rational accounts of political economy. In fact, there would be a tension between the model of globalization that we recognize in a more or less contested way today, as the suppression of alternative world-formation and a *mondialisation* that grew without reason or independent of the reasons of globalized capital.[11]

Our interest here lies less in the issue of globalization than in what it tells us about creation on Nancy's terms. Having sketched out the theological context of thinking the problem of the world. He notes:

> If 'creation' means anything, it is the exact opposite of any form of production in the sense of a fabrication that supposes a given, a project, and a producer. The idea of creation, such as has been elaborated by the most diverse and at the same time most convergent thoughts, including the mystics of the three monotheisms but also the complex systems of all great metaphysics, is above all the idea of *ex nihilio* (and I do not exempt Marx from this, to the contrary: while his understanding of Christian creation is only instrumental, for him value is precisely created…). The world is created from nothing: this does not mean fabricated with nothing by a particularly ingenious producer. It means instead that it is not fabricated, produced by no producer, and not even coming out of nothing (like a miraculous apparition), but in a quite strict manner and more challenging for thought: the nothing itself, if one can speak in this way, or

rather *nothing* growing [*croissant*] as something (I say 'growing' for it is the sense of *cresco*—to be born, to grow—from which comes *creo*: to make something merge and cultivate a growth). In creation, a growth grows from nothing and this nothing takes care of itself, cultivates its growth. (p. 51)

Nancy then offers the arresting statement that 'the *ex nihilio* is the genuine formulation of a radical materialism, that is to say, precisely, without roots'.

This passage will bear some commentary. Nancy is offering us a thorough rethinking of creation and so creativity per se. Creation, and we might say creativity, is not the act of a producer or an outcome from a chain of production or a making ('fabrication' to use Nancy's chosen term here). This, to begin with is to challenge a certain materialist understanding of the world and so of the creative act.[12] Rather, creation is *ex nihilio*, something is created from nothing, this is the trope that runs through the Abrahamic tradition and lands in Marx in more or less explicit ways. There is no producer instead nothing grows as something, a cultivation of nothing as something. The use of '*croissant*' in the French perhaps suggests the lunar cycle, in which a full moon grows out of seemingly nothing. This is then nothing that becomes something, but also something that was always there as nothing growing as something. If it is the basis of a 'radical materialism' it is because it upsets the idea of the 'radical' itself, a radicalism without radicalism, or a radicalism without roots, or, origin. This is another materialism, perhaps a materialism of the Other: this radicalism without origin.

Nancy is then presenting something of a challenge to the other materialisms that dominate the present theoretical scene, this is not the muscular Maoism of a Badiou or a return to political economy.[13] Rather, Nancy points out the moment of difficulty in the Marxist formulation of matter, 'by conceiving of itself as a reversal of the relation of production, Marx's revolution presupposed that this reversal was equivalent to a conversion of the meaning of production (and the restitution of created value to its creator). What we have begun to learn is that it is also a matter of creating the meaning or the value of the reversal itself. Only perhaps this creation will have the power of the reversal' (p. 54). It is not enough merely to reverse the relation of production from Creator to Created in order to upset that relation (and so restore value to the creator). Rather, one must question the value of the reversal itself. The reversal does nothing to dislodge the onto-theological gesture inherent in this understanding of creation, and so creativity. Only an understanding of creativity that started from the premise of questioning the meaning of any reversal can disrupt the onto-theology at the heart of materialism. This is a creativity without origin or roots, without duty or obligation to a certain materialist tradition. We might say that this creativity as the growth of nothing as something is an inscription or grafting (although these are not Nancy's words) of nothing, *ex nihilio*, as something: matter *ex nihilio* matters.

In the second section, 'On Creativity', of this short book Nancy makes a diversion via Kant that illuminates this problem creating value in the questioning act of creation itself. Nancy says, apropos of the *Third Critique*, 'consequently, what indirectly appears as a new problematic of 'creation' is the question of a judgement about ends that would not be only a judgement extrapolated beyond the limits of the understanding, but also, or rather, the judgement of a reason to which is given in advance neither end(s) nor means, nor anything that constitutes whatever kind of 'causality known to us' (p. 66). The issue in understanding creation is not to be found in origins or ends in a chain of production, causality, or intention, but in judging (i.e. critiquing and questioning) the end of creation. By this we mean not only the something Created, grown as/from nothing, but also the end of a certain model of creation, as well as the purpose of creation, to what end does one create? Creation without ends is creativity without purpose or use, at least a purposeless purposiveness.[14] This is art, or, the rose that grows without reason. Accordingly, such a judgement cannot ground itself in reason or end in reason. This judgement exceeds, or cannot be saturated by, rationality, both a madness and an act of faith in the value of the *ex nihilio*. Art exists without reason and cannot be exhausted by rationality. Why did you make this? No reason. Why do you like this? No reason. Nancy continues, 'the judgment about the "ends of all things" must be concerned with a condition of being that would not depend on causality or finality, nor consequently on mechanical consecuation or subjective intention. By destituting the creating God and the *ens summum*—sufficient reason of the world—Kant also makes clear that the reason of the world pertains to a productive causality. He opens implicitly and outside of theology a new question of "creation" (p. 66). This is true up to a point, Kant has given us an opening into creativity as a question that is distinct in orientation from the Abrahamic algorithm that underscores the onto-theology of Marx, for example, but the question of creation can never be disassociated from the metaphysics of religion. There is no escaping the orbit of theology on this question, especially when judgement without rational telos or finitude leaves us in the realm of faith. Faith and reason are not strangers in judgement.[15]

Whenever we begin with the question of creation we are in the midst of a certain vocabulary of the religious and part of the history of a theology that we cannot escape.[16] To say that Kant opens up an understanding or creation outside of religion or to imagine that Nancy's discourse on globalization is anterior to the onto-theology he takes aim at would be to offer a foreclosure that repeats the structure it seeks to outflank. Nancy is, of course, not a creationist. He is not tied to creation as an anchor but instead he works around creation in order to allow another thinking of the material, or, to allow the other to be thought once more in the material. However, it is a useful gesture on Nancy's part to begin the thinking of creation and so creativity without a producer, that is without agency, intention, or appropriation. This is a creativity in which nothing grows as something. Nancy goes on to comment:

> What we have said thus far forces us to posit that the principle, not of all phenomena but of the *totality* of phenomena and of phenomenality itself, or the ontological principle of the phenomenality *of* the thing in itself, precisely cannot be a principle of production; it must be that which appears indirectly as a 'creation', that is to say, a provenance without production. It is neither procession nor providence, nor project, a provenance without a *pro-*, prototype, or promoter—or else a *pro-* that is *nihil* in the very property of *pro*-venance. (p. 66)

A provenance comes with a history; that is the point of such a guarantee of authenticity. Here we have a history and provenance that is literally nothing, a provenance without origin, or a provenance that has its origin in nothing [*pro-venir*, to come from nothing, if you will]. The 'pro-' here also suggesting an advance or projecting forward, a futurity (from *pro-venir* to *a-venir*, a pro-mise not of the past or heritage but of future worth) and also indicating substitution (pro-noun). But this is 'a *pro-* that is *nihil*', a future that comes from nothing or a nothing that grows as a future, a future guarantee ('*pro*-venance') that comes from nothing, a guarantee without guarantee. We have then not only 'provenance without production' as Nancy puts it but a 'pro-duction' that is not a production, something that comes from nothing, or a nothing that grows as something like the prologue to a production of *King Lear*. The stakes here are large, including the 'the *totality* of phenomena and of phenomenality itself', something comes from this nothing, the future is a nothing that grows as something. In fact, everything comes from this nothing. Creation in Nancy is only the beginning, as a starting point for thinking a radical new materialism and phenomenality itself.

However, as we know in the beginning there was not nothing but the word [*logos*] and the word here is 'creation', this most metaphysical and theological of terms that names the beginning. It gives us to think another nothing, not creation out of an absolute vacuum, like a God, but another proposition concerning creativity, which as a phenomenon is not production with origins, ends, and use-value, but a growth as nothing, but a nothing that is something of import and consequence, like Cordelia's claim. There is a whole culture invested in the idea of art as a model of production, with its authors, makers and theorists. But what if the presentation of production where only ever a care for the growth of nothing, art without essence or wellspring or utility? Creativity in this sense would be the process *in media res* of the undoing of process itself. Such an understanding of creation would make it an important moment in the deconstruction of production, insofar as such a deconstruction proceeds from production itself, and is perhaps its most active resource. Any act of creation would be the simultaneous launching and interruption of production that recuperated itself in the presentation of production while equally causing that model of production to wear away as the condition of its presentation. There will be no escape from this onto-theology just as it will be opened and endlessly ruined by creativity. We might say here, that on these terms, creativity is deconstruction. That is not to say, that creativity is an operation that is applied to production but rather the resources within production that escapes the ends of production by demonstrating the divisibility within production, in which its ruin is most active resource. It is for this reason that we encounter in creativity that moment of blindness or unknowing that is the interruption of the self-same by the Other as an event of art. We cannot absolutize this Other, there is nothing mystic about art, this break or intrusion by the Other is part of an economy of recuperation and re-launch but one that cannot secure its origin or satisfy its ends.[17]

This is not a melancholy of making or a negative gesture of withdrawal, rather it is to describe the active and affirmative growth of creativity and creativity as a growth and care for the Other. The Other resides in creativity, opening it endlessly to its own contradictions as its very resource, just as that creation places the Other in an economic relation to the self-same that inscribes both in the work of art as the source and reserve of art itself. Art is then a materiality that has its roots in nothing, a nothing that grows as something, a *creatio ex nihilo* that provides the material for another materiality. A novel, a poem, a painting, a film is not like a kettle, a car, or a house. Their meaning does not depend solely upon matter or even reference to a material world that exists per se. Their meaning as art in fact depends upon the suspension of reference between the reality they present and a material world. No one actually mistakes *Ulysses* for a map of Dublin. A kettle, a car, or a house can be a work of art but its meaning and existence as art is not derived exclusively from their materiality.

The materiality of art is the nothing of creativity, this moment of suspension, blindness, or unknowing, and the interruption and deferral of utility.

However, and equally, one should be careful not to imagine that art in this sense is an aberration, a unique form of signification that stands apart from the material world. If it were it could be dismissed accordingly. Rather, art opens up the material world in productive ways, ones that we seldom see in advance or have barely began to think about. Art is not the supplement to experience in the world but the very way in which experience the world itself. Creativity is then not a special gift or an operation to be enacted in the world but is the means by which the world both presents itself and undoes itself in its presentation. If we stay close to Jean-Luc Nancy for a moment, we might note his comments in the appendix to *La création*, entitled '*Ex nihilo summum* (Of Sovereignty)', in which he says, 'the *ex-nihilo* contains nothing more, but nothing less, than the ex—of existence that is neither produced nor constructed but only existing [*étante*] (or, if one prefers, *étée*, 'made' from the making constituted by the transitivity of being). And this *ex nihilo* fractures the deepest core of nihilism from within' (p. 71). This nothing is not a nihilism but the resource of existence. Existence exists without reason, without origin, or without ends. It is the relation of all things to one another that constitutes that existence, but relation is not production, relation on the contrary is not a thing, it is a question of difference. Meaning, and so existing, lies in the relation, as a nothing that grows as a something, not in the construction or production of objects. It is not an idealism to say that the meaning of a novel and its existence as art does not depend solely upon or even as its construction as ink on bound paper. Its meaning both as art and as an opening of experience is elsewhere. Insofar as, creativity is the resource for the concession of art, it is the means for the active inauguration of experience of the world. It is the condition of being human.

Let there be no misunderstanding here. This is not an argument that dismisses the material in the name of an idealization of an absolute other. Rather, it is one that puts in play another possibility of the material as an experience that grows from the nothing of difference, and finds its most active consideration and translation in the work of creativity that delivers us art in all its complexity. It is in this route to experience that comes from the care for and growth of this significant nothing that we become human and so at the same time separate ourselves from the material not as an escape from it but as a denaturation of it. While the *ex nihilio* defers our ends, existing without reason, the human reinstates them, as a gesture of finitude within a denatured world. In this way, the infinite possibility of creation is recuperated into the self-same of being human within the world. This is the effect and consequence of creativity, both its outcome and its ruin, which impels it to continue beyond itself in a growth that is not necessarily an enlargement or development. Nancy suggests, 'with this becoming human, this movement appears to itself as its own principle and its own end. That is to say, properly without principle and without end since it proceeds from an initial detachment, which one can name 'human condition' and whose permanence involves an extreme instability and mutability of what has thus been detached (contingency forms the necessity of this 'history'). And which is what we can call, feigning to believe that there would have been first a pure and stable 'nature', denaturation. And one could then say that 'humanity' is the indexical name of the indefinite and infinite term of the human denaturation' (pp. 86–7). This denaturation and detachment finds its form in art through creative practice, here *techne* and *praxis* provide the means for an extrication from the world that is also the most profound engagement with the world. It is a separation that does not provide security or certainty of understanding but rather inscribes the instability and mutability of the aporias of art as an effect of difference into the condition of humanity and its history. This is not a pure denaturation but one that leaves us inextricably linked to the material in our extrication as humans while presenting that relation as a relation in the mode of creativity as an experience of the world. Creativity then is not merely the reserve of the artist but the resource of everyday living that finds its humanity in contingency.

The invention of the other

We have just noted the ways in which Jean-Luc Nancy's thinking of globalization might provide us with a set of resources to think about the problem of creation and creativity. Throughout this account of Nancy, I have stressed the role played by the Other, the not-me, in the act of creation to suggest that creativity is always otherwise to itself, disruptive and unpredictable. However, while this is in keeping with the wider terrain of Nancy's thinking, we will not find a reference to the Other in Nancy's book on creation, this will have been an invention of my own. Nancy's reluctance to use that term is notable in this book even if the schema of creation he describes is decidedly one based upon the effects of difference in the world. This may be a consequence of recent theoretical trends in which alterity is very much out of fashion in preference to a return to an certain unquestioned materiality, which views the material as a value in itself, conferring value on the man-made to ward off the seemingly ethereal power of difference.[18] In what we might take as his own account of creativity, '*Psyché: Inventions de l'autre*', Jacques Derrida is not so inhibited about invoking the name of the Other.[19] '*Psyché*' is just one of the moments in Derrida's writing where he treats the question of creation, or, we might say gets creative within creativity. One might think equally well of the reading of *khora* in Plato as it plays out both in Derrida's essay on Hegel of the same name, we addressed in the introduction to this book, and in his mobilization of the term in his collaboration with Bernard Tschumi on an architectural design for the Parc de la Villette in Paris.[20] There is an obvious connection between *khora* as a metaphor of midwifery in Plato and with the *ex nihilio* as a concept of growth and care in making of the world. Both rely upon a feminization of the tropes of philosophy, turning the question of creativity to the matrixial in preference to a model of creator as pro-genitor, producer, or seminal influence. We might note the importance of such metaphors as the way in which our experience of the material is determined by the production of meaning in our everyday lives.

Throughout the pages of this book we have been at pains to identify the moment of doubt, uncertainty and unpredictability that is integral to the creative experience. In so doing, we have not been satisfied to surrender to mysticism or accept a regressive vocabulary of genius as if creativity were some kind of magical practice. Equally, it is not enough to attempt to assemble a meta-language for creativity, which would continue to separate a critical or theoretical discourse from acts of making, production or invention. The whole point of this study is to examine the moments when the borders of theory and practice are erased and fall away in the interesting spaces of creativity in which art and philosophy combine across the demarcations of genres. Rather than establishing another technical terminology for creativity, we are interested in the ways in which metaphor might result in metamorphosis, figures lead to new figurations, and tropes result in new material inscriptions that open themselves up to their own disfiguration in which the condition of their own possibility is their ruin. We are seeking to recover at the edges of idiom and genre, another understanding of praxis that eludes the Western tradition's misreading of Aristotle, in which *episteme* and *techne* would be separated as distinct realms.[21] This is not necessarily a clear or secure place to be, but it is the complex space experienced by makers as theory-practitioners. The struggle to know in the midst of unknowing is the challenge of such a praxis.

Derrida himself is no stranger to the question of another writing beyond the genres of philosophy and literature. We will find this desire to invent a constant theme in Derrida since the 1968 essay on 'The Ends of Man'.[22] However, the text on '*Psyché*' from 1984 provides us with a considered concentration on the issue of what it might mean to create new work in art and philosophy. It begins with a distinction between invention and improvisation. In the case of the latter, there might be nothing new at all, nothing might be more rehearsed than improvisation as anyone who has ever answered a question at a public event might attest. In response to the challenge of inquiry in public, one might fall back upon what one knows already, has said before or rehearsed on another occasion. If you do that sort of thing often enough, there really is no question you have not heard before, and no answer you have not given before. The skill of improvisation lies in making a rehearsed answer seem spontaneous. Invention, on the other hand—let's say an invention worthy of the name—does different work. It begins by assuming a disruption with the past, a breaking with previous modes and conventions. 'An invention', says Derrida, 'always presupposes some illegality, the breaking of an implicit contract; it inserts disorder into the peaceful order of things, it disregards the proprieties' (p. 1). Invention is disruptive. Accordingly, it must spell the end of the old order and herald in another future even if the invention itself cannot survive its own disruption. However, insofar as invention emerges from the old order 'it has to exploit a largely common stock of rule-governed resources and possibilities in order to sign, as it were, an inventive proposition' (p. 4). This is a question then of inheritance, tradition, and history, of who inherits in a legitimate way and who thinks beyond inheritance but with the resources of that tradition. Invention is a question of the illegitimate or the bastard. This is the double bind of invention, it is both natural and unnatural. Invention presupposes originality, engendering, and is associated with genius, thus with genealogy and the natural. While, equally, invention requires a patent, a claim on legitimacy, rights, and a contract. This emphasis on the law and legitimation leads Derrida to suggest, 'there is no natural invention' (p. 5). Invention then opens itself to the other; it requires the countersignature of the other.

Invention is an event, that is to say, on Derrida's terms, it is singular and unrepeatable, unpredictable and arising from nowhere or nothing, but it brings about something new. An invention does not take place without an inaugural event but something comes as a result of that event. Accordingly, the *ex nihilio* of the event inaugurates the future of a possibility, that is to say, one in which the invention is recognized and legitimated through acceptance, convention, and inscription into a common history. Invention then belongs or returns to the culture and heritage from which it first emerged as an illegitimate offspring. Disruption becomes the new normal, as invention is marked from the beginning by its openness to repetition, exploitation, and recuperation, when Napster becomes Spotify, or the avant-garde appears on the university curriculum. It is the event that ties invention to the other. On the one hand, every invention imagines that something comes for a first time, arrives, *avenir*. But equally, for an invention to be unique this first time must also be its last time, after that although it is repeatable, it is no longer an invention. It is recuperated back into the economy of the self-same. This is where the *ex nihilio* of Nancy and the event of Derrida differ. The latter recognizes difference as an effect of a wider play of difference in which the Other initiates but is retrieved by the same resources that enabled its release, the former runs the risk of absolutizing the other as a resource of infinite disruption. In this sense the other would not just be disruptive but it would be wholly destructive and ruinous without limit or possibility of return. Invention, in Derrida's sense, however, would be another term in that chain of non-equivalent substitutes for différance that performed according to a logic of the quasi-transcendental, in which the condition of the possibility of invention is the limit of its own impossibility.[23]

Whenever we talk of invention or the event in Derridean terms, I am reminded of a twelve-line poem by Seamus Heaney, 'Lightenings viii', from the late collection *Seeing Things*.[24] It is part of a longer meditative cycle, 'Lightenings', but stands on its own as an example of the event as a commentary on the event. It is based upon a fabulous incident reported in the annals of the Irish monastery of Clonmacnoise, fabulous both in the sense of the miraculous and of a fable or story to be recorded and retold. It begins:

> The annals say: when the monks of Clonmacnoise
> Were all at prayer inside the oratory
> A ship appeared above them in the air.

The poem opens by referring to its own status as a report, 'the annals say', legitimizing itself through history while contributing to that tradition just as it fakes and departs from that inheritance. The colon after 'the annals say', introduces the rest of the poem as if it were a report or summary of the annals rather than an invention of the poet, who places himself in a tradition of Irish writing, while sitting outside that genealogy as if he were a witness to a report. The *as if*, is crucial to understanding this poem and the idea of the inaugural or invention, which happens *as if* for the first time. It is as if the poet were a scholar or an annalist, as if poetry carried the same legitimacy as history, as if the two idioms could be separated. The poem relies on the performance of the *as if*, to predicate the truth of invention and the invention of truth. While history and historiography might be inseparable from the figurative dimension of language, being every bit as fabulous as the tales of *Tir Na Nog*, this poem, and a contemporary or modern poem at that, separated from this history by centuries, presents itself both as a report from the annals and a fiction that draws its difference from the annals upon a differentiation that itself might not have grounds for legitimation. The confusion is important and necessary as tradition inaugurates its own disfiguration. Invention here draws upon the resources of the very inheritance it both disrupts and re-inscribes.

The monks are at prayer, a state of both contemplation and of beseeching with respect to the future, *je vous en prie*, as the French phrase might render it. One of the aspects of prayer is precisely this request for an alternative future. While the monks are all at prayer, individually or together, they are minding their own business and in a line of direct communication with God. They might have been addressing the future but they were not expecting the one that comes, as the ship appears above their heads in the oratory. It is as if, while speaking to God and keeping themselves to themselves (they have come to Clonmacnoise to address the almighty but also to be away from everyone else) they catch sight in their peripheral vision of an alternative fabulous. This is the sailing ship that moves above them, occupying a space where their prayers were directed, as if it were a result of their bequest and an intervention or intercession that interrupts the line the communication to God. This is a fabulous craft, one that floats not on the sea but in the air, moving not with wind in its sails but through the clouds and across the sky. It has somehow 'appeared' above them, materializing while passing through the solid walls of the oratory, out of a clear blue sky, as it were:

> The anchor dragged along behind so deep
> It hooked itself into the altar rails
> And then, as the big hull rocked to a standstill,

The monks may direct their thoughts to heaven but at least they had the security of imagining themselves to be on terra firma; however, this event disrupts physical and metaphysical planes, as the monks find themselves at the bottom of the ocean relative to the crew of the ship. They are no longer in their oratory, speaking directly to God, but deep below another plane of existence, 'the anchor dragged along so deep' that it hooks the altar rails, their telephone mast to God is lower than anchor of this ship. The altar rails, like debris on the sea floor, impede the journey of this vessel that seems to have wandered into shallows. The monks who were deep in prayer now find themselves deep in trouble, as their contemplation is shown to be inadequate to the marvels of the universe, their depth is just another's shallows, their transcendence is just another's impediment.

Here tradition in interrupted by invention, the monastic life at prayer is disrupted by the appearance of the fabulous air ship, but equally invention is bound and hooked by the altar rails of the oratory, tied and snarled in the old order of convention and routine. Something must be done to break the impasse:

> A crewman shinned and grappled down the rope
> And struggled to release it. But in vain.

The ship has come to a standstill, the forces that drive the ship and cause the big hull to rock as it strains against the brake of the altar rails, create a tension that cannot easily be broken. The struggle is in vain. Like the flying fish in Valerio Adami's '*Portrait après Glas*', which illustrates the principle of the quasi-transcendental in Derrida's book, neither in nor out of the water, ambient in both and mastered by neither, the crewman descends from the ship to encounter the other world that is the real world of Clonmacnoise. His struggle with the rope may equally be a panic at his moment of encounter, this chance meeting with the other. How odd monks at prayer must seem to an ethereal sailor. Yet he cannot escape, there is an inertia that ties one reality to the other:

> 'This man can't bear our life here and will drown',
> The abbot said, 'unless we help him'.

The abbot displays remarkable presence of mind to recognize a struggle as a panic, seeing in the face of the other his own bewilderment reflected back. The traditional must help the new to arrive, the monks must set the sailors free; one plane of existence must facilitate the other.

However, this is not straightforward altruism on the abbot's part. He does not want the sailor to drown on his altar, to die in front of the monks, disrupting further and forever traumatizing their oratory and way of life. The abbot might see immediately that there is more in heaven and earth than he has dreamed of in his theology, but equally he knows straight away that these two worlds cannot coincide. The man will drown here and that would be a terrible responsibility to bear but equally the ship must be set free and allowed to sail on its way. Only then can the monks return to normal and the abbot have any hope of controlling his flock, returning the monks to their routine of contemplation, reasserting the status quo. This disruption will become a permanent parabasis 'unless we help him', and so the resources for invention and the fabulous must come from the routine and the traditional in order to project that invention forward and equally to protect the old order from endless interruption and ruin. It is a decision that the abbot makes in an instant, perhaps without evidence that sailor cannot breathe the air of Clonmacnoise or bear the life of the monks, but he acts nevertheless, making a decision on the basis of faith. It is a faith that is bifurcated, informed at once by a desire to help the drowning man but also a belief in the value of the old order that must be protected from the risk of the fabulous:

> ... So
> They did, the freed ship sailed, and the man climbed back
> Out of the marvellous as he had known it.

The monks act to help the sailor, saving the other from the threat of their own selves.

For the sailor of the airship the monastic life of Clonmacnoise constitutes an encounter with the marvellous, as much an event in the life of the boatmen as it is in the history of the monastery. While the annals will record this moment as a fabulous occasion, equally the sailor will remember this unique moment that appears for the first time but also for the last time. It is the uniqueness of the encounter that makes it marvellous, the sailor's experience of the event ('as he had known it') constitutes the phenomenality of the thing that arrives out of a clear blue sky. The relative perspectives of the monks and the sailors define the relation that makes the event; that is to say, the event as an event is determined by the relation, the nothing, rather than the material circumstance. On another occasion monks freeing the anchor of an airship from their altar rails might be a quotidian occurrence. The monks might find themselves in the flight path, a repeatable or iterable incident, a matter of the ordinary or the established order. This encounter is made marvellous by its unique nature, for the first and last time, for both monks and sailors. At the same time, the poet is re-inventing a fable from the annals, re-recording the records, borrowing a story and presenting it in a lyric form that is entirely predictable both from the longer 'Lightenings' sequence and the extended corpus of Heaney. Indeed, so familiar is the lyric voice here that we might say that it arises automatically from the established poetic technique, working blind with a re-inscription of the material of the Clonamcnoise narrative. By exploiting the resource of the Irish literary tradition, Heaney is securing the authority and prominence of that tradition.

The poem then, while presenting an event as an incident of the fabulous, as an allegory of invention, works on every level to establish that the event relies as much on recuperation as it does on disruption. The old order not only helps the other to arrive but in so doing is taking steps to protect the legitimacy of that order, threatened by the very thing that arrives.

Where is the original invention here? Is it in Heaney's Nobel Prize winning lyric? Nothing could be more tied to the established order of literature and institutions than this.[25] Is it in the annal, which only records what others have witnessed? The annals of Clonmacnoise now only exist in the form of a seventeenth-century copy, another iteration of the event. Is it in the history of Clonmacnoise as a reputed and self-reported site of miracles, self-nomination being a notoriously unreliable mode of designation? Or is it in the incidence of ships sailing through the air, repeated and re-inscribed through Irish literature since Bishop Patrick of Dublin recorded or invented at the end of the eleventh century the *mirabilia* of medieval Ireland, including '*de naui que uisa est in aere*' ('Of a ship seen in the air'):

A king of the Irish once attended an assembly
With quite a crowd, a thousand in beautiful order.
They see a sudden ship sail the sky,
And someone who casts a spear after fish:
It struck the ground, and swimming he retrieved it.
Who can hear of this without praising the Lord above?[26]

This might be the source that Heaney loosely and with poetic invention refers to as 'the annals', although incidents of flying ships appear in the *Annals of Ulster*, *Tigernach*, and the *Four Masters* as well as the seventeenth-century copy of the annals of *Clonmacnoise*.[27] Such literary archaeology can be left to the cultural historians, the origin of the story is not the issue here. Rather, this recording or inventing of the story of King Congalach and another sailor of the sky, who swims through the air to recover their spear, suggests that the event of the fabulous is iterable. This is not to belittle Heaney's poetic achievement or the 'originality' of his verse, rather it is to suggest the complicated relation between invention and tradition, divergence, and re-inscription. Both the English-language poem of Heaney and the Latin verse of Bishop Patrick are fabulous inventions; that is to say, inventions of storytelling and so inventions of language. At the root of fable/fabulous, as Derrida reminds us, is *fari* or *phanai*: to speak 'as inventions of the same and the other, of oneself as (of) the other' (pp. 8–9). The economy between invention and tradition, creativity, and history, might then be a co-creation between the same and the other, between the me and the not-me. Invention is co-invention with oneself as (of) the other. The marvellous in creativity comes not from sailors swimming in the air to spear fish, but in the struggle, in vain, in the inner space of co-invention between self and/as other.

However, this is again not to propose creativity as a form of mysticism or magic. While we invent stories we also invent machines, and the question of creativity cannot be separated from the problem of *techne*, which as we saw in our previous account of Aristotle, might be translated as craft in the sense of Heaney's lyric art, but which we cannot separate here from *poesis* or *episteme*. There can be no easy separation between the *Fabula* or *fictio* on one side of the fence, and *techne, episteme, istoria*, and *methodos* on the other, that is between the fabulous and know-how, knowledge, research, method, and procedure. *Techne* can also be translated as art, which must necessarily incorporate all of these idioms, particularly on those occasions where Theory and Practice explicitly or more openly meet in self-declarations of critical practice. On the one hand, we might begin to suspect that theory-practice is an example of the performative demonstration of the very thing it asserts, and as such contains a tautological element essential to its condition. On the other hand, in theory-practice there is no choice to be made between *techne* and *episteme*, or between the fabulous and the methodological, not because there is no choice to make but because the issue is undecidable. That is 'undecidable' in a strict sense, not as a matter of indecision or delay in seeking sufficient evidence, but rather it is a question of a structural 'infinite and thus untenable acceleration' of undecidability as an impossibility, as Derrida says of de Man (p. 12).[28] This impossibility is the condition of possibility of theory-practice, and we might say of all art more generally. In theory-practice, there can be no easy distinction between the conceptual and its articulation, between meta-language and language. Language must already be conceptual, and the conceptual must be from the start figurative, denomination is figurative language. Accordingly, the crisis for theory-practice, that is its enduring definition, is its own performative contradiction, in that it posits a schema of distinction that its work then sets out to undermine. The end of theory-practice is to undermine any dichotomization between the two realms from which it derives its resources. The untenable acceleration of any distinction between theory and practice is the very purpose of theory-practice, while at the same time taking the metaphysical division as axiomatic for any point of departure. The end of theory-practice must be to annul the need for theory-practice. In such a place, where impossibility makes the possible, we have the conditions for the most decisive and productive understanding of the wider economy between the fabulous and the technical that determines invention, and perhaps art itself, if art were not already part of that traffic.

However, it should also be stressed that the recuperation of invention by the established order is not straightforwardly a victory for tradition or a conservation of the old. Rather, following the accommodation of invention as a repeatable act capable of legitimation or of reinforcing the order from which it emerged, that very order cannot ever be the same again. As the price of conserving itself the order has opened itself to its own ruin. It has become something other than itself and the incorporation of this other within provides the resources for the undoing of the order in its entirety. The something that arrives changes the space that opens itself to it. In the question of theory-practice it is not merely a question of recuperating a new idiom of making within the protocols of institutional literary study or academic art appreciation, the work of theory-practice in this home is to open all the windows and doors to let new light in. This is because theory-practice must place this question of unreadability at the centre of an academy that neither reads nor practices. To say that the academy does not read, is not to say that the academy is not full of busy people in libraries, making copious notes, productive of 'new readings'. Rather, it is to say that the academy does not entertain, indeed it goes out of its way to exclude or expel, the question of reading itself as an impossible act.

Once the principle of unreadability has been established a certain order of the academic is ruined forever. To say that the academy does not practice, is not to say that the academy does not open itself up to art, music, film, writing practitioners. It does, and institutional histories tell us that it always has done. Rather, it is to say that in accommodating practice, domesticating it within academic norms, the academy actively discourages the moment of practice which makes it practice and which escapes academic meta-language, namely the moment of blindness and unknowing that is another experience of unreadability. Nothing could be more at odds with academic protocol than to recognize such a moment and to value it within institutional cultures and hierarchies. Nothing could be more problematic for a machine of reason to entertain something unreasonable, something that reason can approach but cannot account for, something if not irrational then at least non-rational, something other to the discourse of reason that would seek to describe it. Hence, in theory-practice worthy of the name, it is not merely a question of the oscillation between the constative and the performative in order to produce instability in the order of things. Rather, as Derrida says of invention, 'this instability constitutes that very event… whose invention normally disturbs, as it were, the norms, the statutes, and the rules. It calls for a new theory and for the constitution of new statutes and conventions that, capable of recording the possibility of such events, would be able to account for them' (p. 13). The event of invention leaves the established order needing to explain what has just happened to it. In this way, the protocols and dynamics of established discourses must change, 'it calls for a new theory', and a new way of recording and accounting for that which has arrived. Everything has changed even as the established order must work over time to convince itself that everything remains the same. Unreadability and undecidablity are not a question of choice, technique, or method, rather they are a structuring principle of irreducible impossibility central to any creative practice worthy of the name.

Theory-Practice, critical practice, art practice, or, creative practice is in no way belittled by accepting that it is impossible. For any kind of art *possibility* itself is the greater risk, the danger of becoming an approach, a method, or set of rule-governed procedures. This would be the very death of art, including the pedagogy of art, which cannot be reduced to the transmission of technique, laws, or even theory. The pedagogical space of the studio, and perhaps the pedagogical space in general, would be another venue for the arrival of the other as an event (although this would require another book-length study to demonstrate). Rather, the importance of theory-practice lies in its self-declared encounter with the problem of the impossible.[29] To know the impossible would be the only thing worth knowing, and yet experiencing the impossible is the very moment of theory-practice, just as theory-practice would seek to collapse any distinction between experience and knowing. It is this set of ambitions that makes theory-practice impossible, opened in perpetuity by the impulsion to experience something other than itself, constituted as it is by its own nominative aporia. To say that theory-practice is an experience of the impossible is to say that it is an experience of the other, 'the experience of the other as the invention of the impossible, in other words, as the only possible invention' as Derrida puts it in '*Psyché*'.

Psyché is the French term for a distinctive double mirror on a revolving stand. In such a mirror, beauty can be laid bare and the soul reflected back to the sitter. Lacan makes play on the term in his essay on 'the mirror stage'.[30] Similarly, Derrida works with the multiple meanings of '*psyché*' and with its relation to the mythical story or fable of Psyche and Eros in Apuleius's *Metamorphoses* in which Psyche loses her fiancé Eros for wanting to see him even though it is forbidden.[31] Derrida's essay is also a salute to Paul de Man, his own mirror image, the other that installs itself in the history of deconstruction. The reference to '*psyché*' is central to both de Man and Derrida, and to our concerns here. It is a question of the two selves that confront one another in the moment of theory-practice, the me and the not-me, and the distance between them, the impossibility of seeing oneself and touching oneself at the same time. Derrida quotes de Man's reading of Stendhal's *La Chartreuse de Parme* in late text 'The Concept of Irony': 'this novel tells the story of two lovers who, like Eros and Psyche, are never allowed to come into full contact with each other… When they can touch, it has to be in a darkness imposed by a totally arbitrary and irrational decision, an act of the gods'.[32] Clélia has promised the Virgin Mary never to see Fabrice again, so they only meet in the night, under the cover of dark. 'The myth', says de Man, 'is that of the unovercomable distance which must always prevail between the selves, and it thematizes the ironic distance that Stendhal the writer always believed prevailed between his pseudonymous and nominal identities' (p. 19). The lovers in Stendhal's novel manage to have a child, so one wonders how 'unovercomable' a distance this really might have been.

However, the point for de Man is that the distance between the self and the other, that is between the self and the other, of oneself as (of) the other, is a 'permanent parabasis'. That is to say, it is an irresolvable and irreducible interruption. The parabasis is that moment in Greek tragedy when all the actors leave the stage and the chorus addresses the audience. It is a moment of self-reflexivity and alienation. To speak of a permanent parabasis is to suggest a constitutional suspension of referential terms in which the other and the self-look at one another, even address one another, but are constantly alienated from each other in a touching that does not touch and a seeing that does not see. When in the context of theory-practice we are referring both to the other that theory is to practice and to the oneself as the other who creates, there is then a double rupture that runs through this phenomenon. Both theory and practice reflecting each other in a mirror without touching, and a practice that is theory-practice that interrupts itself in an encounter with itself as (of) its own other. And yet, making still takes place, the lovers pro-create in the dark, this 'pro' carrying the sense as outlined for us by Nancy, of a provenance without history. This is then a 'pro-creation', of bastard children, as in Stendhal, in the dark, fumbling blindly, according to memory and technique, to give life to a creation without certainty or security.

The future then depends upon precisely these circumstances of unknowing and of the impossible. The future arrives but is never experienced as such; it always lies ahead of us in an unknowable and unpredictable fashion.³³ Similarly, the possibility of theory-practice relies upon a certain futurity, of the possibility of a future other than the circumstances of the present. Indeed, it is a necessary impulse of invention that it seeks to create another future. The resources it has to give birth to that future are the circumstances of the now, or, the resources of the tradition from which invention emerges. Accordingly, we need to recognize that any invention is hybrid; that is to say, following Bhabha's own inventive mobilization of Derrida, newness enters the world through hybridity, the merger and cross-pollination of the existing.³⁴ In this sense, invention can only ever be a hybridization through procedure, model, or variation. That is a technical manipulation of what already exists. Here we might suggest then that there is something machine-like about invention. We have previously suggested that the condition of unknowing that sits at the core of our investigation is what defines us as human. These aporia and their frustrations are the human condition. However, we must recognize that this experience is importantly machinic and instrumental. If invention is the hybridization of the existing, then the moment of invention does not necessarily require a spark of creative, human genius. It could just as easily come about as a consequence of the random collision of ideas under the appropriate circumstances. A room full of monkeys with type-writers will eventually produce the manuscript of *Hamlet*. The invention of stories and the invention of machines require the same resources and come about in the same way.

The invention of machines and the machine of invention are not easily separated. On these terms, there would be an important and necessary link between invention and death. This would be to take the question of creation further than Nancy who proposes a creation without producer. To have a form of automated invention would be to think of a creativity that was mechanical and random, throwing out invention as a computer generates numbers, algorithmically, in a generation without generation. This would be a creativity that was entirely technical, a *techne* of pure technicity. Such an element clearly resides within the description of invention that we have offered here. It would be a version of invention that re-invented invention itself, or at least, reminded us of the role of the death drive within creation.³⁵ There is much to say about the balance between inspiration and perspiration in creativity and the need to turn up at work every day, in order to produce that masterpiece. Writing, for example, is habitual and has little to do with any Romantic notions of genius or unique talent. The 'practice' in creative practice is probably the more salient of the two terms. On these terms, writing or making would be a repetition compulsion that pointed the way to dusty death, with each page an attempt to delay its onset and a welcome of its warm embrace. If art defines the human condition then it is only on the condition that there is something inhuman installed within it. Invention requires a certain relation to automation, technique, process and method. In this sense, creativity is not just about an encounter with the myself as other to myself, but with the wholly other of the machine.[36] We might say that creation is less a question of intelligent design and more a matter of artificial intelligence.

Recognizing the wholly other within creativity is an important step in moving us beyond the Romantic heritage that informs much of our understanding of creative acts. In practice, if we can use that phrase with all its possible resonances for us, the modes of invention as fabulation and invention as hybridity are inseparable. The point of Derrida's essay, which we could profitably dwell on at greater length, is that invention should not limit itself to what is 'inventible'. That would be to invent what is already possible, predictable, producible, masterable and so on. To make another Super Hero film in an existing franchise or write another Emergency Room based drama is not invention worthy of the name. Invention must do the impossible and invent the uninventible, and in so doing transform the idea and discourse of invention itself. Invention then cannot be tied to what is possible, the uninventive, if you will, of the 'I can'. For Derrida in this essay, the other is not inventible in this sense, it cannot be subject to a masterable possibility under the rule of the I as something that can be invented. Rather, this other impossible invention is of the other, the other is invention. That moment of encounter or arrival of what comes, unpredictable and without conditions, is invention and irreducibly of the other.

In his account of invention Derrida cites examples from art and music but also techno-science and medicine, invention is a multidisciplinary activity for Derrida. For this reason, among others, Derrida prefers the formulation that invention 'finds something for the first time' (p. 23). There is something of the accidental, automatic, and unprecedented that is encapsulated in this idea of the event as an original finding. Accordingly, whether one considers invention as the object that is found or the act of discovering, 'invention does not create an existence or a world as a set of existents, it does not have the theological meaning of a veritable creation of existence *ex nihilio*' (p. 24). Rather, this version of invention discovers what was already there but was not found or produced as *techne* as a configuration of existing or available elements. Here, we might say that something only comes of something, as one of the threads of the heterogeneous modes of invention. We might also note that this sense of the inaugural event in which invention occurs does not create an existence, either invention finds for the first time something that already exists, or, invention of the uniquely fabulous for the first time is also for the last time. Invention, in this sense, would be the reserve of the human, while creation was the act of God. We might also say that Nancy's use of the *ex nihilio* is an attempt, hampered as it is by its own theological flavour, to shift the register of creation away from a model of production that has its roots in the inheritance of monotheism. In Derrida's essay, something must come from something, but that thing, both in the sense of what is created and the resources of creation, is the event of the arrival of the other.

Thinking invention, on these terms, is then a considerable task, one that asks us to imagine new idioms of understanding that see what cannot be seen, touch what cannot be touched, account for what cannot be predicted. This includes the recognition that 'the other' as a concept is an invention of philosophy, and thinking invention creatively will call on us to preserve the work of this term by not wearing it out or setting it in play anew in order to name the experience that cannot be phenomenalised. It will require a significant degree of self-reflexivity and an openness to thought and experience that some modes of creative practice might consider luxurious or self-involved. That does not of course place them outside of the aporias of creativity, rather in turning a blind eye to their own blind spots they demonstrate precisely the need for such an investigation. If theory-practice has a privileged role to play in our consideration of invention and creation then it is because it is itself part of a history and system of conventions and conceptual orders that ties techno-science to the humanities as the heir of the questions of humanism. What it means to be human is the proper subject of theory-practice as a creative art. Accordingly, it must open up the question of the human not in order to repeat the androcentrism of science but to suggest that the idea of the human that runs through humanism and science is inadequate because it does not fully account for what it does in fact mean to be human. In the creative act, for example, we must recognize and understand the role of the other and the irreducible importance of the wholly other in the acts and objects of invention. That is to say, it must question a whole programmatic of invention that runs from fine art to techno-science that seeks to programme, plan or proscribe invention. Invention cannot be invented in this way, nor, can creativity be created. Equally, invention and creativity must, as we have discussed, be recuperated into the history and tradition from which it emerges to disrupt. Accordingly, a true invention that rethought and displaced this enclosure of invention would require its own institutions and other vistas of support for properly creative and critically creative spaces. It would require us to reinvent the conditions of invention beyond programme or proscription and at the same time not surrender to an idealist future that abandoned the academy or the state to its own worst instincts. Theory-practice then has a considerable amount of work to do, transforming and mutating the host, which both sets it in play and inevitably recuperates its inventive possibilities to a regime of measurement and management.

Part Two

In Practice

6

1975 to 1871

If I might be allowed to paraphrase Marx, hitherto this book has only interpreted the world of critical practice, the point is to do it. Accordingly, I could direct the reader towards my own projects with filmmakers that might be considered examples of the sort of theory-practice that was described in the first half of this book.[1] The experience of working on those films with accomplished directors certainly informed the intellectual labour of the previous chapters. This work would be impossible to reproduce in the context of this book, nor should one present one's own activity in an uncritical way. The process, reflection and commentary have been captured elsewhere. However, given all that has been said up until now regarding creative work and the writing practices that take place at the fraying borders of philosophy as a contribution to extending the parameters of theory-practice, it will be necessary to point towards the sort of artistic activity that constitutes this particular category. In the two chapters that follow we will read singular examples of theory-practice. They are not intended as exemplary either of a particular aesthetic sensibility or for their value as philosophical encounters. They must also be read here, unavoidably, in a critical way. This would be the supplement to theory-practice, criticism cannot be circumvented in a book such as this. It is, perhaps, the critical part of the practice announced by the title of this study. If theoretical writing and creative practice can be triangulated in the idiom of artistic work we are identifying as Theory-Practice then that combination calls for criticism; that is, it calls to be read critically and theoretically. Criticism in this sense being another practice that escapes the ambitions of Theory-Practice. It is not the dialectical result of theory's encounter with practice, but it is what persists and cannot be assimilated by the sublation of Theory-Practice, which must face this other practice both as its other and as a critical practice of its own.

Accordingly, if we cannot help but present such work in the mode of criticism then let us embrace that opportunity for what it might tell us, through singular examples, of the work of Theory-Practice. In this chapter we will look at a tableau vivant by Valerio Adami, an artist whose work responds to and countersigns the texts of Derrida, Benjamin, Joyce and others. In the following chapter we will read images by Mark Tansey, an artist who has made concerted material efforts to incorporate the text of theory into his canvases. In commenting on these images by Adami and Tansey, these readings will roam across other artistic and philosophical texts, including contemporary filmmakers, playwrights and seventeenth-century artists. It will also necessarily involve reading the theoretical work that this art responds to and exceeds. In choosing these two limited examples, I do not intend to suggest a set of criteria for 'good' and 'bad' critical practice, but I would like to make a distinction between practice that engages with theory as a provocation or extension of the philosophical text rather than creative works that are 'about' philosophy or are merely illustrative of the truth of theory. There is a real value in telling the stories of philosophy or recounting the biographies of the great thinkers, but this seldom results in what we have called here alternatively critical practice or theory-practice. Adami and Tansey are two theory-practitioners, two philosopher-artists who have something to say about both art and philosophy through their art. There are many other examples we could read, many other pathways to diversity we ought to follow through the rich pantheon of Theory-Practice. However, on this occasion, under the constraints unique to this book, we will need to be content with Valerio Adami and Mark Tansey as exemplars of the sort of work identified in this book as Critical Practice. The resources of this study should allow others to extend an analysis, reading and creative response across the wider and diverse fields of Theory-Practice.

1975

Everything starts with an image. Jacques Derrida and his family would often stay at the house of the artists Valerio and Camilla Adami in Arona on Lake Maggiore in Italy. In an interview with Benoît Peeters, Camilla Adami recalls 'every year, Valerio would direct a tableau vivant inspired by a classical picture, such as *The Miraculous Draught of Fishes*, or *The Massacre of the Innocents*. Jacques cheerfully joined in, with Marguerite and the children'.[2] There is perhaps something a little odd about the idea of cheerfully joining in a tableau of a biblical atrocity, even if one is on holiday with friends and family. The image of the reproduced scene is included in Peeters' biography and has been widely circulated.[3] It is based on

Nicolas Poussin's 1629 oil on canvas (147 cm × 171 cm) now displayed in the Musée Condé de Chantilly in France.[4] It references King Herod's slaughter of children as recounted in the gospel of Matthew.

The Magi, who had followed the Star of Bethlehem to worship the newborn Christ, stopped at the palace of Herod the Great to ask if he knew how they could find the king of the Jews. The paranoid king in a situation of political instability feared for his throne and with seeming innocence asked the wise men to return with news of the Christ child so that he might also pay his respects. However, as Matthew reports, the three Kings were warned by God in a dream not to return to Herod and they left Judea by another route. An angel also appeared to Joseph in a dream and told him to flee with Jesus and his mother to Egypt and to remain there until Herod's rule was at an end:

> For Herod will seek the young child to destroy him ... Then Herod, when he saw that he was mocked of the wise men, was exceeding wroth, and sent forth, and slew all the children that were in Bethlehem, and in all the coasts thereof, from two years old and under, according to the time which he had diligently inquired of the wise men.[5]

Of all the troubling scenes of cruelty in the Bible, the story of the massacre of the innocents, historically accurate or not, has a particular resonance with artists.

While the account of Matthew may be a creative, theological hagiography, concerned with establishing Christ as the Messiah through the seeming accomplishment of Old Testament prophecy, the events implied by the few lines of verse 2:16 speak to an all too familiar political act of violent repression that today we might recognize as calculated, criminal, ethno-religious or genocidal. Equally, the historic Herod, like Richard III, may of course be poorly served by literary and artistic representations: Giotto's fresco of 1305 depicts Herod directing the massacre from his palace; Brueghel the Elder (1566), painting during the wars of religion following the Reformation, renders the soldiers as Habsburg troops attacking Dutch villagers; Tintoretto (1582-7) and Rubens (1611-12) offer tableaus of visceral cruelty that seem to include rape as well as infanticide, in which the mothers of Judea are central to the visual drama. Rubens also returned to this scene with a no less graphic portrayal in 1638. The version of 1590 by Cornelis Van Haarlem is equally kinetic in its depiction of a riotous scene of depravity and assault by naked soldiers. On the left-hand side of the tableau a group of mothers take unforgiving revenge on an isolated soldier. However, for holiday fun, the Adamis and the Derridas recreated a later work by Poussin, which is markedly different from the traditional representation of the scene as a mass outrage of rampaging soldiers. Rather, Poussin concentrates on a single moment in which an individual soldier stands on the throat of a male baby, raising a sword aloft, while holding a mother back by her hair as she screams and attempts to block the path of the killer. In the background another mother of Judea looks to the skies, holding a dead baby in one hand. Further in the distance another woman carries a baby (alive or dead, it is impossible to say) over her shoulder. In the space between the soldier's leg and the ground we can see two other mothers, one of whom looks out at us across the canvas, observing the scene of murder before her but her line of sight is multiple, distracted and distracting.

In the Adami tableau, the imagined classical architecture of Poussin is replaced by the Adami house at Lake Maggiore, itself a sizeable palazzo partly destroyed during the war. Jacques plays the role of Herod's soldier with a cloth draped over his shoulders, kitchen knife in hand, with his foot (wearing sandals) resting on the stomach rather than the throat of his eight-year-old son Jean. Marguerite Derrida enacts the part of the distressed mother seemingly reaching for the knife while her husband holds her back by the hair. Unlike in the Poussin, Marguerite's face turns inwards towards the murder weapon, rather than outwards as the figure screams in despair. Camilla Adami is the other distraught mother, positioned closer to the front of the frame than in the original painting, in line with Marguerite, and without a baby in her hand but with a dog at her feet. In the space under Derrida's raised arm we can see Valerio Adami enjoying his holidays, sitting on a Baroque chair, in contemporary clothes and wristwatch, looking on at the simulation in front of him. It is of course a comic set-up in which the philosopher father holds a knife over his son as his psychoanalyst mother seeks to bar his path. The artist observes in the background and his wife looks out of the window, hands on her head, sunshine on her face, more Norma Desmond than Old Testament Rachel. It is, however, a curious image to choose to while away one of those wet afternoons that so often descend on the northern lakes during the summer months. One might ask whether for all its 'cheerfulness' it is a wholly innocent image?

The eponymous innocent is Jean, born in 1967, and so at least as old as the age of grammatology, forecast in the same year. His brother Pierre is nowhere to be seen but instead a dog lies asleep at his feet in an inventive addition to Poussin's scene of death. He holds his arms above his head like the child in the original painting, but in the Poussin, it seems as if the baby's arms are raised not so much in horror or in surrender but in an involuntary fashion as a result of the weight of the soldier's foot on his throat. There is then little that is innocent about Jean Derrida's pose, for it is precisely that, a pose or posture, a deliberate feint, that carries all the weight of art history, a performance under the heel of the philosophical father. Jean, unlike the infant in the Poussin, is of course covered below the waist: there is only so much family fun you can have. Like Adam and Eve after they have eaten from the tree of knowledge, the young Jean Derrida knows what it would mean to be naked. He is no innocent newborn. This then is a knowing tableau, not an innocent one. It is both a pose and a posture. We might say that it massacres its own innocence in its knowing and ironic performance of the scene it reproduces that places the emphasis on the laughter in slaughter. Marguerite pleads for the life of her son, or the return of the bread knife, while Jacques assumes his position for the camera, hoping that he is neither pressing his foot down too hard on his son nor clutching his wife's hair too tightly. He is acting for all his worth, as he truly murders murder. There would be little that would be innocent about this family drama between philosophy and psychoanalysis, watched on knowingly by the artist directing the scene from his chair, both a seat of learning and a director's chair for a God like mogul. As with the Poussin his line of sight is complex and multiple, looking on to the scene of murder without murder and through it to the outside of the frame. His wife looks off out the window rather than to the heavens, while the dog plays dead, the most convincing performance in the scene.

There is no doubt an innocent explanation for why Adami chose this scene to re-enact – that is a speculation for another biography and another day. However, the summer of 1975, sadly like many summers before and since, was notable for disquiet in the region of Herod the Great. Lebanon, once the site of the French mandate in the Middle East, witnessed the outbreak of a bloody, multi-sectarian Civil War that would last for fifteen years. In Iraq, Saddam Hussein brought down his boot on the throat of the Kurds when the Algiers Agreement between Iraq and Iran saw the Shah withdraw his support for the Kurdish uprising in return for settlement of the border at Shatt al-Arab waterway. Suddenly and unexpectedly without backing from Iran, Israel and the United States, the Kurds were left to the mercy of Saddam, hundreds of thousands were killed or displaced. The Iraqi Army rounded up village after Kurdish village and took the population to a compound in the southern desert where they were forced into huts, the walls of which had 'Dar-al-Fana' ('House of Annihilation') scrawled on the side. This particular massacre of the innocents lead the then US Secretary of State, Henry Kissinger, to explain his cynical withdrawal of support from the Kurds to the Pike House Committee on CIA activity, with the words 'covert action should not be confused with missionary work'.[6] While the slaughter of innocents is a recurring theme in the history of the world, the manipulative treatment of the Kurdish cause by the Western powers is a repeat performance of a tableau we have witnessed many times before: innocence died with Nixon, no innocence after Kissinger, and still today the sacrifice of the Kurds in the Great Game continues.[7]

The Adami house in Piedmont is said to be a place rich in stories and resonant of the history of the region. Perhaps Adami had the words of John Milton in his mind when he posed this scene from Poussin. The 1655 sonnet 'On the Late Massacre in Piedmont' speaks to the poet's anguish at the massacre of the Waldensian protestant sect by the Duke of Savoy. Milton's record of this atrocity bears comparison to the classic tableau of Poussin:

> Avenge O Lord thy slaughtered saints, whose bones
> Lie scattered on the Alpine mountains cold […]
> Slain by the bloody Piedmontese, that rolled
> Mother with infant down the rocks.[8]

The sadly long route of the primal generality of criminal atrocities by soldiers on innocent civilians, marches past the door of many particularities, each in their own way worthy of consideration, each requiring a more patient and considered response to do justice to the individual lives lost across the span of history, from Milton's 'Italian fields' to 'the Babylonian woe' he invokes at the end of his sonnet. And massacres beget massacres, as Milton's ripping up of the Irish peace process in 1649, on the grounds that vengeance was called for after the 1641 'rebellion', paved the way for Cromwell's massacres at Drogheda and Youghal later that year.[9] The question here is not what Valerio Adami was thinking when he set up his holiday tableau but in so doing what it gives us the opportunity to think with respect to the haunting resonance of the scene's title and what it would mean to think of 'innocence' as such. The pose of Derrida standing over his son with a knife most keenly reminds us of the reading of Abraham and Isaac in *The Gift of Death* (dedicated to the Czech philosopher Jan Patočka) in which the slaughter of an innocent child is ultimately substituted for the slaughter of an innocent kid.[10] The question of Abraham's own innocence, compelled and tested by God, is an open one for any observer of that scene. Moreover, God is the one who comes out of that situation least well, having caused such anguish to father and son: how innocent can an all-knowing being be? He directs the scene on Mt Moriah like Adami, while back at home that morning Sarah wondered where all the kitchen knives had gone.

1981

Six years after the tableau vivant at Lake Maggiore, an innocent Jacques Derrida was arrested in Prague on the pretext that narcotics had been found in his luggage at the airport when he was about to leave the country. The facts of the Prague Affair are widely recorded elsewhere but some of the details are worth revisiting in order to understand the complexity of a phrase that would be tantamount to an oxymoron for some: 'an innocent Jacques Derrida'.

Derrida was visiting Prague as vice-president of the Jan Hus Foundation (named after the religious reformer who was burned as a heretic in Constance in 1415, another slaughtered saint). He taught a seminar on Descartes *in camera* for philosophers repressed under Communist rule. He had become increasingly worried that he was under surveillance and in fact decided to abandon the second session of the seminar, checking out of his hotel and going to stay with an aunt of his wife, whose maternal family were of Czech origin. Derrida had taken a risk in his bold act of solidarity with Czechoslovakian intellectuals but that courage did not extend to a double session and prudence (either for himself or for the sake of his hosts) got the better of him. It was when attempting to board his plane to France that the Czech police sprung their trap, finding the drugs they had already concealed in Derrida's suitcase and placing him under arrest.[11]

One way these events have been understood is that the Czechoslovakian state attempted to frame Derrida in order to discourage dissent and to intimidate other foreign intellectuals who might be minded to visit Prague. That is to say, Derrida was targeted because he was Derrida. The reality of the situation was quite different. The facts were confirmed later by Ladislav Hejdanek, a signatory of Charter 77, the human rights movement that had previously requested that the Czechoslovakian government uphold its own legal obligations to freedom, and in whose home Derrida's seminar took place. He explained that a new head of the local police had just been appointed, who wanted to make a name for himself by some innovative act of repression. Acting on his own accord he decided to make an example of the Jan Hus Foundation, coincidentally at the time Derrida was visiting. He knew nothing of Derrida or his place in the world, and was ill prepared for the diplomatic and media row that ensued after Derrida's arrest. After Derrida's release, the police chief was demoted and sent back to his previous provincial duties. Benoît Peeters records that after the Velvet Revolution, the same officer was himself arrested for drug trafficking. The chief of police had considered the whole of the Jan Hus group guilty but had thought he was picking on an innocent man in order to deter further criminality. In fact, his choice was anything but innocent. There is something profoundly Hitchcockian about this set-up, in which rather than an innocent man stumbling onto a scene that leads to his embroilment with intrigue and the police, here we have a police officer who naively picks on an 'innocent' man only to be caught up in an international row.[12] The doubling and inversion are dizzying: the corrupt police chief turns out to be an innocent in the ways of philosophy, the innocent tourist is revealed to be the mastermind of an international network of free thinkers that extended all the way up to the highest echelons of the Élysée Palace. Marguerite Derrida turned to Régis Debray, who at the time was an advisor to President Mitterrand, for help in securing Derrida's release.

The Prague Affair begs a number of questions about the innocence of the philosopher abroad, or, the philosopher who knowingly intervenes in the business of another country.[13] There is a certain complicity that needs to be explored around this question of how innocent, as opposed to how naive Derrida was in undertaking this trip to Czechoslovakia. This is not to question Derrida's motives or to defend the actions of the Prague police; rather it is to raise a question about the absolute innocence of the innocent. Innocence in English, taking its root from the Latin *in-nocentem*, meaning doing no injury, or, free from guilt by doing no harm. The activity of innocence is then based on a certain passivity, its positivity is the result of a negative, doing no harm is not the same thing as doing any good.[14] However, by any recognizable legal criteria we would say that Derrida was the innocent party in this intrigue. On his return to Paris, Derrida wrote to President Gustav Husak demanding an official apology and insisting that he be cleared of the accusations against him. After an eighteen-month delay, the response from the Czech Foreign Ministry simply certified that 'no criminal proceedings had been set in motion'.[15] This, of course, acknowledges that he is technically innocent but there remains within such a statement the whiff of insinuation, that there may have been a case to answer and that the Prague police are themselves innocent of any wrongdoing. To be placed before the Law is immediately to be marked by the Law and in defending one's innocence one is merely drawing attention to the ways in which innocence is necessarily contested.

What would have happened to Derrida had he actually been an innocent? His arrest resulted in the Ambassador of Czechoslovakia in Paris being called to the Quai d'Orsay, and headlines in the world press. This is not the usual response in such circumstances afforded to those who are innocent but who lack celebrity, friends in the media or ex-students in ministries. Derrida was acutely aware of the good fortune of his name in the world. He told the Antenne 2 film crew that met him on his return: 'I hesitate to describe the brutality of the thing, which in one sense was commonplace and in another was reserved for me alone'.[16] That is to say that this was in some ways quite an innocent experience, an everyday experience for thousands of prisoners around the world. In one sense, there is nothing unique or especially cruel about it. Derrida does not want to claim a special privilege for his experience, after all Jan Patočka had been beaten to death while in the custody of the Czechoslovakian regime. It is the Chartists, Derrida went on to say to the press, 'who are struggling for human rights to be respected. Yes, they are the ones I would like to salute, since they are struggling in really heroic—in other words obscure and anonymous—conditions'.[17] The innocence of the Chartists, and so many others like them throughout history, is not secured by their obscurity and anonymity. Every day, the innocent people are found guilty of thought crimes, their experiences are singular to them, and sadly quite ordinary. They lack the intense mediatization of a scene that would lift their case from obscurity to exemplarity, from the particular to the general. How many babies die every day from lack of sanitation or medical facilities it is well within the resources of globalization or nation states to provide for them? But how many must die anonymously and in obscurity before we can speak of a massacre of the innocents, today?

When Derrida returned to Paris, the first visitor to his house was Jean Genet who wanted to ask him about his experience of prison. Genet knew, of course, that there was nothing unique about Derrida's time in the Ruzyne jail in Prague. No doubt Derrida told his friend about the Hungarian gipsy who had been placed in his cell on his first night and who, touched by his companion's distress, helped him clean the cell as best they could and later played noughts and crosses with Derrida on a paper handkerchief. The gipsy may have been more familiar with incarceration than Derrida and his fate after the philosopher's release may have been less certain. However, Derrida's experience in prison in Prague is of course unique, not only in the sense that it was an experience personal to him but that it was also the event of Jacques Derrida's imprisonment. It was one experience among many similar ones experienced repeatedly by literally millions of people, but equally it could never be reduced to one among many.

Prior to these events in Prague, Derrida had been reluctant to share his personal image publicly. When news broke of his arrest the media had few photographs of Jacques Derrida with which to illustrate their articles. The images of Derrida's return to the Gare de l'Est are well known to any scholar of his work. He stands at the centre of a paparazzi scrum, in a sheepskin coat, over an open-necked shirt, his tie undone, looking exhausted and haunted, his hair far from the immaculate coiffeur that some of us associate with him. These are images of a human drama but one that is equally of public interest. After the media tumult at the train station in Paris there could be no return to the obscurity and anonymity of philosophy for Jacques Derrida. He was no longer innocent as far as the media were concerned. Nor could he maintain a certain pretence or a certain innocence with respect to his own mediatization.[18] Innocence would necessarily have to give way to the narcissism of the jealously protected image. We might say that on this occasion the innocence of Jacques Derrida was secured by the complicity of Derrida, his family and supporters in the mediatization of the scene of his release, which was a staged event, a simulacrum of release, not at the gates of the Ruzyne but on the platform of the Gare de l'Est, safely within the perimeter of Paris.

These photographs that spread around the world were very different from those taken days earlier in a Prague jail. As he wrote to Catherine Malabou in Contre-Allée: 'I have never been more photographed in my life, from the airport to the prison, clothed or naked before putting on the prisoner's "uniform".[19] A surveillance state works by having the citizen under its gaze, in its sights, capturing their image in order to arrest, in every sense, the individual. The press photographs of the dishevelled Derrida are very much images of the man laid bare before a judging audience, but they are not the pictures of a naked foreign philosopher held on record by the Prague police. There is no doubt something indecent about both sets of images but one set are public and one set secret. Perhaps Derrida came to realize that there was indeed a safety to be found in a public image, that complicity with the media would preserve his hard-won innocence, and that the fiction of that innocence could be maintained by the media he had previously sought to elude. Prague had surely taught him that there could be safety in the guilt of publicity and danger in the innocence of anonymity. After all Derrida had once been an obscure, innocent Jewish schoolboy in French Algeria expelled from the Lycée and whom, like so many others, no one had spoken up for, just one more victim of a modern sacrifice. For an academic there is a violence worse than the surveillance of the university and that is expulsion from the university. Perhaps, one does not stop being a pupil or an academic after one has been expelled from the institution, at least not in one's own mind, but there is a geometry of formal exclusion that is more outside than in. Anonymous exiles from the university live the life of the mind without a safety net.

If we speak here of a fiction of innocence, it is not to question the moral character of Jacques Derrida or belittle his genuine experiences of incarceration, rather it is to suggest that the presentation of innocence must always be necessarily fictional. When he was finally released from the Prague prison, his assigned lawyer said to Derrida: 'you must have the impression of living in a Kafka story… Don't take things too tragically; consider it a literary experience'.[20] The phrase is ambiguous, did the lawyer mean that Derrida should consider it the sort of experience that a writer like Genet might turn into fiction, or did he mean that all of this should be experienced as if it were coded as literary? In that second sense, there is something more profound in the words of the lawyer, something even a little accusatory. He is saying that the events of the last few days may seem familiar to you from fiction: you know how they will proceed if not how they will conclude, for you as a foreign professor with influential friends who will soon be released to Paris, you can afford the luxury of their fictionality. For us who remain here we must have another relationship to the apparatus of a security state, one that is different from the policing structures of the French philosophical establishment.[21]

The question of innocence cannot it seems, be separated from the question of literature, as Derrida himself might have put it. The possibility that doing no harm is different from an absence of guilt might be closely related to the simultaneous avowal and disavowal that takes place during the suspended reference of literature, of all that can be said publicly under the name of literature.[22] On this occasion we have chosen to read Derrida not, so far, through his philosophical writing, but through events in his life, as if they were a fictional text, a narrative to be deconstructed. No doubt the more meticulous or perhaps scrupulous will object to this strategy but when it comes to imagining Derrida or speaking of the image of Derrida we are never far from the question of the writing of fiction and of the literary, certainly of storytelling and self-narrativization.

1977

Tom Stoppard's play *Professional Foul* was written in 1977, the same year as Ladislav Hejdanek, Jan Patočka and others signed their declaration for human rights and the rule of law in Czechoslovakia. It is another fictional frame for the experiences of Derrida and the Jan Hus Foundation in Prague. It concerns a group of international philosophers invited to a colloquium in the Czech capital during the age of what some insist on calling 'the linguistic turn' in philosophy: 'a lot of chaps pointing out that we don't always mean what we say even when we manage to say what we mean'.[23] The central characters are Professor Anderson, the J. S.

Mill Chair of Ethics at Cambridge University, and Professor McKendrick, a self-declared left-winger who works in Stoke-on-Trent. The former philosophizes in the realm of abstract privilege and is not keen to be drawn into any local dissent, as this would be an act of bad manners against his hosts, the Czechoslovakian government. He has plans instead to attend a World Cup qualifying match being played at the same time between England and Czechoslovakia. The paper he intends to present is entitled 'Ethical Fictions as Ethical Foundations', perhaps a hint at Stoppard's own intentions in the presentation of the drama. McKendrick would be keen to participate in some local action but has no genuine connection to Czech intellectuals, rather his energies are more directed towards attempts to chat up women attending the conference. He is a self-identified Marxist and author of science fiction short stories for pornographic magazines. Anderson's reticence is disturbed when he is visited by one of his ex-students, Pavel Hollar, who asks him to smuggle an essay out of the country that contains ethical arguments contrary to the Communist regime. Hollar is not a professor at Cambridge. In fact, he has become déclassé and is now a cleaner at the bus station, one of those heroes of free thought struggling in obscurity and anonymity: 'I am not a famous dissident. A writer, a scientist … if I am picked up … there is no fuss … but I have something to say – that is all' (p. 142). Anderson does not agree to take the text out of the country as he thinks it would be a breach of politesse with his hosts. He does not want to be put in a difficult position and offers ethical arguments against the direction of Hollar's essay to justify his own inaction. However, he does hold on to the text to prevent his student running the risk of being stopped in the street with dissident material.

The following day, before the football match, Anderson visits Hollar's flat to return the essay only to find that his student has been arrested and that the Prague police are searching his flat. He is detained and misses the match, which England lose 4–0, the first goal coming from a penalty conceded from a professional foul committed by one of the footballers, Broadbent, staying in the same hotel as the philosophers. Anderson is finally released when the police 'discover' foreign currency they have planted in the Hollar residence. Anderson finds himself as a professor of ethics who must now profess an ethical position beyond the 'bun-fights' of philosophical colloquia. During a verbose lecture by an American professor of language theory, McKendrick asks Anderson, 'do you ever wonder if all this is worthwhile?' 'No', replies Anderson, to which McKendrick smiles and says, 'I know what you mean' (p. 148). They are professional thinkers; it would be a foul against the profession to question the value of philosophical conferences in foreign capitals. It would also be a foul against professional ethics to criticize his hosts but having reflected on his situation the priggish Anderson decides to make his own intervention by grounding his ethical abstractions in material actions, if only in the guise of a fiction. He sits up all night to rewrite his paper for the conference with a typewriter he borrows from a football journalist in the room next door. The lecture he gives then follows on from his discussions with his former student about the rights of the individual against the state, noting the freedom of letters as a shared human right. The moderator complains that this is not the paper he submitted prior to the conference. Anderson feigns innocence and carries on with his 'fictional' paper. Rather than allow him to proceed with his talk, a policeman sets off the fire alarm and clears the building.

The closing act of the play sees Anderson and McKendrick moving through customs at Prague airport. A junior colleague, Chetwyn, who is known in the UK for campaigning on behalf of Czech intellectuals, is stopped and arrested for carrying clandestine materials. Anderson also has his suitcase checked but the guards only find the pornographic magazines containing McKendrick's fiction. On the plane back to London, Anderson explains to McKendrick that Chetwyn, 'will be on the next plane. Wouldn't look well with them, all the publicity'. McKendrick says 'he took a big, risk, I wouldn't do it, would you?' Anderson confesses that he knew that he would be searched personally so hid Hollar's essay in McKendrick's suitcase. 'You bastard. You utter bastard', rants McKendrick, 'Not quite playing the game is it?' His colleague replies, 'I thought you would approve ... Ethics is very complicated business. That's why they have these congresses' (p. 179).

A professional foul in soccer is when one player deliberately commits an offence against an opposing player, usually a defender against an attacker, in order to prevent a goal. It is known as a professional foul because it is something that a professional footballer, one who is paid to play the game, is expected to do when faced with such a choice. It is a foul by one professional against another, and among professionals is an accepted part of the game. Now it would earn the player a straight red card, but in 1977 such an act only merited a yellow card. In ethical terms we might say that it is an act of least violence committed by the individual for the sake of the collective. The yellow or red card is a professional hazard, taking one for the team. On this occasion the ultimate professional foul is the risk that Anderson takes by making McKendrick the mule for Hollar's essay. Despite his avowed Marxism, McKendrick is furious that his professional reputation and personal liberty were put at risk for the sake of what he had earlier called 'professors with unpronounceable names' (p. 132). He has a point. He is the only innocent in this whole schema: Hollar and Chetwyn are active dissidents, Anderson is implicated in the intrigue whether he likes it or not. The innocence of Anderson, Hollar and Chetwyn is at least contestable. The ethical calculation that Anderson makes is that the least bad thing to do is to sacrifice McKendrick in a switch that uses his colleague's seeming innocence as a front for smuggling. Ethically and politically, this might be an acceptable thing to do, but this professional foul is not a foul without a victim. The professional foul may be an accepted part of the game, a foul without a foul, as it were, but there is always a consequence, and always someone who is 'brought down' by the foul. It is right, and an equally accepted part of the game, that a penalty be imposed.

The question is whether the penalty is a hard shot lashed at the goal or whether it is what is known in the game as a 'Panenka', a skilful and subtle chip deceiving the goalkeeper, named after Antonin Panenka who won the 1976 European Championship for Czechoslovakia with such an innovative technique. In the Great Game of politics, a professional foul like that committed by Nixon on the Kurds might be laughed off in a memoir but the cynicism rebounds through the decades. The difference between the sacrifice of McKendrick by Anderson and the sacrifice of the Kurds by Nixon is one of magnitude. No doubt Anderson would have thought twice if he had entertained the possibility that McKendrick might have died in prison. What Stoppard's scenario weighs for us is the measure between the private and the public, between philosophy and politics between persons and the people, between a Marxist professor from Stoke and a new Czech Spring for all those professors expelled from the university in the name of Marx. How many innocents can be sacrificed for the greater good? Anderson finally extricates himself from Hollar's flat when he convinces the police captain that he is not there to deliver foreign currency but a philosophical paper. He is dismissed immediately, philosophy being a matter of no consequence to the state, even though it is, in fact, the very reason they are pursuing Pavel Hollar. The question of sacrifice is central to much of later Derrida, notable in relation to questions of sovereignty and economy as a problem of substitution.[24]

'There is a lot of juice left in the fictions question', (p. 132) McKendrick tells Anderson in their opening exchanges on their British Airways flight. This recalls Derrida's exchange with Searle, which seems to hang like a backdrop to Stoppard's fictional conference. Fiction is the idiom in which it is possible to say everything that must be said in the name of truth, just as it can be disavowed as a straightforward or innocent reference to the real world. There is nothing more innocent than fiction, nothing more fictional than innocence, and nothing more complicit than fictionalization. As soon as there is writing, we are guilty. The Czech word for guilt is '*vina*', more strictly meaning fault, but like the German

'*Schuld*' also carrying a sense of 'debt'. There is much made in Stoppard's play of philosophical translation at the international conference. As soon as there is debt we are complicit—to whom does Anderson owe a greater debt? Is it to his student or his governmental hosts or to freedom of speech and the academy? For the Czech-born Stoppard the fiction is pointedly engaged with the real world; in 1977 it presaged issues with which few outside the literary and academic community in the West were familiar. There is no suggestion that Derrida knew his Stoppard, but he was engaged with the Jan Hus Foundation, and was aware of the fictional history of Prague and the literary mediatization of totalitarian Communist states. Writing involves a certain massacre of the innocents, sacrificing their narratives for a purpose beyond their own singularity. How could one make the story of déclassé intellectuals known without offering up individual narratives to a wider audience? Writing is both the nude photograph of a prisoner and the paparazzi scrum in a Paris train station. Either way there is no choice but to submit one's story to exposition, watched over by the other, for the other, as a sacrifice to the greater good, submitting to that gaze in more or less knowing ways. In this sense, there is nothing more public than private anonymity, and nothing more obscure than the public performance of singularity. The individual has the right to cry, 'you utter bastards', but their particularity is always already sacrificed to the mediatization of the political, which is to say the political *tout court*. No politics without media, no media without politics. And philosophy is in no way exempt from this professional hazard. Just as it is an accepted part of the game of Association Football to trip an opponent from behind, it is equally understood that attacking players will attempt to fake a foul in order to gain an advantage or have an opponent sent off. One can be lured into committing a professional foul or indeed be punished for such an offence when one is entirely innocent. In tackling the media, philosophy since Derrida has begun to appreciate that it is increasingly difficult to tell the difference between playing the ball and playing the man.'[25]

1919

In Ken McMullen's *Ghost Dance* made in 1982 (released 1983) a short while after Derrida dropped his prohibition on the image, Derrida offers the following comments about his time in Prague:

> Last year, exactly a year ago, I went to Prague to take part in a private seminar with some dissident Czech philosophers who were banned from the universities.

> I was followed by the Czech secret police who made no secret about it. After the seminar I went for a walk around Kafka's town as if in pursuit of Kafka's ghost who was, in fact, himself pursuing me. I went to see the houses where Kafka lived. There are two in Prague. And I went to his grave. I found out the next day when I was arrested for drug smuggling, supposedly, that it was at the exact time that I was at Kafka's grave and so preoccupied to some extent with Kafka's ghost that the Czech secret police entered my room and planted a little packet of drugs as a pretext for my arrest the next day. When I was interrogated by the police as to why I was in Prague I answered truthfully that I was preparing a paper on Kafka on an extract from Kafka's *The Trial* called 'Before the Law'. So throughout my short interrogation and imprisonment Kafka's ghost was effectively present and Kafka's script was manipulating [*reglé*] the whole scene. The scene being that of *The Trial* as if we were all acting in a film controlled [*programée*] by Kafka's ghost.[26]

Here Derrida is in performance, improvising a character that is both himself and entirely fictional. How honest an answer this was to give to the Prague police is contestable, certainly it was an innocent one if not entirely an innocent one. With his friends and colleagues still in Czechoslovakia, a year later it is perhaps more than a question of good manners not to mention the Jan Hus Foundation. However, if Derrida's time in Prague in 1981 reads like a fiction and screens like a film, it is because since the event it has been thoroughly fictionalized, least of all by Derrida himself in McMullen's film. The events are then both predetermined by fiction and post hoc rationalized as fiction. Here Derrida suggests that the whole thing was a screenplay written by Kafka who sat in the director's chair, like Adami at the Lake Maggiore villa or McMullen on the set of *Ghost Dance*.[27]

The text that Derrida is referring to in McMullen's film is Kafka's 1919 parable, '*Vom dem Gesetz*' that was originally published separately from *The Trial*. Familiar to us from Derrida's essay, it tells the story of a man who comes from the country to seek admittance to the Law but is blocked by one gatekeeper after another who impedes his progress through the doorways of the court. The man spends all his money and several years frustrated in the hallways of the court. As he is dying he asks the final gatekeeper why, if so many seek access to the Law, he has never seen another soul all these years. He is told: 'No one else could ever be admitted here, since this gate was made only for you. I am now going to shut it.'[28] Derrida offers a long reading of this text in relation to the problematics of prohibition in Kant and Freud, which there is no space to elaborate on here. However, Derrida is also concerned with the question of literature. The Kafka text is to be considered literature, a literary phenomenon, if you will, but that literariness is not straightforwardly connected to its fictional status or its narrative form. Rather, it is literary according to certain Laws of the institution of literature but, asks Derrida, 'who decides, who judges, and according to what criteria?'[29]

Like any relation to Law, the law of literature must necessarily involve a singularity, 'a law of singularity which must come into contact with the general or universal law without ever being able to do so' (p. 187). The singular experiences of Jacques Derrida in Ruzyne are his and his alone, as are those of the J. S Mill Professor of Ethics at Cambridge University or the villagers of Iraqi Kurdistan, but they have a relation to a universality that makes them of interest to the generality of Law, its enactment and suspension. The universality of Law requires that, in Derrida's words, it 'must be without history, genesis, or any possible derivation. *That would be the law of the law*' (p. 191). The Law is the general algorithm through which the exemplary is judged. However, just as it disavows its historicity, fictionality, and narrative status, the Law can only rely on individual cases to develop and establish itself. Standing before the Law is the pinch point between singularity and universality. And the rule of Law is multiple: Professor Anderson stands before a categorical imperative as well as the Prague police force; Professor Derrida stands before his accusers in the Czechoslovakian secret service and the immutable law of mediatization. An innocent man may stand before the Law wrongly accused but his relation to the law is always divided. To whom does he owe a greater obligation and according to what criteria, and who will judge? When Derrida recounts in *Ghost Dance* his 'truthful' answer which law is he submitting to – judicial, ethical, literary, or another strange law of the media? His innocence is thus divided, irretrievably ruined by the law that he must both submit to and defend himself from. His innocence, one might say, is both massacred and sacred, split by a différance of infinite complexity, complicity, guilt and debt.

Only an innocent man can pass through the Law, equally, an innocent man can never be done with the law. In his text on Kafka, Derrida recalls the words of his Prague lawyer: 'don't take this too tragically, live it as a literary experience'. He adds to this anecdote that he tells his prosecutor that he had never seen the drugs before. The prosecutor replied: 'That's what all drug traffickers say' (p. 218). He has gone beyond Kafka to *Catch 22*: only an innocent would say that they had never seen the drugs, but by denying knowledge of the drugs he proves his obvious guilt. Derrida is something of a specialist when it comes to double binds and the non-passage from the absence of Law to its fulfilment. Philosophy cannot resolve such a conceptual impasse, it can only dig us deeper into the hole it has dug and that we have dug for ourselves. Only the simultaneous suspension and imposition of the laws of mutability that come with writing can move us to another place.

1940

Professor Anderson has his suitcase checked at Charles Airport in Prague. Despite requests Derrida never had his confiscated valise returned to him by the secret police. These 'fictional' professors carry considerable baggage that makes them a suitable case for study. In their stories they evade the law, give it the slip, and live to profess another day. They return home to the academy. Derrida shared a birthday with Walter Benjamin, who in 1940, pursued by the Law of National Socialism, and with no chair in Cambridge or consulate representative or accompanying camera crew, sat in Portbou in Catalonia, with only a suitcase full of manuscripts, unable to secure passage across the border, and finally understood the weight of the totalitarian and the unbearable lightness of philosophy. This gate was made for him and him alone, and then it shut. He is the subject of Derrida's other great essay on the Law concerning *'Zur Kritik der Gewalt'*. A self-slaughtered innocent captured so sympathetically by Adami in his portrait, another counter signature to an image, another ethical fiction as ethical foundation.

1961

Margarethe von Trotta's excellent 2012 film, *Hannah Arendt*, demonstrates many of the problems of film's encounter with philosophy.[30] This film does not come out of a tradition that seeks to engage film itself as a medium that could be productive of knowledge, rather it wants to tell the story of a philosopher and in order to do so has to find ways of explaining philosophy on screen.[31] It is not true to say that the philosophy is incidental to the story, the philosophy in this case is not a McGuffin that might as well have been otherwise. Rather, the story that the film wants to tell around Arendt depends entirely upon the meaning of her philosophical work. However, this is not an in-depth study of philosophical issues as such, in the way that, say, *The Ister* (2004, dirs. David Barison and Daniel Ross) is a contribution to philosophy through film, or, Kirby Dick and Amy Zeiring's 2002 film on Derrida is a document of reported thought.[32] There is no unpacking or countersigning of Arendt's significant thought on totalitarianism, revolution, violence or human rights.[33] Rather, the film tells the story of Arendt's commission by *The New Yorker* to report on the trial of Adolf Eichmann in Jerusalem and the media scandal that followed as a result.[34] It is then a human story, philosophy as costume drama, in which it is necessary to explain who Arendt is, why she was significant, and what her report on Eichmann actually said. There is a necessary tension in the film between drama and exposition, between action and thought, practice and theory, if you will. The drama is to be found in the biography of Arendt, her youthful affair with Heidegger (told in flashback), her escape from occupied Europe, her domestic arrangements with the unfaithful Heinrich Blucher, her friendship with the ever-loyal Mary McCarthy, her visit to Israel, and the experience of vilification for reporting evidence from the trial of Eichmann that Jewish community elders had assisted in the organization of deportations.[35] The narrative of the film flips in a way that Arendt moves from investigator and reporter to being the persecuted figure on trial. In the final scenes her lecture room at the New School becomes a courtroom in which she has to defend herself in public against accusations of being a Nazi apologist. Between, the domestic interactions and this narrative arc, the film convinces as a drama and so pulls its audience, by no means expected to be expert in philosophy, through the turns of Arendt's thinking in relation to Eichmann. However, as with any similar storytelling on screen, we have elisions and composite characters, the realism is entirely artificial for the sake of capturing a narrative on screen.

In an early scene, the editorial team of *The New Yorker* are gathered in the office of Editor William Shawn as they receive the news that Arendt is interested in covering the Eichmann trial. 'She's not one of those European philosophers is she?' asks journalist Francis Wells. The exposition is clunky but we are through it quickly. However, the important point for the drama here is in fact one of greater significance for the problem of film and philosophy. Wells quips to Shawn, 'philosophers don't make deadlines', and correspondingly we later find Arendt dodging phone calls from her editors and refusing to print her thoughts on Eichmann until her studies are concluded. However, the film itself also plays out the problem of the time of philosophy and the time of media, which are two, not necessarily compatible, separate things.[36] A film of this budget and with this ambition to reach a wide audience must by necessity fall back on the centrality of narrative. It is, in essence, a biopic, and a particularly good one at that. However, having made the choice of the speed of media, which is necessarily reductive to complex thought, the moments when we encounter Arendt's philosophy are therefore elided if not compromised. For example, we see Eichmann make the defence that he was obliged by his oath in the *Feurherprinzip* to follow orders. There is a suggestion here of a conflict between duty and conscience, which Arendt makes something of in her philosophical work as an inheritance of the Kantian categorical imperative in the German tradition of public service.[37] However, this is left veiled in the film, which does not have time to unfold these considerations. Von Trotta has come as close as anyone (including John Huston's *Freud* [1962], Pinchas Perry's *When Nietzsche Wept* [2007], or, David Cronenberg's film on Freud and Jung, *A Dangerous Method* [2011]) to pushing a biographical film about a philosopher in the direction of an exposition of philosophy through dramatic action.[38]

Nevertheless, the speed of film and the speed of philosophy are different. You will learn more about the thought of Arendt by reading one of her books or sitting in a philosophy lecture than you will by watching this film. This does not make it a bad film, on the contrary it is a rather good film, but it is still a film not a text of philosophy, and a film that would be recognizable as such to both philosophers and filmmakers. Von Trotta's interest in Arendt does not extend to her philosophical work impacting the director's own practice as a filmmaker. There is little in Von Trotta's back catalogue to suggest that she is engaged on the cusp between theory and practice, seeking new idioms for the articulation and representation of complex thought. However, she is a skilful filmmaker who delivers a compelling drama in her film of Hannah Arendt. This is not Theory-Practice but rather a technical consideration from the side of an industry professional of how to represent thinking on screen. Thinking in this sense being a problem for the screen as it is essentially invisible.

However, the story needs to tell us that Arendt is thinking, this is why she is late with her copy for *The New Yorker* and why it is so good when it finally arrives. The film has to discover within the resources of the sound-image a way of representing the quality of thought: why thinking about your article for a long time will make it better than rushing to a pressroom deadline. Philosophy, in this sense, is value-added thinking, which does not negate the need for editorial deadlines outside of the Ivory Tower, but demonstrates why we need the thinking that goes on in the Humanities Faculty as well as the newsroom. Accordingly, we see Hannah (Barbara Sukowa) smoking, lying on her ottoman in the afternoon, lying on her ottoman in the dark, smoking and lying on her ottoman, sitting at her typewriter, smoking at her typewriter, smoking outside the New School: a woman lost in thought. We see Martin Heidegger tell the young Hannah that 'thinking is a lonely business', and we see her thinking by herself in venues across the tri-state area and Israel. Heinrich (Axel Milberg) is sneaking out the door, perhaps hurrying to a liaison with a lover, when Hannah catches him. He responds, 'never disturb a great philosopher when they are thinking'. Hannah tells him, 'but they can't think without kisses'. Heidegger might not have advocated that view, but this after all is a *female* philosopher and this is the movies. Hannah's deep thought is in contrast to Eichmann who as a banal bureaucrat of the Third Reich did not think about what he was doing. The young Hannah sits in the front row of a lecture given by Heidegger in which he tells us that thinking does not lead to knowledge, instead we think because we are thinking beings. In the final lecture room scene at the New School Hannah makes a defence of thinking, repeating Heidegger's view that thinking does not produce knowledge but instead enables us to tell right from wrong and so to avoid catastrophes. It would seem that she privileges *phronesis* over *episteme*, or judgement over pure reason.

However, what links Eichmann in the courtroom and Arendt's tormentors in the lecture room is the inability to think. It is also her own Achille's heel, she failed to think through what would happen when she published her critique of the *Judenrat*.[39] Her thinking exists in a differently mediatised frame from those who received it second hand, in summary and without reading what she had actually written, even though it appeared in the most prominent and canonical media space possible, *The New Yorker* magazine. She did not see it coming and even when she is in the middle of the hurricane can only think of it as a storm in a teacup. The speed of philosophy and the speed of media are very different. The film then thematizes the same dichotomy it performs, namely the gap between thinking and showing, between thought and its representation, and so between theory and practice. It does so at a level that does not consciously challenge that binary as a self-reflective Theory-Practice might have done so, but as a text, like any other text, this film accomplishes its own disarticulation regardless. The value of the film is its attempt to show the value of thinking that it cannot possibly show. Further, as a feature film that took longer to make than it took Arendt to write *Eichmann in Jerusalem*, it demonstrates its own value and values according to a different index. The reductive speed of media can in fact be longer than the time of philosophy. The gearing is different, one is not a more advanced mode of the other; their orbits are not concentric. It shows film and philosophy to be distinct just as it combines them within a single film about philosophy. It sits in a spectrum with theory-practice, filmosophy, and 'films about philosophy', a range that has considerable overlap and is constituted by several shades of grey.[40] However, Theory-Practice cannot be reduced to a question of thematic content or style, it is rather a matter of a critical attitude that compels a work into self-reflection at the abyss and border between philosophy and art.[41] Perhaps, neither Von Trotta nor Stoppard are critical practitioners in the way that Adami and McMullen are, or that Benjamin and Derrida might be, the study of Theory-Practice is not easily rendered as a competition in aesthetic value.[42] That does not delegitimize or lessen their contribution to philosophy on screen. On the contrary it makes it necessary, the necessity arising from their difference. Telling the stories of philosophy is too important only to be left to philosophical storytellers.

1867

Everything starts with an image.

Edouard Manet made several attempts to paint the execution of Emperor Maximilian of Mexico. The work refers to his death by firing squad that brought an end to the abortive Second Mexican Empire, after Napoleon III of France withdrew French troops that had been propping up his puppet ruler. Manet painted the scene four times. One version now hangs in the Kunsthalle Museum in Mannheim, painted between 1868 and 1869 but dated in the corner with Manet's signature as 1867.[43] An earlier version from 1867–8 exists in the form of fragments in the Nation Gallery in London. It is thought that Manet cut the painting himself and parts of it were sold separately after his death. The existing fragments were brought to London by Edgar Degas in 1918 but were not combined as a single canvas until 1992. A third, unfinished oil version from 1867, can be found in the Museum of Fine Arts Boston. It is smaller than the Mannheim canvas, but not as small as a fourth version now in the Ny Carlsberg Glyptotek in Copenhagen. This version formed the basis of a 50-impression lithograph run in 1869, prints from which can be found in the Metropolitan Museum of Art in New York, among other galleries.[44] In the Boston version the soldiers wear the clothes of the Mexican peasantry, in the Mannheim canvas and the Copenhagen oil they wear uniforms and can be easily or deliberately mistaken for soldiers of the French army. The paintings were never exhibited in France during the reign of Napoleon III, with the first appearance of the Mannheim version appeared in New York and Boston in 1879 six years after the death of Louis-Napoleon.

In a short film entitled '1867' Ken McMullen responds to a commission from The Programme for Art, sponsored by Channel Four, the Metropolitan

Museum of New York and the Ghetty Foundation to document the creative process through the eye of the artist.[45] He chooses to produce a 15-minute film of single uninterrupted shot that tracks the walk of Maximilian from his prison cell to his execution via the studio of Manet. The short film is a response of one painter (McMullen) to another (Manet) that is also a documentation of process in general. It records the path from historical event to its iterations in art, commenting on a practice through the ambition of a single shot as the chosen vehicle for McMullen's own critical practice. This is process that takes account of process, a visual mis-en-abyme that places the representation of history within the history of representation.

There is a double movement within the short film. A column of troops accompanies Maximilian and his two loyal generals from a castle on a hill to a courtyard where they will become a firing squad. They march past the window of Manet's fictional studio where he has assembled the resources for the contemplation of this scene and where a tableau has been established of another fictional firing squad, which provide the models for Manet's painting. Historically, Manet used real French soldiers to paint the Mexican firing squad for additional authenticity. McMullen doubles these doubles with actors and simulacra, painting over verisimilitude with the genre of realism, and doubling the artifice. Manet used actors to pose as Maximilian and his generals, McMullen raises the stakes by having actors play the part of actors posing as historic figures. It is a film that works with the image as much as it works the imagination, doubling an ambiguous genitive as it shows the creative process through the eye of the painter: both that of Manet and of McMullen who reimagines the scene of the Emperor's death and the scene of production of the work of art that represents that death. This after all is McMullen's studio, the studio set of a film director and not the actual studio of Manet the artist. It is the studio of the artist McMullen, the artist who works in the medium of film but who trained as a painter. He 'paints' for us both the studio of Manet and another version of the execution of Maximilian, one more to countersign the work of Manet. The maker of this 1867 is someone like McMullen-Manet, a director-painter, an author of the image and worker in the imagination.

The camera takes us through a history of art, citing the influence of anxiety in Gericault's *The Raft of the Medeusa* and Goya's seminal *The Third of May*.[46] A voice-over reading from Manet's notes, states 'at last I have a subject of history worthy of the salon'. The Goya shows the shooting of peasants, the Manet shows the shooting of an Emperor. The one constant is the French army providing the bullets. The two paintings rifle home a message about the Napoleonic legacy; in contrast the prolonged run on McMullen's camera takes aim before it fires off its missive. In the case of the painting we have an instant caught on canvas, at the speed of a bullet, in the case of the film we have a sweep of history and several minutes to understand several centuries. As the Manet narration tells us it took him one and a half years to paint these four canvases, McMullen takes 15 minutes, in a single take, to reproduce Manet's process. The film ends, surprisingly perhaps for the non-specialist (there for the art rather than the history, at least there for the art history) with Maximilian addressing his firing squad in German. This provides a sharp incongruity to the setting of Frenchmen in Mexico (the scene was actually shot in Portugal). McMullen's shooting is a distant echo of the guns of the French army, swapping one sort of action for another. As Maximilian and his generals are shot, by the firing squad, they pose for the camera, capturing the artifice of the original action picture, the painting that arrests history as a still image rather than a flow of time, reducing depth to surface and achieving depth through mere surface. Maximilian and his generals freeze, their time is over, while a stray dog moves around the square where McMullen films. There is then nothing natural about this history. The moving image and the still image contrast and complement, McMullen's single shot against the random volley of the gunfire, McMullen's compressed whole against Manet's four attempts at the scene, McMullen's freeze against Manet's friese, McMullen's unbroken track against the torn fragments on display in the Nation Gallery in London.

This is not to suggest a privileging of McMullen over Manet as a painter of the historic process. The medium is different, the intention is different, the outcomes are mutually beneficial. Manet finds little possibility of closure in his obsession with this moment, as demonstrated by his repeated return to the scene of the crime. Equally, and despite appearances, McMullen is just as obsessed, just as at sea with respect to the flow of history. This short film, *1867*, is in fact a companion piece to McMullen's feature film on the Paris Commune, *1871*.[47] Painted a few years earlier, the Manet painting plays a role in feature, as the object of attention of a salon run at the Café Anglais by the revolutionary General Cluseret during the siege of Paris. The later *1867* short is then both a prologue and an epilogue to the longer work of *1871*. It stands before and after the history of the film and the filming of history. The film *1867* is part of the prehistory of *1871*, the *préhistoire* in French specifically names a historic period 'avant l'apparition de l'écriture', before the appearance of writing.[48] The film *1867* is in some way prehistoric, primordial and fundamental to McMullen's practice, like cave painting to the Sistine Chapel on *1871*. It designates a period before writing, that is to say, before the architecture of McMullen's practice in the feature film, which is a profound engagement with texts, the writing of texts, the imagining and imaging of texts, not as an adaptation, translation, or illustration but as an active writing of their future. McMullen is a writer-painter who feels his way along the path of images and texts, assembling and editing, in a practice tethered to an idea of history. That *1867* was made after *1871* is immaterial to this material practice, as an origin it can never be originary enough, coming as it does after the main feature. A short should of course always be watched before the feature. The temporality here speaks of a return rather than of progress.

The shorter film on the process of Manet is then part of the process of McMullen and part of a process that fails to progress. It cannot account for, this unaccountable scene that remains resistant to capture and heterogeneous to measurement. Nor can it process resistant material in a psychoanalytic sense, the execution of Maximilian remains a resistant core that returns as a symptom to be read again and again. This is a process that fails to process. Instead it obsesses, stewing in the juices of history, unable to achieve exit velocity sufficient to understand itself in any other way as art history, and part of the art history it comments on. The combination Art-History, like Theory-Practice, in this sense would be a contradiction in terms, both an approximation and record of the truth and a suspension of reference, given over to the realm of the other. For McMullen and Manet their Art-History is an impossible conjuration, the touching of an asymptote where art caresses history as they both tend to infinity, working towards each other but never wholly making a connection. Instead we have another version of the material, the material represented through the materials of the artist, that is both irreducibly historic and irreducibly art without ever being fully history or solely art. In this Art-History telling a story is as important as capturing a fact. Maximilian and his generals did not process past Manet's studio window, but in adding this procession to the process of Manet, McMullen creates another frame for understanding and experiencing the making of Art-History. The performative and the constative sit within this single frame, which takes a new angle, a camera angle, on this established scene.

This is a process that like all creative process starts from a position of not-knowing. The Art Programme cannot programme, it can only project a programme, an episode, one programme among many that tells its own story from the perspective of a single artist McMullen-Manet, which is not reducible to either Manet or McMullen or even McMullen's other Manets. The seeming coherence of a single shot masks the work of assembly and creation that leads to that moment of action, the artifice of the edit, or the serendipity of the take. The film is shot on 35-mm celluloid, a procedure that was unusual and expensive even in 1990. On the occasion of the first take, having tracked the passage of Maximilian from his cell to the spot of his execution, and everything having run smoothly up until then, at the last moment as the Emperor gave his speech in German, a gust of wind blew off his sombrero and the dog chased after it. 'Cut!' screamed the frustrated director.[49] Two takes is a better hit rate than the four attempts of Manet, but this cut is as deep as the scores that separate the sections of the painting in the National Gallery. In the gaps between the fragments of Manet's painting we will find the questions of the abyss between art and history, performance and epistemology, practice and theory, and between what presents and what persists. These problems fall in the gap between *1867* and *1871*.

1871

Ken McMullen's film of the Paris Commune is less a document of communism and more an account of the impossibility of filmmaking. Before the reader decides to flick through the following pages, disgusted at the idea of the blood and spirit of the Commune erased in preference to the undecidable performative, they might reflect how obviously true the previous sentence is. McMullen's 1990 film may be a document of Thatcherism but it is hardly to be taken as a historical record of the events of Paris 1871. It is a glorious fiction, that leans but not too heavily on Zola's *La Débâcle*, also a fiction in the Rougon-Macquart series.[50] It is one thing to salute comrade McMullen for his interest in the Commune, which is far from equivocal (the staging of the show trial of General Cluseret, for example) and quite another to mistake his narrative for a documentary. Instead, the film places us in that zone, which McMullen occupies in films such as *Zina* and *Partition*, namely, that of Art-History, where proximity to historical truth, whatever that might mean here, occurs within the idiom of an undecidable, suspended reference that insists upon reference regardless.[51] Reference that must be taken seriously as reference but nevertheless is irreducibly suspended. This is also, of course, the space that a writer such as Zola occupies. If I am concerned here with the work of Ken McMullen in this book, it is not just because of my own proximity to his films, which cannot be denied but rather must be embraced and understood, nor is it just because in McMullen we will find an exemplary case of Theory-Practice that mobilizes the thought of Marx, Freud and Derrida along the path of making cinema, but because the films of Ken McMullen are a test case (no more exemplary than any other example, to be sure) of this splice or graft between the constative and the performative. McMullen's films are about history and filmmaking and the impossibility of both, there is a well-developed sense of theory and a considerable artistic practice, but the grain of a McMullen film is to watch the asymptote of art tend towards the point of contact with history, but for the two never to touch, and in the gap between the two, the film takes place. This is what makes film art and not a Xerox of the historical record. It is the decisive index of the dehiscence between practice and theories of practice.

The film begins and ends in a considerable degree of self-referentiality. It is bookended with sequences set in 1873 at the London Cyclorama, an early technology of the moving image that combined cinema and theatre to tell a story through a panoramic representation. The opening shot of two male figures, one inside the Cyclorama, projecting, the other looking in, as both audience and participant in the drama, will return at the end of the film when we are more familiar with the significance of the two characters. From here we move to a title sequence that places the front credits within the frame of a proscenium arch. Like Marcel Carné's *Les Enfants du Paradis*, this is a film about the theatre.[52] It is the story of a set of characters who work in the theatre or who move in and out of the theatre as a space of entertainment and business. Timothy Spall's Ramborde is the impresario who treads a fine line between running a theatre and a brothel, frequented by, among others, the Prince of Wales (Ian McNeice) and the British secret agent Lord Grafton (played with colour-blind casting by Roshan Seth). The theatre is home to Maria (Maria de Medeiros) and Séverine (Ana Padrao) actresses in Ramborde's burlesque productions who survive through their relations with the men who pass through the theatre, including O'Brien (John Lynch) an Irish nationalist. The theatre provides a microcosm for the economic bubble and crash that comes with Napoleon III's free-market policies ('capital must flow and flow') and later becomes the site of an imaginary last stand of the Paris Commune, as the theatre troop are mowed down by the troops of the French national government. The action takes place on the stage, in the wings of the theatre, in the dressing rooms, in the fly system, and front of house. The film uses story cards, musical numbers, and live stage productions. It is a drama about drama, about the theatricality of staging politics, and the undecidable pretence between performance and action.

The exception to the story of love and revolution set in Ramborde's brothel-theatre is a number of episodes featuring Napoleon III (Dominique Pinon). Here we see the Emperor as a writer (completing his biography of Julius Caesar) and as an object of art, as he has his portrait painted as his hero, dressed in a toga.[53] We are privy to his inner monologue and we find that he is haunted by the ghost of Karl Marx, played in full-beard by the Algerian actor Med Hondo.

Marx stands over the Emperor's soldier and delivers sonorous lines from *The Eighteenth Brumaire of Louis Napoleon*, 'Men make their own history, but they do not make it just as they please; they do not make it under circumstances chosen by themselves, but under circumstances directly encountered, given and transmitted from the past. The tradition of all the dead generations weighs like a nightmare on the brain of the living'.[54] These lines become a refrain in the film as the events of the Commune play out against this theatrical backdrop. Napoleon III prefers the great man of history model of historical agency to Marx's formulation of the dialectical path of socio-economic circumstance, but he is, as Marx wrote in his unpublished novel of 1837, *Scorpion and Felix*, more like the playacting Octavianus left behind by the hero Caesar.[55] If McMullen's film has an explicit relation to discrete theoretical texts, it would be this; testing his practice against these words of Marx, telling the story of lives that make history, make up history, and made up lives that make up history wearing the make-up of the theatre.

However, this film is a work of art of considerable complexity, it is no patronage portrait of the Emperor dressed as Caesar. It is not a propaganda advert for the Marxist position as an application or illustration of a theory. Nor is it the Emperor's new clothes. Rather, as a film it must stand on its own as a film, generative of the affect proper to film, or it is worth very little almost nothing, as un-credit worthy as the *envois* [invoices/letters] of the crashed Paris Stock Exchange that ruins Ramborde and the Emperor. *The Eighteenth Brumaire* is a text about Napoleon III's own history; it discusses the coup of 1851 in which Louis-Napoleon Bonaparte assumed dictatorial powers before claiming the throne as Napoleon III in 1852. It takes its title from the earlier coup of 18 Brumaire in which Napoleon Bonaparte seized power from the revolution in 1799. In it Marx offers one of his most famous formulations regarding the predictive power of history: 'Hegel remarks somewhere that all great world-historic facts and personages appear, so to speak, twice. He forgot to add: the first time as tragedy, the second time as farce. Caussidière for Danton, Louis Blanc for Robespierre, the Montagne of 1848 to 1851 for the Montagne of 1793 to 1795, the nephew for the uncle'. While Napoleon III sees himself as the new Caesar, these words echo in his mind, by the time of the Second French Empire in the years before its collapse at the end of the Franco-Prussian War, the usurping nephew as Emperor is now removed further still, in another space where farce repeats itself as farce like Ramborde's theatre. The comic Pinon plays the Emperor as a dwarf in giant's robes, a fool whose laissez-faire drive for speculation and easy wealth leads his country to ruin. The capital of his empire is ruined by the capital of his empire. As the Prussian's advance and the stock market collapses, the city falls under siege. It moves from a city of light to a place of darkness. While the citizens starve, the elite dine on the animals in the Paris zoo in a symbolic exchange in which the swan swing we see early on in a burlesque production of the story of Leda, is swapped for the roast swan's wing of the secret elite dinners ('deprivation is never a universal condition'). Swan [*cygne*] and sign [*signe*] sharing the same homonym as a signifier, pointing us to the ways in which farce can also repeat itself as tragedy. The theatrical farce of Ramborde's shows turn to the last stand of the Commune, using the same repertory company, who literally die on stage.

This is a film about the pageant and aesthetics of the political, from Ramborde's nationalist musicals that encourage consumption and the path to war, to the staging of the 'Internationale', with full chorus and flag waving, from an Emperor who plays at dressing up, to spies in disguise and actors who take centre stage. It is about the extravagant play of politics, the extravagance of the players, the gaming of the political, and the excess of a performativity that leads to real material hardship and historical catastrophe. McMullen shows us not so much that history must have blood, but that the blood of history could just as well have been otherwise and is always the result of the actions of men, under circumstances of their own choosing or not. In this sense, the film's narrative of singular loves challenges Marx's thesis on world-historic forces. As Ramborde tells the Marquise de Gallifet, as he arranges a firing squad for the theatrical workers, 'they don't mean it, they are just a bunch of stupid actors who get over excited when they dress up'. Ramborde is trying to both save his livelihood and to make a last-ditch attempt to save the lives of his actors, presenting the Commune as a benefit gig for a trendy cause gone wrong. The actors go down performing, singing in the face of death, pitting an aestheticization against the materiality of the bullet, and so projecting the Commune into a future, swapping the barricades for an auditorium, to give voice to an idea that cannot die with their own mortality. In the meanwhile, the professional revolutionaries Cluseret and O'Brien escape Paris disguised as priests, living to foment another day. But the Irishman cannot escape the denouement of his own drama. The film closes with a return to the Cyclorama, two years later, where O'Brien recognizes Grafton, the English aristocrat and spy, who was his rival for the love of Séverine during the months of the Commune. O'Brien takes revenge on Grafton, shooting him, on a cinematic set, where all the characters of the film 'live on' in the panorama, not out of ideological purpose but out of sexual jealousy. *Eros* trumps *polis*, within the frame of the aesthetic. That's the movies, if not the Marxist playbook.

In the centre of all this is the Café Anglais, where Cluseret exhibits Manet's 1871, accompanied by the testimony of a French soldier who reports on the disaster of the Franco-Prussian war. The restaurant is raided but the subversive painting has been swapped for a portrait of the Emperor. The image of the execution of Maximilian is a *mis-en-abyme* within the *mis-en-scéne*, like a door in an advent calendar that if opened would lead us down a wormhole into the process of the director and into the studio of an artist named McMullen-Manet-Zola. In Art-History, for the history-artist, 'the tradition of all the dead generations weighs like a nightmare on the brain of the living'. Manet and Zola are part of a history of art, a history of history in art, which McMullen cannot escape from. Instead, he advances on it with his revolutionary battalions, not to overthrow it but to surrender to it. Manet and Zola are as much his nightmare as his muse, the weight of their significance pressing on his creative brain. In this sense, the history-artist is never free to do just as they please. History and the makers of history (its artists more than its actors) leave their traces in the texts of the living, imposing themselves in images and words, signs rather than wonders. If it were appropriate to paraphrase Marx, we might say that McMullen's art-history shows us that men make films but not under circumstances of their own choosing.

7

Derrida Queries de Man

In the previous chapter, we considered examples of a critical visual practice in the case of Valerio Adami and Ken McMullen, and read these across a ranging textual landscape, including Margarethe von Trotta's *Hannah Arendt*. One of the issues that emerge from reading examples of Theory-Practice is the attempt to understand when and how a work of art is contributing to the field of speculative labour. There are works that illustrate philosophy in a reflective way, drawing upon an idea or a story in order to present their own work as complex and compelling texts. In such cases the use of philosophy may be entirely instrumental, just the latest novelty for a genre or media practice hungry for fresh material. In other work, however, there is a different attitude of reflection, one that presents itself to philosophy as an alternative mode of questioning. In this sense, the sort of critical practice that concerns us in this study is an attitudinal proposition with respect to philosophy, one that knows itself and interrogates itself on the horns of the dilemma between art and speculation. In this chapter, we will continue to explore this difficulty through an all too brief consideration of the theory-paintings of Mark Tansey. The aim is not to provide an exhaustive account of Tansey or even come close to opening up the collected problems of Theory-Practice through the metonymic use of Tansey's work. Rather, it is to begin the task of thinking about how some of the resources and insights of the first half of this book might be used to think about singular examples of Theory-Practice. Here we will return to the pages of Kleist and de Man, for example, that occupied us in chapters 2 and 3 of this study as a way of understanding Tansey's own theoretical sublime. As this present inquiry draws to a close, the reader is left with the task of multiplying questions and connections between texts and images to carry on the work of making and reading critical practice.

The material of the letter

In *Theory at Yale: The Strange Case of Deconstruction in America*, Marc Redfield closes his volume with a reading of two works of art by Mark Tansey.[1] The first, 'Derrida Queries de Man' (1990), is a homage to an illustration in *The Strand Magazine* by Sidney Paget (1893) to the Sherlock Holmes' short story 'The Final Problem' in which Holmes and Moriarty wrestle above the Reichenbach Falls.[2] The second, 'Constructing the Grand Canyon' (1990), is a landscape in the American sublime style in which de Man and Derrida sit at the perspectival centre of the painting directing the construction and deconstruction of the national landmark.[3] In this chapter, while saluting Redfield's detailed reading of the two artworks, I do not intend to repeat the work so meticulously detailed in his 2016 study. However, I would like to use it as a point of departure for some consideration of the group of artworks by Tansey from around 1990 that Redfield calls 'theory-paintings', and then for a wider consideration of questions about the relationship between de Man and Derrida from the perspective of scholarship and art practice in the academy of 2017.

However, let me first recount an anecdote about 'reading' the Tansey painting 'Derrida Queries de Man'. The artwork itself is large at over three square-metres, monochrome in a blue-green hue, with a landscape made from blurred silkscreen lines of printed text, some of which is identifiable as pages 146–7 of de Man's *Blindness and Insight*. On a precipice two figures wrestle, or dance, or embrace, in the style of the Paget illustration, as mist and spray rises and falls from the cascade of water that runs through the centre of the image, separating two sides of a gorge. The two figures are of significance here, as Redfield describes the scene in his text, 'Paul de Man faces away from us, toward Jacques Derrida and the abyss' (p. 160). This is Redfield's starting point for everything that follows, there is seemingly little doubt in his mind that de Man is the figure with his back to the viewer, and Derrida is the one facing us. However, I recall sitting around a table in a farmhouse in upstate New York with Marc Redfield and Kevin Newmark, where the three of us had gathered to work on editing the correspondence between de Man and Derrida for future publication. The conversation came round to discussing Marc's book, which had just appeared that year, and in particular the closing chapter on these two works of art. Kevin Newmark was unfamiliar with the Tansey paintings but obviously familiar with the persons of both Paul de Man and Jacques Derrida. Redfield opened his laptop and showed Newmark some high-resolution versions of 'Derrida Queries de Man' that he had obtained for inclusion in the book. Our co-editor sat looking at the image for some time, looking this way and that, blowing up details, and shifting in his seat to secure different vantage points. When he eventually broke his silence, he asked 'which one did you say de Man was?'

For Newmark it was not at all certain which of the two figures was de Man and which was Derrida. This was more than the obvious ambiguity of two figures wrestling or dancing, but a genuine unreadability of the image on the part of an observer who had known both de Man and Derrida well during their lifetimes. Nor, do I think it was just contrariness on Newmark's part to want to ask a question of Redfield's seemingly, secure interpretation of the image. The more one looks at the scene, the more difficult it becomes to be certain which figure is which. The one with his back to the viewer has black hair with a side parting (to my mind it looks much more like Michael Naas than either Paul de Man or Jacques Derrida). The figure facing us has grey hair, gathered higher on the head and slightly receding, it could be taken as suggestive of Derrida's sometimes meticulously maintained bouffant but it might equally denote the later de Man of his final years at Yale. There is genuine confusion here, intentionally or not, significant or not, and once observed it insists and persists in a way that cannot simply be resolved by a designation of one figure by a proper name and the other by the alternative. It would seem that the tile of the work 'Derrida Queries de Man' does not just name a scene in which two suited figures wrestle and/or embrace risking a precipitous fall into an abyss, but describes the set-up of a scene of unreadability in which figures cannot be easily distinguished but nevertheless demand our attention.

Redfield comments of the painting that, 'we must beware the temptation to reduce this texture-text to a message—the temptation, that is, of imagining that if we consult *Blindness and Insight*, or, more specifically, 'Literary History and Literary Modernity' (the chapter within which page 146 appears) we will access the hidden meaning of the painting' (p. 164). This is a strong gesture on Redfield's part, as he instead points his reader towards the problematic legibility of the lines within the texture of the painting, suggesting that the scene is not a stable allegorical structure but one replete with warning signs and 'posted danger signals'. However, while we could do worse than to heed Redfield's concerns, I think it would be equally problematic to refuse altogether the significance of the pages that Tansey uses here. In the modernist tradition of *objet trouvé*, the found object can be presented and reframed, and made to signify other than itself, but also and in doing so, perform *itself* as art. Marcel Duchamp's 'Fountain' is both a work of art and a urinal. It is importantly a urinal – this is what gives it meaning as an art object. Equally, we might say of the lines from de Man's text that Tansey presents as his landscape, they are both the material for a layering in a representation of a craggy outcrop, and the words of pages 146–7 of Paul de Man's *Blindness and Insight*. This is the aporia that the work of art presents, like the abyss of the Reichenbach gorge it presents, and we risk life and limb if we do not tread carefully on this slippery surface. Another name for the painting might have been 'Impasse' had Tansey not given us the direction of 'Derrida Queries de Man', which he inscribes in the lower right hand corner, the words running up the other side of the gorge, with the grain of the rock, as legible as the title of de Man's book that runs in the opposite direction on the other side of the abyss, where the ground gives way beneath the feet of the two figures. *Blindness and Insight*, as a title names a specific aporia important to the work of de Man, a conceptual but productive impasse that brings him into contact with Derrida and in this book, it is de Man who queries Derrida not the other way around.

Accordingly, while as Redfield points out due to the blurring and the easing of word over word and paint over word, we cannot be certain that all of the text used to layer the landscape comes from these pages by de Man, we really ought to attend to what the pages actually say in *Blindness and Insight*. After all they would seem to be the ground upon which our figures are set upright, as well as the abyss into which they are imminently about to fall. Figure and ground here should be taken to mean not just the penned characters against a suggested ravine, but the organizing principle of perception in art in which objects are distinguished from their background, as the composition of *gestalt* and affect. Equally, for those with ears to read de Man today, 'figure' here refers to figuration and disfiguration as the dynamic of meaning that de Man begins to lay out in the chapters of *Blindness and Insight* but more fully in *Allegories of Reading* and later work. In this sense, Tansey literally (and we also need to say figuratively) gives us a ground composed of figures, in which it is impossible to figure out which figures have been mixed, blurred and ground into the ground.

This then is a work of art that also operates at a high level of self-referentiality, produced by an artist familiar with all those de Man-inspired readings of the 1980s, which in the words of Barbara Johnson, 'enabled readers to become sensitive to a number of recurrent literary topoi in a new way. Texts have been seen as commentaries on their own production or reception through their pervasive thematizations of textuality—the myriad letters, books, tombstones, wills, inscriptions, road signs, maps, birth-marks, tracks, footprints, textiles, tapestries, veils, sheets, brown stockings and self-abolishing laces that serve in one way or another as figures for the text to be deciphered or unraveled or embroidered upon'.[4] Tansey's work of art takes that tradition of reading further by translating print into screen-print in a visual tableau, using the actual critical text itself as the material for its own surface. This artwork adds to its own 'pervasive thematization of textuality' (the figures of de Man and Derrida in the landscape, the reference to Sherlock Holmes) to incorporate, perhaps one might say here 'to inscribe', a literal textuality into the body of the artwork. Where de Man spoke of the materiality of the letter, Tansey makes the letter the material of his art. This is, of course, a practice familiar to us from Braque and Picasso who also incorporated material objects into the surfaces of their paintings in order to thematize the constructed nature of art and the artificial flatness of the surface of a painting (*papier-collé, collage*). Like his surrealist and cubist forebears Tansey closes the gap between representation and the represented by incorporating the object of art into the artwork itself. Here Tansey is not merely illustrating an idea from Theory, in the way that Sidney Paget 'illustrates' a passage from Conan Doyle's short story, rather he is erasing the gap between illustration and art, between reference and referentiality, between commentary and creating, and between Theory and Practice.

The work of art presents a ravine with two sides of rock, the one to the right and in the background of the landscape is a sheer face, lightened by the water that sprays up from the ravine below; the second has an outcrop where the two men implausibly grapple, with only the suggestion of the most precarious of paths along which the figures have met. This is in contrast to the Paget original where although progress along the path seems impossible, it is evident how Holmes and Moriarty got there and ultimately how one of them might get back down again, even if Conan Doyle would have us believe in this story that the two men meet their end in the thunderous water below. In the Tansey, the path to the point where de Man and Derrida are positioned looks decidedly insecure. Who could walk such a path, one that is made up of mostly illegible text, leading to a point of no return? On the sides of the cliff in the foreground, the text of *Blindness and Insight* runs sheer into the abyss; its readability made possible through the light afforded by the spray of the water that divides the ravine in an *Aufklarung* that is also a falling.

These are, following Paget, the Reichenbach Falls, as depicted by Turner before Paget, located high in the Alps in the centre of Europe, inseparable now from their literary significance and history. Or perhaps these falls are in the gorges of Ithaca ('a place built by and on gorges'[5]) above Cornell University, where de Man taught before he moved to Yale and were sections of *Blindness and Insight* will have been written. While at Cornell de Man also held an appointment at the University of Zurich, a mere two-hour drive from the Reichenbach Falls, where in Tansey's imagination Derrida always already seems to have been waiting for him. These falls are strictly of the imagination, of the image and the imago, the term Freud uses for an unconscious idealized image of someone, especially a parent, which influences conscious behaviour, and which he, Sachs and Rank used to name their journal in Vienna in 1912, whose later successor was established by Freud and Sachs as *American Imago* in 1939, now published by John Hopkins, another of de Man's haunts. 'American Imago' might well have been another title of Tansey's artwork. However, it is called 'Derrida Queries de Man' and dates from 1990. Therefore, it might be said not to reference or to illustrate a point of Theory to be found in *Blindness and Insight* or related texts, such as 'The Rhetoric Blindness' the central essay in the collection in which de Man takes to task Derrida's reading of Rousseau in *Of Grammatology*.[6] Rather, this is another scene set in a different landscape, the Theory world of 1990, after the so-called de Man affair, the revelation, publication and commentary on de Man's wartime journalism. These waters that cascade through the mind and the middle of Tansey's art are of another order: they are Yale Falls. 'Yale Falls' could be another title for this work.

In 1990 Yale had fallen and the name of deconstruction had, if you pardon the phrase, fallen off a cliff. If Derrida ever queried de Man it was in the posthumous scene of elegy, in which classically the lost loved one is reunited with the poet in the landscape they knew well when together. In this sense, the landscape here is that of the abyss and the impasse, hewn from the very words and letters of de Man's texts. In Tansey's painting the two men meet again in the pages of *Blindness and Insight* in a scene that could be one of embrace and forgiveness or one of accusation and repercussion. The image references Conan Doyle, but in this sense it might equally suggest Dante, this is the landscape of the afterlife of Theory, following the path through the Falls that appear in the third round of circle VII in the Inferno, marking the realm of the Sodomites (Eve Sedgwick will have had something to say about the homosocial, murderous pursuit of query and quarry in Holmes and Moriarty, and in Tansey's image of the wrestling de Man and Derrida).[7] It would not be too much later that Derrida would in fact query de Man in the texts '*Le Parjure*' and 'Typewriter Ribbon', where for the first time he attempts to put some distance between his own work and that of de Man.[8] The first of these essays provides an autobiographical disclosure concerning the novel by Henri Thomas and its fictional representation of de Man's supposedly bigamous marriage in America. The acolyte and witness who accompanies the novel's anti-hero, Stéphane Chalier, across the United States offers us the notable refrain, 'after all it was not me'. One cannot help but feel that Derrida's presentation of these words in one context are also intended to resonate across to other histories he had with de Man, in which the Belgian may have forgotten to mention certain facts.[9]

In the second essay, Derrida returns to the question of Rousseau, where all of this began, reading de Man reading Rousseau in *Allegories of Reading*, just as *Blindness and Insight* revolves around de Man reading Derrida reading Rousseau, another Swiss who found a home in the Alps. Derrida is more robust with de Man in 'Typewriter Ribbon', an account of the 'Excuses' chapter of *Allegories*, than he is anywhere else across their iterative relationship. These two essays are another scene of 'Derrida Queries de Man', of interrogative elegy, old friends reunited in the landscape of Rousseau, in which Derrida has a final say, letting us know one last time that 'after all it was not me who forgot to mention certain facts'. To address the question, whether we should read these essays as Derrida returning fire or as another passage in the complex dance/embrace/wrestle that Tansey captures, would require a space greater than the one afforded to me here.[10] They post-date the Tansey painting but provide a frame for a work of art, the choreographed encounter identified by the name 'Derrida Queries de Man', which might speak to a certain performativity as well as a particular methodology or means of progressing through a textual landscape. In other words, it would name a certain deconstruction, both a moment of deconstruction, a singular and significant, long-awaited reading, and a staging of deconstruction, a performance of its performativity, in an encounter between Derrida and de Man, orthodox and reform, legitimate and bastard, legal and renegade. The allusion to Holmes and Moriarty suggests a conflict between uncanny doubles, nemesis and rival, between an evil genius and a lawman who often crosses the line, acting in a criminal fashion to uphold the law. As Kevin Newmark's comments remind us, it is not clear which would be Derrida and which would be de Man, two sides of the same coin erased in the pockets of old philosophers. However, if Tansey accurately captures a sense that de Man and Derrida are bound together on the edge of a precipice, these two later essays by Derrida, to my mind, speak of a wish on Derrida's part that if Yale falls then de Man is not taking Derrida down with him. After all, in the Sherlock Holmes stories, the detective rises again from the Reichenbach waters, having faked his death and offering his co-terminal fate with his Other as a ruse for his readers. After Yale falls, Derrida rises again. In many senses we might recognize Derrida querying de Man as 'The Final Problem' for the author of '*Le Parjure*'.

The violence of the letter

A second Tansey painting from this same period, 'Under Erasure', offers a related visual scenario and might be thought of as a companion piece to 'Derrida Queries de Man'.[11] Here we have a close up of a waterfall cascading off of a rock face comprised of pages 112–13 of Derrida's *Of Grammatology*, the water flows down the middle of the pages in a space that Derrida identifies in Dissemination with the hymen.[12] The flow of liquid obscures the edges of the text and the resulting spray renders the pages ever more illegible as we descend into the depths below. 'Under Erasure' here then also refers to the literal practice of Tansey's screen-printing technique. The image is cropped before cliffs and torrent reach the bottom. Perhaps, this is the waterfall that stands behind the two figures in 'Derrida Queries de Man', the *Grammatology* irrigating the pages of *Blindness and Insight* further down the ravine. However, the spray behind the two figures in the Derrida-de Man painting would seem to be of a different order of force than the stream in this painting. Rather, the one we have here is reminiscent of the Lake District, so familiar to de Man's *ursprung* Wordsworth, where the flow is dependent upon the seasons and are seldom as significant as the waterfalls in the Alps or the sort of Niagara that Tansey places behind the figures of America's Paul de Man and Jacques Derrida in his other artwork. In either case, the cascade erases, over time, the words inscribed on the mountainside doing literal violence to the letter. The questions of erasure, deletion and forgetting are entirely germane to work of Tansey's art.

While Marc Redfield warns us against reading too much into the painting, 'Derrida Queries de Man', i.e. to read literally the text that forms the material surface of the work of art. He himself resists his own very good advice and comments on the pages from *Blindness and Insight*, suggesting that foregrounding of a page 'that cites Nietzsche on memory and forgetting may be adduced as, among other things, a discreet tracking device, orientated toward the media storm that marks the culminating point of the phantasmatics of theory in America' (p. 173). He is not wrong in his assessment of these pages. However, in his attempt not to read literally, he may be reading far too literally. Tansey may be channelling Derrida, channelling the acolyte in Henri Thomas's novel when he tells Chevalier that he was not the one who forgot to mention certain facts. There is undoubtedly a part of that in the painting, or at least we can now read it in this way because Tansey, like most of us in 1990, was unlikely to have been familiar with the novel. There is also a certain forgetting that will need to take place for deconstruction to reach the heights it once commanded after it has fallen off the cliff edge of the de Man affair. However, it is the 'other things' that Redfield alludes to here that interests us in this present commentary.

These paragraphs from de Man's book may have been chosen at random by the artist and the merged and blurred lines may come from other parts of the book, or another book entirely, it is importantly undecidable. However, it is just as likely that they were chosen deliberately by an artist who is familiar with his Theory and works knowingly within the conceits of art history. Either way the intention is unimportant, rather what is of significance is that which the artwork presents in its affect and gives us as a singular insistence to read. Therefore, it is entirely relevant for a certain reading that these pages come from this particular section of *Blindness and Insight*, and while they might not be sending us a message they are certainly leaving a trace. It is significant that Braque uses a metro ticket to form the surface of his artwork, it is not merely a commentary on the practice of art and the art institution (although it is also this) but it is the incorporation of the metro ticket that makes the art object art. It is from here that it derives its significance. Equally, it is the fact that Tansey embeds a text by de Man in his artwork that makes it art. The meaning and performativity of the artwork cannot be separated from these pages as a citation and a sighting and a siting, raising Tansey's work beyond mere illustration into reframing and iteration. It is the very thing that makes Tansey's work from this period something like, what Redfield calls, 'Theory-Painting'. To attempt to set aside the significance of de Man's text here seems wilful, if not obscure, then perhaps 'literalist' on Redfield's part. It is odd that Redfield does not want to leave a mark on Tansey's artwork when there are so many marks already involved in this scene. So, what does de Man say in these pages? Why is it of importance to the question of theory-painting? And how is it related to the pages from *Of Grammatology* that Tansey uses in 'Under Erasure', which we must treat in an equally literal way by reading them as having some significance to the work of art. Attempting to provide satisfactory answers to these three questions will guide this present inquiry to a close.

Firstly, the paragraphs in question run over from an argument that begins on the previous page (p. 145) as we enter into the second movement of the essay 'Literary History and Literary Modernity'. In the opening salvos of the text de Man has set up a series of non sequiturs suggesting that literature and modernity may be incompatible concepts and that history and modernity may be even more at odds. At stake here is a questioning of the value that academic workplaces on historicization as a justification of its own institutional formation: 'only an exceptionally talented and perhaps eccentric member of the profession could undertake [the task of putting the term history seriously into question] with sufficient energy to make it effective, and even then it is likely to be accompanied by the violence that surrounds passion and rebellion' (p. 145). He cites Nietzsche as a philologist turned academic maverick as someone who questioned a culture based on the disciplines of history, challenging a historical consciousness based on periodization and an obsession with the past. As the page turns from 145 to 146, de Man is in mid-sentence suggesting that an emphasis on modernity in the academic framing of history is an effect of this consciousness that Nietzsche's 'cultural criticism' would directly address, 'modernity is a descriptive term that designates a certain state of mind' (p. 146). Accordingly, for de Man, the more dynamic approach that Nietzsche takes to understanding the problem of modernity is to oppose history to 'Life'. De Man unpacks this proposition in the paragraphs that follow, in the pages Tansey utilizes as the surface material of his artwork. We might then say, that what de Man is discussing in these important pages is, the meaning of 'Life'. That is no ordinary question for a philosopher or a philologist, and it is hard to imagine that this was lost on the sly artist Tansey.

The meaning of 'Life' is quite specific here. Nietzsche conceives of the term not just in biological terms but in temporal ones, 'as the ability to *forget* whatever precedes a present situation' (p. 146). The definition arises from Nietzsche's opposition to the Romanticism of Rousseau, which de Man is keen to emphasize as in fact a Rousseauistic pattern itself. De Man glosses a quote from Nietzsche on the animal's ability to forget by saying: 'this ability to forget and to live without historical awareness exists not only on an animal level. Since 'life' has an ontological as well as biological meaning the condition of animality persists as a constitutive part of man. Not only are there moments when it governs his actions, but these are also the moments when he re-establishes contact with his spontaneity and allows his truly human nature to assert itself' (p. 146). De Man is doing little more here than following Nietzsche's line of argument as it reflects the Rousseau he ostensibly opposes. However, in so doing he foregrounds a formal problem that looms large in the later thought of de Man associated with his work published, anachronistically under the collective title *Aesthetic Ideology*, as de Man's final problem.[13] I am thinking here in particular not of one of the essays collected in Andrzej Warminski's significant editorial endeavour but in the text 'Aesthetic Formalization: Kleist's *Über das Marionettentheater*' which dates from 1983 and is closely related to those texts gathered together in the *Aesthetic Ideology* volume, as the second of the Messenger Lectures de Man delivered at Cornell, somewhere among the gorges and waterfalls.[14]

In this text, de Man identifies what he sees as a misreading of Kant in Schiller's *Letters on Aesthetic Education*.[15] At stake, as we have seen, is the pivot between Theory and Practice, or between Critique and 'Life', the difference between thought and action, and the necessary forgetting that inserts itself between the two in order for action or making to take place. This insertion happens not in order to dichotomize the choice between Theory and Practice but occurs over an abyss on the very edge of a precipice, constantly risking a fall, while carving out a landscape in which the sheer cliffs of Theory and Practice reflect and supplement one another. To go too quickly, and to recap the argument of chapter 2 of this book, the crucial moment comes in Schiller's translation of Kant's mathematical and dynamic sublime into his preferred terms the 'theoretical' and 'practical' sublime. The distinction in Kant arises from a desire to understand two possible failures of representation. In Schiller, according to de Man, the slippage in terminology arises from a desire to prefer one flavour of sublimity to the other. There then follows from Schiller a tradition that favours the practical over Ivory Tower-bound theory. However, Schiller makes his choice because as a playwright and artist he finds the dynamic performance of terror a greater draw to an audience than the mathematical consideration of magnitude. Terror makes better art, as the grappling figures in Conan Doyle and Tansey demonstrate. All of this must be read here in the context of Tansey's work (including his sublime landscapes of American theory) as an artist, a maker like Schiller, or perhaps a theory-painter who attempts to straddle the chasm, while Schiller chooses to plant his flag firmly on the side of the utility of philosophy for making art. There is then, importantly, a serious forgetting at work in the Schillerian gesture that takes a leap beyond the impasse of Kant's categorization of the sublime. The artist must forget the immobilizing fear or prudence of Theory and jump into the beyond, forgetting that there is an abyss beneath their feet. Neither the cliff face of Theory nor the sheer drop of the artwork provides secure footing or refuge from the terror of the abyss but forgetting allows the leap and in the leap, the process of the jump or fall, we find the moment of art. It is here, in the terms Nietzsche offers us via the slopes of *Blindness and Insight*, that 'Life' is affirmed at its fullest, at that moment when we struggle at the edge of the abyss with an impossible opponent who as our Other and double can only ever be ourselves. This is a moment of experience that was surely known to Nietzsche, de Man and Derrida, and which Tansey presents in the sublimity of a six-foot-long canvas that brings the Theory of the philosophers to Life, as it were.

This problematic in the essay on Kleist is indicative of the wider problematic that de Man develops in the Messenger Lectures around what we now call the materiality of the letter, namely, and to go too fast once again, as we have by now covered this argument extensively in previous chapters and we are approaching the end of our study, the confusion between the signifier and the signified as the inscription of ideology in the material world and so as the very experience of the material world. Schiller mistakes the effect of terror in his theatre as an adequate formalization of terror, even though a far more terrifying non-understanding lies beneath in the abyss below his stage. Similarly, the 'Life' that Nietzsche promotes depends upon a forgetting of what led to this moment of affirmation. And yet just as Schiller must forget to make theatre, Nietzsche must forget to feel alive, if it is an aberration it is one necessary to the human condition. De Man notes on page 147 of *Blindness and Insight*: 'Moments of genuine humanity thus are moments at which all anteriority vanishes, annihilated by the power of an absolute forgetting. Although such a radical rejection of history may be illusory or unfair to the achievements of the past, it nevertheless remains justified as necessary to the fulfilment of our human destiny and as the condition for action'. It would be a very poor literal reader who took de Man's words as some sort of an exculpation of his own personal history. Rather, he is describing via Nietzsche a remarkable insight into practice (in all its senses), writing, art, and living. If you think him blind to the splinter in his own eye, then let that be your prerogative on this occasion and completely in keeping with arguments advanced by de Man in his writing and by Mark Tansey in this artwork that inscribes this argument into his own theory-painting. I am not suggesting that Tansey is familiar with the essay on Kleist and its relation to these pages from *Blindness and Insight*. Rather, the point is that this textual constellation forms the surface of Tansey's artwork, making the materiality of the letter the very material of the visual. In his own way, Tansey must jump across the abyss between Theory and Practice to make art, and so his painting will have forgotten more than it ever knew in order to perform its status as 'theory-painting'.

The final third of page 147 of *Blindness and Insight* moves on from a consideration of forgetting and history to a commentary on fashion as the only mode appropriate to modernity or of a consciousness that privileges modernity. While these lines may be legible to only the most patient or obsessed of Tansey's viewers they can surely not be ignored in relation to Tansey's presentation and commentary on the Yale School and the de Man affair: falling out of fashion is the final problem of the avant-garde. These paragraphs were perhaps closer to the front of Tansey's mind when making his art object than the argument of the Messenger Lectures. It is telling that in 'Derrida Queries de Man' and 'Under Erasure' he mobilizes lines from the two most prominent texts from the deconstructive canon during the 1980s, which is not to question Tansey's scholarship (although I suspect as an artist he might snort at the very idea) but to suggest that as someone who may be familiar with a limited range of texts by de Man and Derrida that he is an astute close reader of Theory. His piece, 'Close Reading', also from 1990 presents a mountaineer of the extreme sports variety, dressed in what we might be tempted to call a Lyotard, climbing a sheer face of rock composed from lines from *Blindness and Insight*. This is not a climber dressed against the elements to ascend the Swiss Alps but a Californian, like Tansey, trying to find a foothold in the sheer face of Theory. By 1990, after its fall from grace at Yale, deconstruction had made a new home and was rising again at the University of California, Irvine, where J Hillis Miller had taken a chair and Derrida with him.

There is much to say about this artwork and the related painting that Redfield addresses, 'Constructing the Grand Canyon'. Tansey also uses the same pages from Derrida in the silkscreen background of 'John the Baptist Discarding His Clothes in the Wilderness (after Domenico Veneziano)' also from the 1990 theory sequence. Equally, the artist also uses either single page 146 or 147, or the double spread from Blindness and Insight in the theory-paintings 'Close Reading', 'Bridge over the Cartesian Gap', 'Incursion', 'a', and 'Reader', all from 1990.[16] The persistent return of these pages from the same texts by Derrida and de Man surely point to more than the material convenience of their use as 'background' in this series of paintings. Rather, they are calling attention to themselves, over and over again, and require to be read, theoretically and critically as part of the experience of the art object. On another occasion, I will return to this to examine the run of Tansey's theory-paintings at greater length, but by way of closing and, in order to balance the scales with de Man, lest they topple and fall, on this occasion allow me to turn to the pages in *Of Grammatology* that Tansey inscribes in the artwork 'Under Erasure'.

To go too quickly once more and to be positively sprinting now in the space that remains, these pages come from the first chapter of Part II of the *Grammatology* in Derrida's reading of Lévi-Strauss enroute to another scene with Rousseau, perhaps waiting to meet him at the Creux-du-Van on the way to Motiers in the Swiss Alps to initiate another query in a quarry. Lévi-Strauss in this respect, like Nietzsche in the de Man, fails to escape the gravitational pull of the Rousseau-esque enterprise he seeks to exceed. If we were to credit Tansey with the same readerly insight as we afforded him with respect to de Man, we would say that again he has chosen a significant moment in the text of Derrida that is worthy of consideration. Here, Derrida recalls the way in which the anthropologist inculcates himself in the 'aboriginal' scene, in order to leverage a scientific commentary that in fact reproduces the very discourse of violence it seeks to observe. This violence comes with the rights of naming in which the privilege reserved for adults in the community does violence to the children under observation and is then outflanked by the extrinsic violence of the anthropological observation, 'the intimacy of proper names can be opened to forced entry. And that is possible only at the moment when the space is shaped and reoriented by the glance of the foreigner' (p. 113). These pages are often read as a condemnation of the anthropologist; however, they are better understood as a description of the violence and ex-appropriation involved in all naming. Once we are in language there is only the unavoidable violence of the otherness we present to ourselves, 'the eye of the other calls out the proper names, spells them out, and removes the prohibition that covered them' (p. 113). In this sense the violence of the letter in Derrida is very similar to the materiality of the letter in de Man, naming is both a necessary gesture of reason and another mystification, just as forgetting is a necessary break from impasse and another re-inscription of aporia. In both de Man and Derrida we have an understanding that an opening is just another step to possible foreclosure, like two cliff edges tempting the solitary walker to jump. The significance of these pages for Tansey might lie in the act of erasure, the forgetting of the violence of the letter, worn away by the constant fall. In naming his own artworks, Tansey enters into his own anthropological moment that attempts to arrest the flow from the source of de Man and Derrida into the stream of writing that heads towards the rapids and spray of Tansey's chiaroscuro of figures and ground. Throughout this text I have offered alternative names for some of Tansey's art, to note that they might as well signify otherwise as allegories of painting. One could play this game for any length of time, but it has a point. One should be careful to attribute proper names to figures in writing or in painting when the impossibility of figuration is the very frame of the work in question. Or at least one should be aware of the violence one will be doing to history when, for example, one identifies the configuration of Theory in America with the proper names of Jacques Derrida and Paul de Man. This would, in many respects, be the whole point of Redfield's remarkable and important book.

I will conclude with three observations. Firstly, that while Derrida and de Man, orthodox and reform, have their salient differences as they wrestle over the proper name of deconstruction (e.g. Derrida has little interest in Romanticism or Modernity as categories) from the position of a reader of today unfamiliar with the history of Yale and its distant affairs, if there is to be a recovery of and reconnection with deconstruction then it will come around a return to the question of the Other as an interruption of a too hasty formalization of the material.[17] Secondly, it is interesting to note the work that an artist like Tansey puts de Man and Derrida to in his art. Tansey unlike Redfield may well have only read two books by the men, but he has read them really well, and opens them up in surprising and inventive ways. While there is something in Redfield's account that for all its scholarship begins to look like a foreclosure that is also, despite intentions, a historicization. Thirdly, the lesson that de Man and Derrida might have to teach an artist today is that (1) there is history but then there is deconstruction, but then, (2) get over it, because (3) there is art, (4) but get over that because there is also Theory-Practice. It is just a pity that so few in the academy make it beyond part 1 of that lesson.

Notes

Introduction: Practice Is Not What You Think

1. The title of this introduction is a reference to Geoffrey Bennington, 'Deconstruction Is Not What You Think', *Art and Design*, 4 (3/4), 1988, pp. 6–7.
2. See, *Love in the Post: From Plato to Derrida* (Heraclitus Films, 2014), dir. Joanna Callaghan, and *Oxi: An Act of Resistance* (Scape Films, 2015), dir. Ken McMullen.
3. See *Creative Criticism: An Anthology and Guide*, eds. Stephen Benson and Clare Connors (Edinburgh: Edinburgh University Press, 2014).
4. See Lisa Tickner, *Hornsey 1968: The Art School Revolution* (London: Frances Lincoln, 2008).
5. See Nigel Llewellyn, ed. *The London Art Schools: Reforming the Art World, 1960 to Now* (London: Tate Publishing, 2015); Malcolm Quinn, *Utilitarianism and the Art School in Nineteenth-Century Britain* (London: Routledge, 2016).
6. See Anthony Easthope, *British Post-Structuralism: Since 1968* (London: Routledge, 1988).
7. Jorge Luis Borges, 'On Exactitude in Science', in *Collected Fictions*, trans. Andrew Hurley (London: Penguin, 1988).
8. See for example, Katy MacLeod and Lin Holridge, eds., *Thinking through Art* (London: Routledge, 2005); Estelle Barratt and Barbara Bolt, eds., *Practice as Research: Approaches to Creative Enquiry* (London: I.B. Tauris, 2006); Hazel Smith and Roger T. Dean, eds. *Practice-Led Research, Research-Led Practice in the Creative Arts* (Edinburgh: Edinburgh University Press, 2009); Graeme Sullivan, *Art Practice as Research: Inquiry in Visual Arts* (London: Sage, 2009); Robin Nelson, ed. *Practice as Research in the Arts: Principles, Protocols, Pedagogies, Resistances* (London: Palgrave Macmillan, 2013); Shaun Mcniff, *Art as Research: Opportunities and Challenges* (London: Intellect, 2013).
9. Chris Rust, Judith Mottram and Jeremy Till, 'Review Report: Practice-Led Research in Art, Design and Arcjitecture', http://arts.brighton.ac.uk/_data/assets/pdf_file/0018/43065/Practice-Led_Review_Nov07.pdf.
10. Angela Piccini, ed., 'An Historiographic Perspective on Practice as Research', http://www.bris.ac.uk/parip/t_ap.htm.
11. Advice to prospective PhD students at the University of Surrey, posted under the title 'AHRC Guidance Is as Follows', https://www.surrey.ac.uk/fass/research/studentships/ahrc/practice-based-research/.

12 Friedrich Schiller, *On the Aesthetic Education of Man, in a Series of Letters*, trans. E.M. Wilkinson and L.A. Willoughby (Oxford: Clarendon Press, 1967).
13 Later in this book we will attend to Paul de Man's extended reading of Schiller's Aesthetic Education, my comments here stay close to the spirit of that reading in its early pages.
14 See my account of Schiller in 'Paul de Man and Art History I: Modernity, Aesthetics and Community in Jacques Ranciere', in *Reading Ranciere: Critical Dissensus*, eds. Paul Bowman and Richard Stamp (London: Continuum, 2011).
15 Paul de Man, *The Rhetoric of Romanticism* (New York: Columbia University Press, 1984).
16 In Chapter 5 of this book we will attend in greater detail to Derrida's treatment of innovation in *Psyche: Inventions of the Other*, Vol. 1, eds. Peggy Kamuf and Elizabeth Rottenberg (Stanford: Stanford University Press, 2007).
17 Derrida, *Psyche: Inventions of the Other*, p. 30.
18 Jacques Derrida, *The Post Card: From Socrates to Freud and Beyond*, trans. Alan Bass (Chicago: University of Chicago Press, 1980).
19 Benoît Peeters offers some biographical context to the 'Envois' in his *Derrida: A Biography* (Cambridge: Polity Press, 2013).
20 Jacques Derrida, 'The Ends of Man', in *Margins of Philosophy*, trans. Alan Bass (Chicago: University of Chicago Press, 1972), p. 135. I have discussed this passage in Derrida at length in 'Extraordinary Rendition: Derrida and Vietnam', in *Deconstruction after 9/11* (New York: Routledge, 2009).
21 On this confusion see my 'New (Improved) French Feminism', in *Deconstruction without Derrida* (London: Bloomsbury, 2014).
22 Hélène Cixous, *Insister of Jacques Derrida*, trans. Peggy Kamuf (Edinburgh: Edinburgh University Press, 2007); *Portrait of Jacques Derrida as a Young Jewish Saint*, trans. Beverley Bie Brahic (New York: Columbia University Press, 2005); *Manhattan: Letters from Prehistory*, trans. Beverley Bie Brahic (New York: Fordham University Press, 2008); *Hyperdream* (Cambridge: Polity, 2009).
23 Hélène Cixous, 'The Laugh of the Medusa', trans. Keith Cohen and Paula Cohen, *Signs*, 1 (4), 1976, pp. 875–93.
24 Hélène Cixous, *Love Itself: In the Letter Box*, trans. Peggy Kamuf (Cambridge: Polity, 2008).
25 Augustine of Hippo, *The Complete Works of Saint Augustine*, ed. Philip Schaff, trans. Marcus Dods, Rose Elizabeth Cleveland and J.F. Shaw (Edinburgh: T&T Clark, 1871).
26 Soren Kierkegaard, *The Seducer's Diary*, trans. Howard V. Hong and Edna Hong (Princeton, NJ: Princeton University Press, 2013); *Either/Or: A Fragment of Life*, ed. Victor Ermita, trans. Alastair Hannay (London: Penguin, 1992).
27 Walter Benjamin, *The Storyteller: Tales Out of Loneliness*, eds. Sam Dolbear, Esther Leslie and Sebastian Truskolaski (London: Verso, 2016).

28 Roland Barthes, *A Lover's Discourse: Fragments*, trans. Richard Howard (Chapel Hill, NC: Hill and Wang, 1979); *Mourning Diary*, trans. Richard Howard (Chapel Hill, NC: Hill and Wang, 2012).
29 Didier Eribon, *Returning to Reims*, trans. Michael Lucey (New York: Semiotexte, 2013); Guy Debord, *Mémoires* (Paris: Allia, 2004); *Panegyric*, trans. James Brrok and John McHale (London: Verso, 2009); *Cette mauvaise réputation* (Paris: Gallimard, 1993).
30 Geoffrey Hartmann, *A Scholar's Tale: Intellectual Journey of a Displaced Child of Europe* (New York: Fordham University Press, 2009); Bernard Steigler, *Acting Out*, trans. David Barison and Daniel Ross (Stanford: Stanford University Press, 2008).
31 Alain Badiou, *Ahmed the Philosopher: 34 Short Plays for Children and Everyone Else*, trans. Joseph Litvak (New York: Columbia University Press, 2014); *Almagestes* (Paris: Editions du Seuil, 1964); *Portulans* (Paris: Editions du Seuil, 1967).
32 Jean-Luc Nancy, *Noli me tangere: On the Raising of the Body*, trans. Sarah Clift, Pascale-Anne Brault and Michael Naas (New York: Fordham University Press, 2008).
33 Mahasweta Devi, *Breast Stories*, trans. Gayatri Chakravorty Spivak (New York: Seagull, 1997); *Imaginary Maps*, trans. Gayatri Chakravorty Spivak (New York: Routledge, 1995); *Chotti Munda and His Arrow*, trans. Gayatri Chakravorty Spivak (Oxford: Blackwell, 2002).
34 Jean-Jacques, Rousseau, *Le devin du village* [The Village Soothsayer] (1753) translated into English by Charles Burney and performed as *The Cunning Man* (1762), parodied by a twelve-year-old Mozart in *Bastien und Bastienne* (1768) following a commission by Franz Mesmer; *The Pervert's Guide to Cinema*, dir. Sophie Fiennes (Amoeba Films, 2006); *The Pervert's Guide to Ideology*, dir. Sophie Fiennes (Blinder Films, 2012).
35 Nicholas Royle, *Quilt* (Brighton: Myriad, 2010); *An English Guide to Birdwatching* (Brighton: Myriad, 2017).
36 Susan Sellers, *Virginia and Vanessa* (Edinburgh: Two Ravens Press, 2008); *Given the Choice* (Manchester: Cillian Press, 2013).
37 David Farrell Krell, *Nietzsche: A Novel* (New York: SUNY University Press, 1996); *Son of Spirit: A Novel* (SUNY University Press, 1997).
38 Kelly Oliver, *Jessica James Mysteries*, vols. 1–3 (*Wolf, Coyote, F.O.X.*) (New York: Kaos Press, 2017).
39 Frank Lentricchia, *After the New Criticism* (Chicago: University of Chicago Press, 1981); *The Dog Killer of Utica* (Brooklyn, NY: Melville House, 2014); *Lucchesi and The Whale* (Durham and London: Duke University Press, 2003); *The Sadness of Antonioni* (Albany: SUNY University Press, 2011).
40 Patricia Duncker, *Hallucinating Foucault* (London: Serpent's Tail, 1996).
41 Terry Eagleton, *Saint Oscar and Other Plays* (London: John Wiley & Sons, 1997); *Wittgenstein* (London: BFI Publishing, 1993); *Saints and Scholars* (London: Verso,

1987). See also, my 'Irish Eagleton: Of Ontological Imperialism and Colonial Mimicry', *Irish Studies Review*, 10 (1), 2002, pp. 29–38.

42 See for example, Willy Maley and John Maley, *From the Calton to Catalonia* (Glasgow: Calton Books, 2014); Willy Maley, *The Lions of Lisbon* (Glasgow: Luath Press, 2017).

43 Lars Iyer, *Spurious* (London: Melville House, 2011); *Dogma* (London: Melville House, 2012); *Exodus* (London: Melville House, 2013); *Wittgenstein Jr.* (London: Melville House, 2015).

44 John Schad, *Someone Called Derrida: An Oxford Mystery* (Brighton: Sussex Academic Press, 2007).

45 George Eliot, *Middlemarch: A Study of Provincial Life* [1871] (London: Penguin, 1994); Leo Tolstoy, *War and Peace* [1869] (London: Penguin, 1982).

46 Gilbert Adair, *The Death of the Author* (London: Heinemann, 1992); John Banville, *Shroud* (New York: Alfred A. Knopf, 2003); John Banville, *Ancient Light* (New York: Alfred A. Knopf, 2012); Bernhard Schlink, *Homecoming* (New York: Pantheon, 2008).

47 Mary McCarthy, *The Groves of Academe* (New York: Harcourt Brace, 1952); Henri Thomas, *Le Parjure* (Paris: Gallimard, 1964).

48 Jed Rubenfield, *The Interpretation of Murder* (New York: Henry Holt, 2006); Irving Stone, *The Passions of the Mind: A Biographic Novel of Sigmund Freud* (Garden City, NY: Doubleday, 1971).

49 Terry Johnson, *Hysteria: Or Fragments of an Analysis of an Obsessional Neurosis* (London: Methuen, 1993).

50 Brenda Webster, *Vienna Triangle* (New York: Wing's Press, 2009); Selden Edwards, *The Little Book* (New York: Dutton Penguin, 2008); Angela von der Lippe, *The Truth about Lou* (Berkeley, CA: Counterpoint, 2006).

51 Irvin D. Yalom's *When Nietzsche Wept* (New York: Basic Books, 1992); *The Schopenhauer Cure* (New York and London: HarperCollins, 2006); *The Spinoza Problem* (New York: Basic Books, 2012).

52 Goce Smilevski, *Freud's Sister* (London and New York: Penguin, 2012).

53 Hanif Kureishi, *Something to Tell You* (London: Faber and Faber, 2008); Salley Vickers, *The Other Side of You* (New York: Picador, 2006).

54 Laurent Binet, *The 7th Function of Language* [2015], trans. Sam Taylor (New York: Farrar, Strauss and Giroux, 2017); Philip Kerr, *A Philosophical Investigation* (New York: Farrar, Strauss and Giroux, 1992).

55 Alain de Botton, *Essays in Love* (London: Picador, 2006).

56 George Santayana, *The Last Puritan: A Memoir in the Form of a Novel* (1935), published as *The Works of George Santayana*, Vol. IV, eds. Henry J. Saatkamp, Jr., William G. Holzberger and Donna Hanna-Calvert (Boston: Bradford Books, 1995).

57 Iris Murdoch, *A Severed Head* (London: Chatto & Windus, 1961).
58 Umberto Eco, *The Name of the Rose*, trans. William Weaver (Boston and New York: Houghton Mifflin Harcourt, 1980) to *Numero Zero*, trans. Richard Dixon (Boston and New York: Houghton Mifflin Harcourt, 2015).
59 Christine Brooke-Rose, *Remake* (Manchester: Carcanet, 1996).
60 Raymond Queneau, *Sunday of Life* [1952], trans. Barbara Wright (London: Alma Classics, 2012); *Zazie in the Metro* [1959], trans. Barbara Wright (London: Penguin, 2001).
61 Zoë Wicomb, *Playing in the Light* (Cape Town and New York: Random House, 2006); Tom McCarthy, *Remainder* (London: Vintage, 2007).
62 Drusilla Modjeska, *Poppy* (London: Serpent's Tail, 1990).
63 The topic of architecture has great significance to the questions posed by critical practice and requires patience and its own space to be read properly in all its singularity. I will return to this issue on another occasion. For discussions between philosophy and architecture see for example: Bernard Tschumi, *Architecture and Disjunction* (Boston: MIT Press, 1996); Peter Eisenman, *Eisenman Inside Out: Selected Writings, 1963–1988* (New Haven: Yale University Press, 2004); Jacques Derrida and Peter Eisenman, *Chora L Works*, eds. Jeffrey Kipnis and Thomas Lesser (New York: Monacelli Press, 1997); Daniel Libeskind, *Radix-Matrix* (New York: Prestel, 1997); Daniel Libeskind, *The Space of Encounter* (New York: Universe Publishing, 2001); Mark Wigley, *The Architecture of Deconstruction: Derrida's Haunt* (Boston: MIT Press, 1993).

Chapter 1

1 Immanuel Kant, 'On the Common Saying: That May Be Correct in Theory, but It Is of No Use in Practice', in *Practical Philosophy* (Cambridge: Cambridge University Press, 1997).
2 See Paul de Man's comments to this effect in *Allegories of Reading: Figural Language in Rousseau, Nietzsche, Rilke and Proust* (New Haven: Yale University Press, 1982), p. 50.
3 For an extending reading of Kant in this vain see Paul de Man, *Aesthetic Ideology* (Minneapolis: University of Minnesota Press, 1996); also Andrzej Warminski, *Ideology, Rhetoric, Aesthetics: For de Man* (Edinburgh: Edinburgh University Press, 2013); and *Material Inscriptions: Rhetorical Reading in Practice and Theory* (Edinburgh: Edinburgh University Press, 2013).
4 Aristotle, *The Nicomachean Ethics*, ed. Lesley Brown, trans. David Ross (Oxford: Oxford University Press, 2009). For reasons that will become clear in the discussion of the operation of terms in the *Ethics*, I have adapted the translation of the text in line with existing scholarship. References to the text to use with other standard

translations can be traced through the section and line numbers provided in the body of this chapter.
5 I am indebted here and in the philosophical etymology that follows to the monumental work of Barbara Cassin, her editors and translators in the *Dictionary of Untranslatables: A Philosophical Lexicon* (Oxford and Princeton: Princeton University Press, 2014).
6 Karl Marx and Friedrich Engels, *The German Ideology*, vols. 1–2 (London: Lawrence & Wishart, 1965).
7 Saint Augustine, *Confessions*, trans. Henry Chadwick (Oxford: Oxford University Press, 2008).
8 Jean-Jacques Rousseau, *Emile: Or On Education*, trans. Barbara Foxley (London: Penguin, 2007).
9 Jean-Paul Sartre, *The Age of Reason*, trans. Eric Sutton (London: Penguin, 2001).
10 Madame de Staël, *Delphine*, trans. Simone Balaye (Chicago: Northern Illinois University Press, 1995); Voltaire, *Candide and Other Stories*, trans. Roger Pearson (Oxford: Oxford University Press, 2008); Jacques Derrida, *La Carte Postale: De Socrate à Freud et au-delà* (Paris: Flammarion, 1980).
11 The field of philosophers and theorists speculating on film in order to read individual films as exemplary of philosophical knowledge is vast. Examples might include: Robert Sinnerbrink, *New Philosophies of Film: Thinking Images* (London: Continuum, 2011); John Mullarkey, *Philosophy and the Moving Image: Refractions of Reality* (Basingstoke: Palgrave Macmillan, 2010); Stephen Mulhall, *On Film* (London: Routledge, 2015); Felicity Colman, *Deleuze and Cinema: The Film Concepts* (London: Bloomsbury, 2011); Thomas Wartenberg, *Thinking on Screen: Film as Philosophy* (New York: Routledge, 2007).
12 On the development of philosophical approaches to performance see Laura Cull and A. Lagaay, eds. *Encounters in Performance Philosophy* (Basingstoke: Palgrave Macmillan, 2014).
13 Plato, *Timaeus and Critias*, trans. Desmond Lee (London: Penguin, 2008).
14 Plato, *Republic*, trans. Robin Waterfield (Oxford: Oxford University Press, 1993).
15 I will be using the term figurative as it is used throughout the work of J. Hillis Miller and Paul de Man, see Allegories of Reading as a good example.
16 Hegel is quoting from *Metaphysics* B 4, 1000a 18–19; Aristotle's passage refers to Hesiod, not to Plato.
17 Jacques Derrida, 'Khora', in *On the Name*, ed. Thomas Dutoit, trans. David Wood, John P. Leavey, Jr. and Ian McLeod (Stanford: Stanford University Press, 1995). A shorter version of this text also appears in the documentation of Derrida's architectural collaboration with Peter Eisenman, *Chora L Works*, eds. Jeffrey Kipnis and Thomas Lesser (New York: Monacelli Press, 1997).
18 See Julia Kristeva, *Revolution in Poetic Language* (New York: Columbia University Press, 1984); Martin Heidegger cites khora in a brief section of the *Introduction to Metaphysics* (Garden City, NY: Doubleday, 1961), p. 55.

19 'Von denen, welche mythisch philosophieren, ist es nicht der Mühe wert, ernstlich zu handeln', Hegel, *Vorlesungen über diw Geschichte der Philosophie, Einleitung*, 8, 2b, *Verhåltnis der Philosophie zur Religion, Werke* 18 (Surhrkamp: Frankfurt a. M.), p. 103.
20 These references also quoted and translated in Derrida, 'Khora'.
21 See Roland Barthes, *The Neutral: Lecture Course at the College de France (1977-1978)*, trans. Rosalind Krauss and Denis Hollier (New York: Columbia University Press, 2008).
22 While I will use the term 'deconstructive' here in the context of Derrida's writing, in general I have shied away from mobilizing the word 'deconstruction' in this book. This is not out of a concern for the validity of that work, on the contrary this volume is replete with the influence of this way of thinking. Rather, it is a conscious attempt to find other ways to describe the action and character that resides in creative practice and which could easily be attributed the precise and economic term 'deconstruction'. Some will recognize the action but not appreciate the term deconstruction, and vice versa. This exercise is as much a challenge to myself to avoid the default of a specialist vocabulary that assumes a reservoir of knowledge and familiarity with a library of texts when describing a set of experiences common to many students and artists without this training.
23 A reader who wished to explore the work of Derrida further would do well to familiarize themselves with, Simon Morgan Wortham, *The Derrida Dictionary* (London: Continuum, 2010).
24 See Dan Edelstein, 'Hyperborean Atlantis: Jean-Sylvain Bailly, Madame Blavatsky, and the Nazi Myth', *Studies in Eighteenth-Century Culture*, 35, 2006, pp. 267–91.
25 See Jacques Derrida, *Monolingualism of the Other, Or, The Prosthesis of Origin*, trans. Patrick Mensah (Stanford: Stanford University Press, 1998).
26 D. Nails, *The People of Plato: A Prosopography of Plato and Other Socratics* (Cambridge: Hackett Publishing, 2002).
27 Fragments of Critias's writing can be found in the 'Demonax: Hellenic Library Beta', website http://demonax.info/doku.php?id=text:critias_of_athens_fragments.
28 See Geoffrey Bennington, *Legislations: The Politics of Deconstriction* (London: Verso, 1994).
29 Here I am using the term 'undecideability' in a strict Derridean sense, not as ambiguity or a matter of choice but as an experience without assurance of any criteriology on which to base decision, but the impossibility of which becomes the condition of possibility for the event of decision. See Jacques Derrida, 'The Force of Law', trans. Mary Quaintance, in *Deconstruction and the Possibility of Justice*, ed. Drucilla Cornell et al (New York: Routledge, 1992), pp. 3–67.

Chapter 2

1. Henrich von Kleist, *Selected Writings*, ed. and trans. David Constantine (Cambridge: Hackett Press, 2004), pp. 411–17.
2. See also Chapter 3 of this volume, which deals with Hélène Cixous' reading of the Kleist text and Carol Jacobs, *Uncontainable Romanticism: Shelley, Brontë, Kleist* (Baltimore: Johns Hopkins University Press, 1989); Cynthia Chase, 'Telling Truths', *Diacritics*, 9 (4), 1979, pp. 62–9; Andrzej Warminski, 'A Question of an Other Order: Deflections of the Straight Man', *Diacritics*, 9 (4), 1979; see also Jacques Derrida's comments in 'Typewriter Ribbon', in *Material Events: Paul de Man and the Afterlife of Theory*, eds. Tom Cohen, Barbara Cohen, J. Hillis Miller and Andrzej Warminski (Minneapolis: University of Minnesota Press, 2001).
3. Derrida discusses the problem of the 'as if' most notably in *Politics of Friendship*, trans. Georges Collins (London: Verso, 1998).
4. William Butler Yeats, 'Amongst School Children', in *Collected Poems of W.B. Yeats*, ed. Richard J. Finneran (New York: Simon & Schuster, 1983).
5. See Pierre Bourdieu in *Distinction: A Social Critique of the Judgement of Taste*, trans. Richard Nice (Cambridge, MA: Harvard University Press, 1984).
6. Novalis, *Philosophical Writings*, ed. and trans. Margaret Mahony Stoljar (New York: SUNY Press, 1997).
7. von Kleist, *Selected Writings*, pp. 405–10. See also *An Abyss Deep Enough: The Letters of Heinrich von Kleist with a Selection of Essays and Anecdotes*, ed. and trans. Philip B. Miller (New York: Dutton Adult, 1982).
8. *An Abyss Deep Enough*, p. 413.
9. The quote is attributed without source.
10. See Martin Heidegger, 'Only a God Can Save Us: The Spiegel Interview' (1966), in *Heidegger: The Man and the Thinker*, ed. Thomas Sheehan (New York: Transaction Publishers, 1981).
11. The phrase 'permanent parabasis' comes from Paul de Man's 'The Concept of Irony', we will have recourse to mobilize it several times in this study, see *Aesthetic Ideology*, ed. Andrzej Warminski (Minneapolis: University of Minnesota Press, 1996), pp. 163–85.
12. See also Jacques Derrida, 'Choreographies: An Interview with Christie V. McDonald', *Diacritics*, 12 (2), 1982, pp. 66–76.
13. See Milan Kundera, *The Unbearable Lightness of Being*, trans. Michael Henry Heim (London: Faber and Faber, 1984).
14. *An Abyss Deep Enough*, pp. 421–2.
15. There are several to choose from, Joachim Maass, *Kleist: A Biography* (New York: Farrar, Straus & Giroux, 1983); Peter Michalzik, *Kleist: Dichter, Krieger, Seelensucher—Biographie* (Berlin: Ullstein Taschenbuchvig, 2012); Rudolf Loch,

Kleist: Eine Biographie (Berlin: Wallstein, 2003); Jens Bisky, *Kleist: Eine Biographie* (Berlin: Rowohlt, 2007); Gerhard Schulz, *Kleist: Eine Biographie* (Berlin: C.H. Beck, 2007); Günter Blamberger, *Heinrich von Kleist: Biographie* (Berlin: Fischer Taschenbuch, 2012). See also, Stefan Zweig, *The Struggle with the Daemon: Hölderlin, Kleist and Nietzsche*, trans. Eden Paul and Cedar Paul (New York: Pushkin Press, 2012).

16. *An Abyss Deep Enough*, p. 98.
17. *An Abyss Deep Enough*, p. 100.
18. *An Abyss Deep Enough*, Letter to Ernst von Pfuel, 7 January 1805.
19. *An Abyss Deep Enough*, p. 101.
20. See Samuel Taylor Coleride, *Biographia Literaria* (1817), ed. John T. Shawcross (Oxford: Oxford University Press, 1907).
21. Paul de Man, 'Kant and Schiller', in *Aesthetic Ideology*, p. 130.
22. de Man, 'Kant and Schiller', p. 131.
23. Ibid., p. 133.
24. Immanuel Kant, *Critique of Pure Reason* (1781) for example in A254/B310, 'The concept of a noumenon, i.e. of a thing that is not to be thought of as an object of the senses but rather as a thing-in-itself', *Critique of Pure Reason*, ed. and trans. Paul Guyer and Allen Wood (Cambridge: Cambridge University Press, 1998), p. 362.
25. Paul de Man, 'Kant and Schiller', p. 138; *Schiller Weke*, 20, pp. 174–5.
26. See Immanuel Kant, *Critique of the Power of Judgment* (1793), ed. and trans. Paul Guyer and Eric Matthews (Cambridge: Cambridge University Press, 2002), sections 25–9.
27. Paul de Man, 'Kant and Schiller', p. 139; '*Vom Erhabenen*', *Schiller Weke*, 20, p. 174.
28. de Man, 'Kant and Schiller', p. 140.
29. Friedrich Schiller, *Mary Stuart* (1799), trans. J.F. Lamport (London: Penguin, 1969); *On the Aesthetic Education of Man* (1794), trans. Keith Tribe (London: Penguin, 2016).
30. Paul de Man, 'Kant and Schiller', p. 141.
31. Friedrich Schiller, *Don Carlos*, trans. Hilary Collier Sy-Quia (Oxford: Oxford University Press, 1996); *Turnadot*, trans. Sabilla Novello (New York: Dodo Press, 2009).
32. Paul de Man, 'Kant and Schiller', p. 141.
33. Friedrich Schiller, *An die Freude* (1785), 'Ode to Joy'; *William Tell* (1804). trans. William Peter (New York: Forgotten Books, 2012).
34. Paul de Man, 'Kant and Schiller', p. 142.
35. Ibid., p. 142.
36. Paul de Man, 'Aesthetic Formalization: Kleist's *Uber das Marionettentheater*', in *The Rhetoric of Romanticism* (New York: Columbia University Press, 1984). An audio recording of the full set of Messenger Lectures is available through The

London Graduate School here http://backdoorbroadcasting.net/2013/10/paul-de-man-the-messenger-lectures-1983/. My thanks to Sam Weber, Patricia de Man and René Wolf for making this resource possible.
37. I discuss this easy and its relation to a politics of pedagogy elsewhere, see my 'Paul de Man and Art History I', in *Reading Ranciere: Critical Dissensus*.
38. 'On the Gradual Fabrication of Thoughts While Speaking', in *An Abyss Deep Enough*, pp. 218–23 ['Über die allmähliche Verfertigung der Ganken beim Reden', Sämtliche Werke und Briefe, ed. Helmut Sembdner (Munich: Hanser, 1961), pp. 319–24].
39. For an extended reading of Kleist see J. Hillis Miller, 'Just Reading: Kleist's 'Der Findling', in *Versions of Pygmalion* (Cambridge, MA: Harvard University Press, 1990).
40. Kant, *Critique of Pure Reason*, A134/B173.
41. *Oxford English Dictionary*.
42. *Oxford English Dictionary*.
43. *Toy Story*, dir. John Lasseter (Pixar Animation, 1995).
44. John Milton, *The Complete Works of John Milton*, eds. John K. Hale, J. Donald Cullington, Gordon Campbell and Thomas N. Corns (Oxford: Oxford University Press, 2012).
45. See Jacques Derrida, 'Faith and Knowledge: The Two Sources of "Religion" at the Limits of Reason Alone', in *Acts of Religion*, ed. Gil Anidjar (New York and London: Routledge, 1996).
46. Samuel Beckett, 'Worstward Ho' (1983), in *Nohow On: Three Novels* (London: Grove Press, 1989).
47. Milton, *The Complete Works of John Milton*.
48. Ibid.

Chapter 3

1. Roland Barthes diagnosed the cult of the humanist author fifty years ago, little has changed. See 'The Death of the Author', in *Image-Music-Text*, trans. Richard Howard (Chapel Hill, NC: Hill and Wang), pp. 143–8.
2. Martin Heidegger, 'Origin of the Work of Art', in *Off the Beaten Track*, ed. and trans. Julian Young and Kenneth Haynes (Cambridge: Cambridge University Press, 2002), pp. 1–56.
3. See our commentary on Aristotle in Chapter 1 of this study.
4. See previous chapter 1, n. 11, p. 216.
5. See 'Grace and Innocence: Heinrich von Kleist', in *Readings: The Poetics of Blanchot, Joyce, Kafka, Lispector and Tsvetayeva*, ed. and trans. Verena Conley (Minneapolis:

University of Minnesota Press, 1991), pp. 28–73, and 'The Last Chapter in the History of the World', in *Prénoms de personne* (Paris: Editions du Seuil, 1974).
6 *Oxford English Dictionary*, 2nd ed., 1969.
7 On the question of touching see, Jacques Derrida, *On Touching—Jean-Luc Nancy*, trans. Christine Irizarry (Stanford: Stanford University Press, 2005) and the two volumes of essays reading touch in Derrida and Nancy, edited by myself, *Derrida Today*, 1 (2), 2008, and 2 (1), 2009.
8 I discuss this term in relation to Derrida's 'Ends of Man' in my 'Extraordinary Rendition', in *Deconstruction after 9/11*.
9 For a further discussion of innocence, see Chapter 6 of this study.
10 Cixous discusses this frequently in her writing, see Hélène Cixous and Jacques Derrida, *Veils*, trans. Geoffrey Bennington (Stanford: Stanford University Press, 2002); Hélène Cixous, *Photos de Racines* (Paris: Editions des Femmes, 1994), translated as *Rootprints: Memory and Life Writing*, trans. Eric Prenowitz (London: Routledge, 1997).
11 Hélène Cixous, 'Writing Blind: Conversations with the Donkey', trans. Eric Prenowitz, in *Stigmata: Escaping Texts* (London: Routledge, 1998).
12 On the topic of blindness see, Jacques Derrida, *Memoirs of the Blind: The Self-Portrait and Other Ruins*, trans. Pascale-Anne Brault and Michael Naas (Chicago: University of Chicago Press, 1993); Paul de Man, *Blindness and Insight: Essays in the Rhetoric of Contemporary Criticism*, rev. ed. (Minneapolis: University of Minnesota Press, 1983).
13 On writing and blindness see Nick Royle, 'Night Writing', in *The Uncanny* (Manchester: Manchester University Press, 2003).
14 On blindness in philosophy see Denis Diderot, 'Letter on the Blind for the Use of Those Who Can See' ['Lettre sur les aveugles à l'usage de ceux qui voient', 1749], in *Blindness and Enlightenment: An Essay*, ed. Kate E. Tunstall (London: Continuum, 2011).
15 King James Version.
16 Music by George Gershwin, lyrics by Ira Gershwin, 'It Ain't Necessarily So', in *Porgy and Bess* (1935).
17 See also her comments on Tiresius in 'Castration or Decapitation?', trans. Annette Kuhn, *Signs*, 7 (1), 1981, pp. 41–55.
18 On secrets, see Jacques Derrida and Maurizio Ferraris, *A Taste for the Secret* (Cambridge: Polity Press, 2001).
19 On death and the question of storytelling see, Ursula K. Le Guin, 'It Was a Dark and Stormy Night; Or, Why Are We Huddling about the Campfire?', *Critical Inquiry*, 7 (1), 1980, pp. 191–9, and Peter Brooks, *Reading for the Plot: Design and Intention in Narrative* (New York: Alfred A. Knopf, 1994).
20 See also, Hélène Cixous, *Poetry in Painting: Writings on Contemporary Arts and Aesthetics*, eds. Joana Masó and Marta Segarra (Edinburgh: Edinburgh University Press, 2012).

21 On handwriting and phenomenology, see Jacques Derrida, 'Geschlecht II: Heidegger's Hand', trans. John P. Leavey, Jr., *Deconstruction and Philosophy: The Texts of Jacques Derrida*, ed. John Sallis (Chicago: University of Chicago Press, 1987), pp. 161–96.
22 On touch and philosophy see, Maurice Merleau-Ponty, *Phenomenology of Perception*, trans. Donald A. Landes (New York: Routledge, 2012); *The Visible and the Invisible*, trans. Alphonso Lingis (Evanston: Northwestern University Press, 1968).
23 See the work of novelist–theorist David Farrell Krell, 'Heidegger's Singular Hand', in *Phantoms of the Other: Four Generations of Derrida's Geschlect* (Albany: SUNY University Press, 2015).
24 For example, see the work of the collective Art & Language over several decades.
25 Johann Gottfried Herder, *Plastik* (1778); *Sculpture: Some Observations on Shape and Form from Pygmalion's Creative Dream*, trans. Jason Gaiger (Chicago: University of Chicago Press, 2002).
26 See for example Derrida's comments on Heidegger, the animal and the world in *Of Spirit: Heidegger and the Question*, trans. Geoffrey Bennington (Chicago: Chicago University Press, 1989).
27 See Jacques Derrida, *The Beast and the Sovereign*, vols. 1–2, trans. Geoffrey Bennington (Chicago: University of Chicago Press, 2009 and 2011).
28 Pseudo-Apollodorous, *Bibliotheca* 11.1.3, Apollonius Rhodius 1.112, Ovid, *Metamorphoses* 1.624.
29 On the question of pros-thesis, see David Wills, *Prosthesis* (Stanford: Stanford University Press, 1995).
30 See my 'Toucher I: (The Problem with Self-Touching)', in *Deconstruction without Derrida*.
31 See the previous chapter of this study.
32 Catherine Malabou, as *The Future of Hegel: Plasticity, Temporality and Dialectic*, trans. Lisbeth During (London and New York: Routledge, 2004).
33 In the English translation of Derrida's *Spectres de Marx*, Peggy Kamuf renders '*la démocratie à venir*' as 'the democracy-to-come', the pun between '*l'avenir*' and '*à venir*' that creates play in Derrida's concept is implied in the French noun. For example, the 2016 Isabelle Huppert film, *L'avenir*, was released in the English-speaking world as *Things to Come*.
34 See Catherine Malabou, *Plasticité* (Paris: Éditions Léo Scheer, 1999); *Plasticity at the Dusk of Writing: Dialectic, Destruction, Deconstruction*, trans. Carolyn Shread (New York: Columbia University Press, 2009); *The New Wounded: From Neurosis to Brain Damage* (New York: Fordham University Press, 2012).
35 On figuration, see Paul de Man, 'Shelley Disfigured', in *The Rhetoric of Romanticism*.
36 See my comments on the non-dialecticity of the dialectic in *Deconstruction without Derrida*.

37 See Catherine Malabou, *La Chambre du mileu, de Hegel aux neurosciences* (Paris: Hermann, 2009); *La Grande Exclusion, l'urgence sociale, thérapie et symptômes* (Paris: Bayard, 2009).
38 Elsewhere, Derrida writes of 'the time of reflection is also the chance for turning back on the very conditions of reflection, in all the sense of that word, as if with the help of a new optical device one could finally see sight, could not only view the natural landscape, the city, the bridge and the abyss, but could "view" viewing. As if through an acoustical device one could "hear" hearing, in other words, seize the inaudible in a sort of poetic telephony.' 'The Principle of Reason: The University in the Eyes of its Pupils', in *Eyes of the University: The Right to Philosophy*, vol. 2 (Stanford: Stanford University Press, 2004), p. 154.
39 See Derrida's reading of Hegel in 'From Restricted to General Economy: A Hegelianism without Reseve', in *Writing and Difference*, trans. Alan Bass (London: Routledge and Kegan Paul, 1978), pp. 317–50.
40 William Shakespeare, *Hamlet*, Act I Scene V, 190.
41 Malabou's work follows on from Derrida's *Spectres de Marx* (Paris: Galilee, 1993) which revists Kojève in light of the Francis Fukuyama's *The End of History and the Last Man* (New York: Free Press, 1992). The surprise resides in revisiting arguments from the 1950s, the lack of surprise comes in the continuation of Derrida's commentary.
42 See Raymond Queneau's novel, *The Sunday of Life*, discussed in the introduction to this study.
43 See also, Jacques Derrida, *The Work of Mourning*, trans. Pascle-Anne Brault and Michael Naas (Chicago: University of Chicago Press, 2001).
44 Jacques Derrida, *Glas*, trans. John P. Leavey, Jr. and Richard Rand (Lincoln: University of Nebraska Press, 1986).

Chapter 4

1 Ovid, *Metamorphoses*, ed. E.J. Kenney, trans. A.D. Melville (Oxford: Oxford University Press, 2008).
2 Hesiod, *Theogony and Works and Days*, trans. M.L. West (Oxford: Oxford University Press, 2008).
3 See Miller, *Versions of Pygmalion*; Victor I. Stoitchita, *The Pygmalion Effect: From Ovid to Hitchcock* (Chicago: University of Chicago Press, 2008).
4 Jean-Jacques Rousseau, *Pygmalion, Edition augmentée* (Paris: Arvensa Editions, 2014).
5 William Shakespeare, 'Venus and Adonis' (1194).
6 See Derrida, *The Work of Mourning*.
7 On the wholly vegetal other, see Jacques Derrida, *The Animal That Therefore I am*, ed. Marie-Louise Mallet, trans. David Wills (New York: Fordham University Press, 2009).

8   On Venus and sexual difference see Hélène Cixous, *Tomb(e)*, trans. Laurent Milesi (Chicago: Seagull Books, 2014).
9   Paul de Man, *Allegories of Reading: Figural Language in Rousseau, Nietzsche, Rilke and Proust* (New Haven and London: Yale University Press, 1979).
10 Jean-Jacques Rousseau, *Narcissus, or The Lover Himself*, trans. Daniel Boden (London: Contra Mundum Press, 2015).
11 For a visual representation of the paradoxes of creation, see Edwin Long's 1878 oil on canvas, 'The gods and their creators', Burnley, UK, Towneley Hall Art Gallery and Museum.
12 The *as if* appears as an important trope in Derrida, *Politics of Friendship* (1997).
13 On the suspension of meaning, see Paul de Man, 'Literary History and Literary Modernity', in *Blindness and Insight: Essays in the Rhetoric of Contemporary Criticism*, 2nd ed. (London: Methuen & Co, 1983).
14 See 'The Foundling', in *The Marquise of O, and Other Stories*, ed. Heinrich von Kleist, trans. David Luke and Nigel Reeves (London: Penguin, 1978).
15 On use, see Georges Bataille, 'The Use Value of D.A.F. de Sade (An Open Letter to my Current Comrades)', trans. Allan Stoekl, in *Visions of Excess: Selected Writings, 1927–1939* (Minneapolis: University of Minnesota Press, 1985).
16 See *Material Events: Paul de Man and the Afterlife of Theory*, eds. Tom Cohen, Barbara Cohen, J. Hillis Miller and Andrzej Warminski (Minneapolis: University of Minnesota Press, 2000).
17 See Geoffrey Bennington's comments on politics in *Legislations: The Politics of Deconstruction* (London: Verso, 1994).
18 See also, J. Hillis Miller, *Speech Acts in Literature* (Stanford: Stanford University Press, 2002).
19 The subtitle of Herder's reflections on sculpture, his *Plastik*, is 'Some Observations on Shape and Form from Pygmalion's Creative Dream'.
20 Of the trilogy known as the Prometheia, we have *Prometheus Bound* but the texts of *Prometheus Unbound* and *Prometheus the Fire-Bringer* only exist in fragments. There may also have existed a fourth play, *The Fire-Bearer* that would have made a tetralogy by preceding *Prometheus Bound*.
21 Percy Shelley, 'Prometheus Unbound' (IV, 573–4), in *The Complete Poems of Shelley* (London and New York: Random House, 1994).
22 Mary Shelley, *Frankenstein: Or, the Modern Prometheus* (London: Penguin, 2003), vol. 15, p. 8.
23 See Gaston Bachelard, *The Psychoanalysis of Fire*, trans. Alan C.M. Ross (London: Routledge & Kegan Paul, 1964).
24 I of course borrow the phrase 'permanent parabasis' from Paul de Man, 'The Concept of Irony', in *Aesthetic Ideology*.
25 Franz Kafka, 'Prometheus', in *The Complete Stories*, trans. Willa and Edwin Muir (New York: Schocken Books, 1995).

26 Sigmund Freud, 'The Acquisition and Control of Fire', in *The Standard Edition of the Complete Psychological Works of Sigmund Freud*, ed. James Strachey (London: The Hogarth Press, 1932), vol. 22, pp. 183–94.
27 Aeschylus, *Prometheus Unbound and Other Plays*, trans. Philip Vellacott (London: Penguin, 2001).
28 See 'The Prometheus Complex', in Gaston Bachelard, *The Psychoanalysis of Fire*.
29 'Reading the morning newspaper is the realist's morning prayer. One orients one's attitude toward the world either by God or by what the world is. The former gives as much security as the latter, in that one knows how one stands.' Georg Wilhelm Friedrich Hegel, *Miscellaneous Writings*, trans. Jon Bartley Stewart (Chicago: Northwestern University Press, 2002), p. 247.
30 Friedrich Hölderlin, *The Death of Empedocles: A Mourning-Play*, trans. David Farrell Krell (New York: SUNY Press, 2009).
31 Diogenes Laertius, *Lives of Eminent Philosophers*, trans. R.D. Hicks (London: Loeb Books, 1989), vol. 8, p. 2.
32 Bernard Stiegler, *Technics and Time, Vol. 1: The Fault of Epimetheus*, trans. Richard Beardsworth and George Collins (Stanford: Stanford University Press, 1998).
33 Jean-Pierre Vernant, 'A la table des hommes', in *La cuisine du sacrifice*, ed. J.-P. Vernant (Paris: Gallimard, 1979).
34 Plato, *Protagoras*, trans. C.C.W. Taylor (Oxford: Oxford University Press, 2009).
35 See also, Bernard Stiegler, *Technics and Time*, vols. 2–3, trans. Stephen Barker (Stanford: Stanford University Press, 2008).
36 Hesiod, *Homeric Hymns, Epic Cycle, Homerica*, trans. H.G. Evelyn-White (London: William Heinemann, 1914), Loeb Classical Library, vols. 57, 82.
37 Stiegler quotes Vernant in a footnote, 'the immortality of the Promethean liver corresponds to the mode of existence of those nature phenomena that, without ever disappearing can only subsist in fact through periodic renewal' ('A la table des hommes', p. 90).
38 See Immanuel Kant, 'Perpetual Peace' (1795), in *Political Writings*, ed. Hans Reiss, trans. H.B. Nisbet (Cambridge: Cambridge University Press, 1991).

Chapter 5

1 See Rob Pope, *Creativity: Theory, History, Practice* (London: Routledge, 2005).
2 See James Engell, *The Creative Imagination: Enlightenment to Romanticism* (Cambridge, MA: Harvard University Press, 1981).
3 William Shakespeare, *King Lear* 1.1.87.
4 Terry Eagleton comments on the nothing of this scene in his *William Shakespeare* (London: John Wiley & Sons, 1986).

5. See F.M. Cornford, ed., *Parmenides' Way of Truth and Plato's Parmenides* (London: Routledge & Kegan Paul, 1969).
6. Lucretius, *The Nature of Things*, ed. Richard Jenkyns, trans. Alicia Stallings (London: Penguin, 2007), 1.156–7.
7. See Gerhard May, *Creatio Ex Nihilo: The Doctrine of 'Creation Out of Nothing' in Early Christian Thought*, trans. A.S. Worrall (London and New York: Continuum, 2004).
8. Jean-Luc Nancy, *The Creation of the World or Globalization*, trans. François Raffoul and David Pettigrew (New York: SUNY Press, 2007).
9. In his poem known as 'Without Why', Silesius writes '*Die Ros ist ohn warum; sie blühet sie blühet/Sie acht nicht iher selbst, fragt nicht, ob man sie siehet*', 'The rose is without why. It blows because it blows/It thinks not of itself, and no display it shows'. Nancy translates the opening phrase as '*rien de raison*', which in turn Raffoul and Pettigrew render as 'without reason'. The best we can say here is that the modern English-language version is removed from its source material.
10. See Jacques Derrida, *Paper Machine*, trans. Rachel Bowlby (Stanford: Stanford University Press, 2005), p. 118. For a summary of the relevant references and debates Victor Li, 'Elliptical Interruptions: Or, Why Derrida Prefers *Mondialisation* to Globalization', *The New Centennial Review*, 7 (2), 2007, pp. 141–54.
11. I have considered this aspect of Nancy's thought before in greater detail in the text 'Deconstruction and Globalization: The World According to Jean-Luc Nancy', in my *Deconstruction without Derrida* (London: Continuum, 2012).
12. The classic discussion of *Produktionsweise* comes in the introduction to Marx's *Grundrisse: Foundations of the Critique of Political Economy*, trans. Martin Nicolaus (London: Penguin, 1993).
13. For example, see Adrian Johnston, *Prolegomena to Any Future Materialism, Vol. 1: The Outcome of Contemporary French Philosophy* (Evanston, IL: Northwestern University Press, 2013). See also Simon Morgan Wortham's criticism of this understanding of materialism in his 'The Pig's Head', *Radical Philosophy*, p.187, September–October 2014.
14. Sometimes translated as 'purposiveness without purpose', see Immanuel Kant, *Critique of Judgment*, trans. John H. Bernard (New York: Cosimon Hafner Publishing, 1951), S.81, p. 204.
15. See Derrida, 'Faith and Knowledge', in *Acts of Religion* (2002).
16. See Derrida's comments on Nancy's relation to religion in *On Touching—Jean-Luc Nancy*, trans. Christine Irizarry (Stanford: Stanford University Press, 2005).
17. On the risk of absolutizing the other see Simon Morgan Wortham, 'There Shall Be No Mourning', in *Desire in Ashes: Deconstruction, Psychoanalysis and Philosophy*, eds. Chiara Alfano and Simon Morgan Wortham (London: Bloomsbury, 2016).
18. For example, Alain Badiou, *Theoretical Writings*, ed. and trans. Ray Brassier and Alberto Toscano (London: Continuum, 2004).

19 Derrida, *Psyche: Inventions of the Other*.
20 See Derrida, 'Khora' and Derrida and Eisenman, *Chora L Works*, discussed in the introduction to this book.
21 See the discussion of *The Nicomachean Ethics* in the introduction to this book.
22 See my 'Derrida and Vietnam', in *Deconstruction without Derrida*.
23 See Derrida's discussion of such terms in *Of Grammatology*, trans. Gayatri Chakravorty Spivak (Baltimore: John Hopkins University Press, 1974).
24 Seamus Heaney, *Seeing Things* (London: Faber & Faber, 1991).
25 Seamus Heaney, *Crediting Poetry: The Nobel Lecture* (London and New York: Farrar, Straus and Giroux, 1996).
26 From his poem, *De mirabilibus Hibernie* [On the Wonders of Ireland]. The Latin is from *The Writings of Bishop Patrick of Ireland, 1074–1084*, ed. S.J. Aubrey Gwynn (Dublin: The Dublin Institute of Advanced Studies, 1955), pp. 64–5; the translation, http://www.inthemedievalmiddle.com/2013/09/seamus-heaney-and-ships-that-sail-air.html.
27 See the corpus of texts made available online by University College Cork, https://celt.ucc.ie/transpage.html.
28 On the undecidable see, Jacques Derrida, *Aporias*, trans. Thomas Dutoit (Stanford: Stanford University Press, 1993).
29 On the impossible see Derrida, 'The Force of Law', in *Deconstruction and the Possibility of Justice*, pp. 3–63.
30 Jacques Lacan, 'The Mirror Stage as Formative of the Function of the I', in *Ecrits: A Selection*, trans. Bruce Fink (London: Tavistock Press, 1977).
31 Apuleius, *The Golden Ass or Metamorphoses*, trans. E.J. Kenney (London: Penguin, 1998).
32 Stendhal, *The Charterhouse of Parma*, ed. Roger Pearson, trans. Margaret Mauldon (Oxford: Oxford University Press, 2009); Paul de Man, 'The Concept of Irony', in *Aesthetic Ideology*.
33 On the future, see our previous discussion on 'l'avenir' in relation to Catherine Malabou, and Jacques Derrida, *Spectres of Marx: The Work of Mourning, the State of the Debt, and the New International*, trans. Peggy Kamuf (London and New York: Routledge, 1994).
34 See Homi K. Bhabha, 'How Newness Enters the World: Postmodern Space, Postcolonial Times and the Trials of Cultural Translation', in *The Location of Culture* (London: Routledge, 2004).
35 See Robert Rowland Smith, *Death Drive: Freudian Hauntings in Literature and Art* (Edinburgh: Edinburgh University Press, 2010); Nicholas Royle, 'The Death Drive', in *The Uncanny*.
36 See Geoffrey Bennington, 'De Man and the Machine', in *Reading de Man Reading*, eds. Lindsay Waters and Wlad Godzich (Minneapolis: University of Minnesota

Press, 1989); Michael Naas, *Miracle and Machine: Jacques Derrida and the Two Sources of Religion, Science and the Media* (New York: Fordham University Press, 2012).

Chapter 6

1. See Joanna Callaghan and Martin McQuillan, eds., *Love in the Post: The Screenplay and Commentary* (London: Rowman and Littlefield International, 2014); Ken McMullen and Martin McQuillan, *Oxi: An Act of Resistance, Screenplay and Commentary* (London: Rowman and Littlefield International, 2015).
2. Benoît Peeters, *Derrida: A Biography*, trans. Andrew Brown (Cambridge: Polity Press, 2012), p. 266.
3. Valerio Adami, 'The Massacre of the Innocents', tableau vivant, 1975, available in Peeters, 2012, and at http://s-hayashi.tumblr.com/post/79710829720/tableau-vivant-of-the-painting-the-massacre-of#notes.
4. Nicolas Poussin, 'Le Massacre des Innocents', c.1628–9, 171 × 147 cm, Musée Condé, Chantilly, France, https://www.wikiart.org/en/nicolas-poussin/the-massacre-of-the-innocents-1629.
5. *The Holy Bible*, King James Version, Cambridge Edition (1769); King James Bible online, 2017. www.kingjamesbibleonline.org [Matthew 2:13, 16].
6. John Prados, *Safe for Democracy: The Secret Wars of the CIA* (New York: Amsterdam Books, 2009), p. 394.
7. See also Jacques Derrida, *Rogues: Two Essays on Reason*, trans. Michael Naas and Pascale-Anne Brault (Stanford: Stanford University Press, 2002).
8. John Milton, *The Major Works*, eds. Stephen Orgel and Jonathan Goldberg (Oxford: Oxford University Press, 2008), p. 80.
9. See Elizabeth Sauer, 'Tolerationism, the Irish Crisis, and Milton's *On the Late Massacre in Piedmont*', *Milton Studies*, 44, 2005, pp. 40–61.
10. See Jacques Derrida, *The Gift of Death*, trans. David Wills (Chicago: Chicago University Press, 1996).
11. See Jacques Derrida, 'The Rhetoric of Drugs', in *Points.... Interviews, 1974–1994*, ed. Elisabeth Weber (Stanford: Stanford University Press, 1995), pp. 228–54. This event also discussed in Peeters, *Derrida: A Biography*.
12. See Tom Cohen, *Hitchcock's Cryptonymies*, vols. 1–2 (Minneapolis: University of Minnesota Press, 2004).
13. See Jacques Derrida, 'The Ends of Man', *Philosophy and Phenomenological Research*, 30 (1), 1969, pp. 31–57.
14. On innocence in general, see Chapter 3 of this book and Hélène Cixous, 'Innocence and Grace in Kleist's Marionette Theatre', in *Readings: The Poetics of Blanchot, Joyce,*

Kafka, Kleist, Lispector and Tsvetayeva (Minneapolis: University of Minnesota Press, 1991). On lies and perjury see Jacques Derrida, *Without Alibi*, trans. Peggy Kamuf (Stanford: Stanford University Press, 2002).

15 Peeters, *Derrida: A Biography*, p. 340.
16 Ibid., p. 338.
17 Ibid., p. 339.
18 See also Jacques Derrida, 'Above All, No Journalists!', in *Religion and Media*, eds. Hent de Vries and Sam Weber (Stanford: Stanford University Press, 2001).
19 Jacques Derrida and Catherine Malabou, *Counterpath: Travelling with Jacques Derrida*, trans. David Wills (Stanford: Stanford University Press, 2004), p. 173.
20 Derrida and Malabou, *Counterpath*, p. 173.
21 See Derrida, 'The Force of Law', in *Deconstruction and the Possibility of Justice*; and his comments in *Limited Inc.* (Evanston, IL: Northwestern University Press, 1990), pp. 135–6.
22 See Jacques Derrida, *Geneses, Genealogies, Genres and Genius*, trans. Beverley Bie Brahic (Edinburgh: Edinburgh University Press, 2006).
23 Tom Stoppard, *Squaring the Circle with Every Good Boy Deserves Favour and Professional Foul* (London: Faber & Faber, 1984), p. 130.
24 See Jacques Derrida, 'La Sacrifice', in *L'éternel éphémère*, ed. Daniel Mesguich (Paris: Verdier, 2006), pp. 143–54.
25 For comments on Derrida's own career in football, 'We used to play until it was pitch dark: I dreamt of becoming a professional footballer', see Geoffrey Bennington and Jacques Derrida, *Derridabase/Circumfession* (Chicago: University of Chicago Press, 1993).
26 Ken McMullen, dir., *Ghost Dance* (London: Channel 4 Films, 1983).
27 Derrida's profound engagement with spectrality and Marxism, following his meeting with McMullen, is of course recorded in Derrida, *Spectres of Marx*.
28 See Derek Attridge, ed., *Acts of Literature* (London: Routledge, 1992), p. 184.
29 Attridge, *Acts of Literature*, p. 187.
30 Margarethe von Trotta, dir., *Hannah Arendt* (Heimatfilm, 2012).
31 See also Margarethe von Trotta, dir., *Rosa Luxemburg* (Bioskop Film, 1986).
32 David Barison and Daniel Ross, dirs., *The Ister* (Black Box Sound and Image, 2004); Kirby Dick and Amy Zeiring-Kofman, dirs., *Derrida* (Jane Doe Films, 2002).
33 The film mentions *The Origins of Totalitarianism* [1951] (London: Penguin, 2017) but centres on the writing of *Eichmann in Jerusalem: A Report on the Banality of Evil* [1963] (London: Penguin, 2006).
34 See editions of *The New Yorker*, 16 February–16 March 1963.
35 Other representations of the Arendt–Heidegger relationship can be found in the novel Catherine Clement, Martin and Hannah (New York: Prometheus Books, 2001). See also Hannah Arendt and Martin Heidegger, *Letters: 1925–1975*, ed.

Ursula Ludz (New York: Harcourt, 2004); Elzbieta Ettinger, *Hannah Arendt/Martin Heidegger* (New Haven: Yale University Press, 1997).

36 See Jacques Derrida, 'Punctuations: The Time of a Thesis', in *Eyes of the University*; Jonathan Culler and Kevin Lamb, eds., *Just Being Difficult? Academic Writing in the Public Arena* (Stanford: Stanford University Press, 2003).

37 See my 'Unfinished Business: Muriel Spark and Hannah Arendt in Palestine', in Michael Gardner et al eds. *Scottish Literature and Postcolonial Literature: Comparative Texts and Critical Perspectives* (Edinburgh: Edinburgh University Press, 2011).

38 John Huston, dir., *Freud* (Universal Pictures, 1962); Pinchas Perry, dir., *When Nietzsche Wept* (Millennium Films, 2007); David Cronenberg, dir., *A Dangerous Method* (Recorded Picture Company, 2011).

39 See Chapter 7, *Eichmann in Jerusalem*.

40 See for example, John Mullarkey, *Refractions of Reality: Philosophy and the Moving Image* (London: Palgrave Macmillan, 2008); Daniel Frampton, *Filmosophy* (London: Wallflower, 2006).

41 See my remarks on Cultural Studies in *Roland Barthes* (London: Palgrave Macmillan, 2011).

42 See Walter Benjamin, *The Storyteller: Tales Out of Loneliness*, ed. Esther Leslie (London: Verso, 2016).

43 See John Elderfield, *Manet and the Execution of Maximilian* (New York: Museum of Modern Art, 2006); Pierre Bourdieu, *Manet: A Symbolic Revolution*, trans. Peter Collier (Cambridge: Polity Press, 2017).

44 Edouard Manet, *Execution of the Emperor Maximilian* (1867). Oil on canvas, 6' 5 1/8" × 8' 6 1/4" (195.9 × 259.7 cm). Museum of Fine Arts, Boston. Gift of Mr. and Mrs. Frank Gair Macomber, 30.444; Edouard Manet, *The Execution of Maximilian* (1867–8). Oil on canvas, 6' 4" × 9' 3 13/16" (193 × 284 cm). The National Gallery, London. Bought, 1918; Edouard Manet, *The Execution of the Emperor Maximilian* (1868–9). Lithograph on chine collé, plate: 13 3/8 × 17 1/4" (34 × 43.8 cm). The Metropolitan Museum of Art, New York. Rogers Fund, 1921 (21.48); Edouard Manet, *The Execution of Maximilian* (1868–9). Oil on canvas, 18 7/8 × 22 13/16" (48 × 58 cm). Ny Carlsberg Glyptotek, Copenhagen; Edouard Manet, *The Execution of Emperor Maximilian* (1868–9). Oil on canvas, 8' 3 3/16 × 9' 10 7/8" (252 × 302 cm). Kunsthalle Mannheim.

45 Ken McMullen, dir., *1867* (Antelope Productions, 1990).

46 Goya, *The Third of May 1808* [1814], oil on canvas, 106' × 137' (268 cm × 347 cm). Museo del Prado, Madrid.

47 Ken McMullen, dir., *1871* (Channel 4 Films, 1990).

48 See Hélène Cixous, *Manhattan: Letters from Prehistory*, trans. Beverley Bie Brahic (New York: Fordham University Press, 2007).

49 As related to me by Ken McMullen.
50 Emile Zola, *La Débâcle*, trans. Elinor Dorday (Oxford: Oxford University Press, 2000).
51 Ken McMullen, dir., *Partition* (Channel 4 Films, 1987); *Zina* (Looseyard Productions, 1985).
52 Marcel Carné, dir., *Les Enfants du Paradis* (Sociétié Nouvelle Pathé Cinéma, 1946).
53 Napoleon III, *History of Julius Caesar* (New York: Harper & Brothers, 1865).
54 Karl Marx (1869), *The Eighteenth Brumaire of Louis Bonaparte* (Moscow: Progress Publishers, 1968), chap. I, p. 10.
55 'Supplementary to Dedicated Verses: Some Chapters from *Scorpion and Felix: A Humoristic Novel*', in *Marx-Engels Collected Works, Vol. 1: Marx, 1835–1843*, eds. Karl Marx and Frederick Engels (New York: International Publishers, 1975), pp. 616–32.

Chapter 7

1 Marc Redfield, *Theory at Yale: The Strange Case of Deconstruction in America* (New York: Fordham University Press, 2016).
2 Mark Tansey, 'Derrida Queries de Man', oil on canvas (212.7 × 139.7 cm), collection of Mike and Penny Winton, Gagosian Gallery. Sidney Paget, 'The Death of Sherlock Holmes', 1893. Image Select/Art Resource, NY.
3 'Constructing the Grand Canyon' (1990), oil on canvas (88 ¼ × 127 ¼") collection of the Walker Art Center, Minneapolis, gift of Penny and Mike Winton.
4 Barbara Johnson, 'Rigorous Unreliability', in *A World of Difference* (Baltimore and London: John Hopkins University Press, 1987), p. 18.
5 '"We Have Flipped over the Candle": Interview with Ellen S. Burt', in *Love in the Post*, p. 149.
6 Jacques Derrida, *Of Grammatology*, trans. Gayatri Chakravorty Spivak (Baltimore: John Hopkins University Press, 1974).
7 See Eve Kosofsky Sedgwick, *Between Men: English Literature and Male Homosocial Desire* (New York: Columbia University Press, 1985).
8 See Jacques Derrida, *Without Alibi*, trans. Peggy Kamus (Stanford: Stanford University Press, 2000).
9 Henri Thomas, *Le Parjure* (Paris: Gallimard, 1964). Shortly to appear in English-language translation as a critical edition through Rowman & Littlefield International, London.
10 I have treated these essays and this problematic in greater detail elsewhere, see Deconstruction after Derrida (London: Bloomsbury, 2014).
11 Mark Tansey, 'Under Erasure', oil on canvas 1990. See Danto, *Visions and Revisions*, p.115.

12 Jacques Derrida, *Dissemination*, trans. Barbara Johnson (London: Athlone, 1983).
13 Paul de Man, *Aesthetic Ideology* (Nebraska: University of Minnesota Press, 1996).
14 Paul de Man, 'Aesthetic Formalization: Kleist's *Über das Marionettentheater*', in *The Rhetoric of Romanticism*. Audio recordings of the full Messenger Lectures are available on The London Graduate School website http://www.thelondongraduateschool.co.uk/blog/listen-to-paul-de-man-the-messenger-lectures-1983/.
15 See Chapters 2 and 3 of this book.
16 For extended accounts of Tansey's work see also Arthur C. Danto, *Mark Tansey: Visions and Revisions*, ed. Christopher Sweet, notes and comments by Mark Tansey (New York: Abrams, 1992), and Mark C. Taylor, *The Picture in Question: Mark Tansey and the Ends of Representation* (Chicago: University of Chicago Press, 1999); Judi Freeman, *Mark Tansey: With Essays by Alain Robbe-Grillet and Mark Tansey*, Exhibition Catalogue, Los Angeles County Museum of Arts (San Francisco: Chronicle Books, 1993).
17 See Simon Morgan Wortham's recent engagements with materialism in work such as *Modern Thought in Pain: Philosophy, Politics, Psychoanalysis* (Edinburgh: Edinburgh University Press, 2015).

Index

Abelard, Peter   40
aberration   25, 28, 99, 116, 118, 121–2, 146, 206
Abrahamic tradition   142–3
abstraction   26–7, 29, 34, 37, 45–6, 65, 177
abyss   6, 10, 62, 74, 83–5, 88–9, 110, 123, 186, 190, 196–200, 205, 206
academics   1–3, 5–8, 10, 14, 16–17, 19, 27–8, 54, 65, 67, 73, 156, 174, 179, 203–4
accident   43, 55, 102–4, 106–8, 110, 112, 115–16, 135, 160
Ackerman, Chantal   20
Adair, Gilbert   16
Adami, Valerio   152, 166–70, 180, 182, 186, 195
Adonis   114–16
Adorno, Theodor   15
Aeschylus   125, 129–31, 134, 136
aesthetics   1–2, 9, 54–6, 59, 61, 63, 65, 67–72, 74, 83, 95, 98, 165, 186, 193, 204–5
agriculture   50, 132, 134
alchemy   5
aletheia   33, 35
algorithms   29, 35, 55, 58, 84, 143, 159, 181
alterity   90, 147
Althusser, Louis   15
America   7, 176, 196, 200, 202, 205, 208
Andreas-Salomé, Lou   17
angels   76–7, 79–81
animal   26, 36, 60–1, 90, 95–6, 101, 104, 114–15, 132–5, 193, 204
annihilation   102, 139, 169
anthropology   43, 50, 96, 208
aporia   25, 42, 54, 58, 64, 69, 77, 82, 84–5, 93–4, 100, 121, 123, 125, 133, 147, 157, 159, 161, 198, 208
Apuleius   157

architecture   7, 20, 27, 33–4, 101, 168, 188
Arendt, Hannah   182–5, 195
Aristotle   32–40, 44, 47, 148, 155
Artaud, Antonin   13
artillery   29, 33–4
artists   1–3, 5, 7–8, 18, 27, 53, 55, 61–2, 65, 69, 75, 82–4, 87–9, 94, 99–100, 113–14, 117–19, 121, 123–4, 138, 147, 165–9, 173, 187, 189, 191, 194, 198, 203–5, 207, 209, 217
Arts and Humanities Research Council   7–11, 67–8
art schools   1–3, 25, 84
asymptote   55, 84–7, 90, 92, 94, 101, 189, 191
Athens   13, 40, 42, 47–52
Atlantis   42, 47–51
Augustine of Hippo   14, 20, 26, 40, 82
Aurelius, Marcus   14
Australia   7, 19
autobiography   12–13, 15, 17, 19, 121, 200

Bachelard, Gaston   15, 130–1
Bacon, Francis   14
Badiou, Alain   15, 142
ballet   58–9
banality   60, 129
Banville, John   16
Barrison, David   20
Barthes, Roland   15, 18, 44–5
Bataille, Georges   15, 41
Baudrillard, Jean   15
beauty   97, 115–16, 157
Beckett, Samuel   78, 108
Benjamin, Walter   11, 15, 41, 166, 182, 186
Bergman, Ingmar   20
Berlin   53, 62
Bhabha, Homi K   159
bible   80–1, 91, 166–7

Bigelow, Katherine 20
bildungsroman 40
Binet, Lauren 18
Bishop Berkley 122
Blake, William 85
Blanchot, Maurice 15, 41
blindness 66, 82, 85, 87, 89–91, 93–5,
  97–101, 106, 113, 116, 136, 146, 156,
  196–203, 205–7
Boethius 14, 40
Borges, Jorge Luis 4
Braques, Georges 199, 203
Brook-Rose, Christine 19
Brueghel the Elder 167
budget 73, 183

Caesar, Julius 191–2
calculation 10–11, 30, 37, 57, 77, 112,
  126, 167, 178
camera 8, 169, 171, 182, 187–9
Camus, Albert 15
capital 16, 51, 107, 138, 140–1, 175–6,
  191–3
Carné, Marcel 191
Catalonia 182
Cavani, Liliana 20
celluloid 112, 189
chance 11, 35, 37, 56, 61, 92, 152
choreography 60, 201
cinema 1, 20, 41, 124, 190–1, 193
Cixous, Hélène 13, 16, 41, 84–93, 101
class 18, 56, 73, 176, 179
classical 36–7, 51, 72, 95, 98, 101, 110,
  113, 131, 140, 166, 168, 170, 200
classification 20, 35–6
cognition 29, 31, 63–4, 102, 116, 119,
  122, 161
Cohen, Leonard 4
Coldstream Report 2
Coleridge, Samuel Taylor 63, 138
colonialism 6, 19, 48–9, 214
communism 171, 176, 179, 190
Conan Doyle, Arthur 199–200, 205
Confession 12, 14, 40, 82
consciousness 58–9, 61, 91, 104, 117,
  204, 206
conservatoire 27, 156
contingency 10, 30, 37, 103, 106–8, 147
Cornell University 71, 199, 204

craft 1, 32, 34, 36, 55, 59, 93–4, 124,
  151, 155
creative writing 1–5, 7–8, 16, 20, 27, 40,
  52, 73–5, 84, 87, 89–90, 93–5, 100, 115,
  121, 165
creativity 10–11, 42, 44, 69, 73, 75, 85,
  87, 90, 101–4, 107–8, 112–13, 123,
  125–7, 129, 136, 138, 142–4, 145–8,
  154–5, 159–61
criticism 2, 9–10, 13, 16, 27, 61, 71, 83,
  165, 204
critique 9, 28, 39–41, 62, 108, 127,
  143, 185
Cromwell, Oliver 170
Cronenberg, David 184
culture 1–3, 8, 10, 13, 15, 17, 26–7, 36,
  52, 56, 62, 65, 86, 101, 132, 134, 141,
  145, 156, 204, 217

dance 4, 27, 30, 35–6, 54–61, 75, 88, 93,
  196, 201
Dante 200
Danton, Georges 192
death 17–18, 58, 63–4, 69–70, 76, 79,
  92–3, 98, 105, 107–8, 110–12, 114–15,
  117, 131, 134, 136–7, 157, 159–60, 168,
  170, 173, 186, 193, 201
death drive 107, 159
De Beauvoir, Simone 15, 41
Debord, Guy 15
De Botton, Alain 18
Debray, Régis 172
deconstruction 12, 18, 145, 158, 196,
  200–2, 207–9
Delueuze, Gilles 26–7
De Man, Paul 9, 15, 17, 57, 63, 69, 116,
  157, 196–8, 202, 208, 212
denomination 116, 155
Derrida, Jacques 10, 12–13, 16–17, 20,
  41, 43–7, 51, 94, 108–12, 138, 148–50,
  152, 154–61, 166–75, 178–82, 190, 195,
  197–202, 205–9
Derrida, Marguerite 166, 168–9, 172
Desmond, Norma 168
destiny 63, 139, 206
De Tocqueville, Alexis 14
dialectic 25, 38, 44, 63, 70, 72, 101–3,
  105–8, 110–12, 117–18, 123–5,
  165, 192

Index

Dick, Kirby 20, 182
Diderot, Denis 14, 40, 94–5
diegesis 42, 116, 120
Diogenes Laertius 131
disciplinarity 1, 3, 7–8, 13, 27, 40, 42, 204
dissemination 3, 115, 202
divinity 4, 36, 38, 51, 113, 116, 118, 122, 129–30, 134, 140
documentary 8, 15, 190
documentation 8, 187, 216
drama 4, 13–15, 17, 27, 50, 54, 57, 116, 120, 140, 160, 167, 169, 174, 176, 183–4, 191, 193
dreams 33, 96–7, 99, 116, 124, 152, 167
Duchamp, Marcel 197
Duncker, Patricia 16

Eagleton, Terry 16
Eco, Umberto 19
economy 11, 32, 85, 87, 117–18, 138–42, 145, 150, 154–5, 178
editing 5, 19, 53, 189, 196
education 2–3, 7, 9, 40, 60, 63, 65, 67–71, 73, 101, 205
Edwards, Selden 17
Egypt 13, 42, 47–9, 167
Eichmann, Adolf 183–5
Eisenman, Peter 20
Empire 48–50, 186, 192
empiricism 30, 32, 64–5, 67, 70, 108, 117, 130, 137
enclosure 54, 108, 111, 162
enlightenment 39, 49, 53
epistemology 3–4, 10, 14, 53, 56, 100, 123, 190
Epithemeus 125, 131–5
Erasmus, Desiderius 14
erasure 14, 36, 202–3, 206–8
Eribon, Didier 15
eros 115, 157–8, 193
error 10, 30, 58, 60, 63, 65, 67, 77, 96, 114, 117–18, 133, 135, 137
ethics 32–3, 35–8, 40, 176–8, 181–2
Europe 2, 19–20, 26, 40, 47–9, 51, 95, 178, 183, 199
Evola, Julius 48
experiment 12, 14–15, 19, 27–8, 52

fable 72, 74, 104, 150, 153–4, 157
fabrication 72, 74, 92–4, 99–100, 108, 122, 141–2
faith 31–2, 75, 77–9, 81, 87, 90, 131, 140, 143, 153, 183
Fanon, Franz 15
fantasy 119–20
fate 31, 51, 57, 62, 114, 125, 128–30, 133, 136, 173, 201
Fathy, Safaa 20
feminism 13, 16
fencing 60, 69, 80, 89
Feuerbach, Ludwig 38–9
fiction 12–18, 42–4, 47, 49–50, 52–3, 56, 69, 71, 73, 75, 99, 151, 174–82, 187, 190, 200
Fiennes, Sophie 15, 20
figuration 2, 15, 17, 27, 34, 36, 41, 43–6, 49–51, 54, 57, 60, 64, 87, 91, 97, 101–2, 104, 108, 117–19, 125, 127, 129–30, 138, 151, 160, 208
filmmaking 1, 3, 73, 82, 94, 117, 165–6, 184, 190–1
fire 126–30, 132–4
Fontaine, Jean de la 72, 74, 133
football (soccer) 57–8, 176–7, 179
formalization 3, 9, 11, 44, 53, 71–2, 74, 204, 206, 209
Foucault, Michel 11, 16
foundations 5, 9, 25, 48, 50, 74, 77, 97–8, 113, 171, 175–6, 179, 180–2, 187
Freud, Sigmund 12, 15, 17–19, 26, 66, 127–8, 180, 184, 190, 200
Friedrich, Casper David 70

gaze 90, 92, 98, 106, 174, 179
gender 19, 116, 119, 121, 149
genealogy 115–16, 139, 149–50
Genet, Jean 173, 175
genius 1, 148–9, 159, 201
genre 13–16, 18–19, 25, 30, 40–2, 45–6, 53–4, 73, 104, 116, 148–9, 187, 195
geometry 34, 87, 174
Gericault, Théodore 187
Giotto di Bondone 167
globalization 140–1, 144, 147, 173
Goddard, Jean-Luc 20, 114, 116, 118
Godwin, William 14
gospel according to Matthew 79, 167

government 6–8, 10, 30, 51, 171, 178–9, 191
grace 59–61, 71, 80, 84–6, 114, 207
Greek 33, 36, 39–40, 43, 48, 51, 83, 85, 102–4, 116, 158
Guilford School of Art 2

Hamlet (Prince of Denmark) 29, 105, 159
haptology 92, 94–6
Hartman, Geoffrey 15
Heaney, Seamus 150, 153–5
Hegel, G. W. F 16, 19, 44, 47, 54, 71, 101–10, 112, 130, 148, 192
Heidegger, Martin 16, 83–4, 131, 183–5
Hercules 79, 130
Herder, Gottfried v, 95–9, 101
hermeneutics 9
Hermes 98, 137
Hesiod 113, 125–7, 131, 133–5
Higgs boson 6
history 1, 3, 8, 13, 15, 18, 28, 40, 42, 45, 49, 51, 54, 62, 64, 78, 82, 84, 86, 88, 94, 106, 108–9, 111, 115–16, 118, 123, 136, 138, 140, 143–4, 147, 149–51, 153–4, 158, 161, 169–70, 173, 179, 181, 187–94, 197, 199, 203–4, 206, 208–9, 212
Hobbes, Thomas 14, 138
Holmes, Sherlock 196, 199–201
Homer 14
Hornsey School of Arts 2
humanism 82, 105, 161
humanities 3, 7, 9–11, 16, 26–7, 40, 62, 67–8, 75, 82, 161, 184
Huston, John 184
Hutchinson, Francis 14
hybridity 18, 108, 159–60

idealization 66–7, 146
ideology 9, 51, 67, 70–1, 82, 122, 193, 204, 206
imagination 59, 64–5, 67, 75, 134, 138, 187, 200
impossibility 10–11, 56–7, 59–60, 65, 67–71, 77–8, 84–5, 87–90, 94, 100, 106, 111, 117–18, 126–7, 136–7, 150, 156–8, 160, 165, 168, 189–91, 198–9, 205, 208, 217 n.29

infinity 61–2, 65, 84–5, 87–9, 189
inhuman 59–60, 118, 160
innocence 6, 59–61, 77, 84–90, 93, 134, 167, 169–70, 172–5, 177–8, 181
intelligible 43, 91, 94, 100
intention 58, 74, 103–4, 143–4, 176, 188, 197, 208–9
interruption 68, 72, 88, 145–6, 153, 158
invention 10–11, 49, 58, 73–5, 111, 129, 134, 136–8, 147–57, 159–62
Irish literature 150, 153–4, 170, 191, 193
iterability 124, 153–4
Iyer, Lars 16

Jarman, Derek 20
Jerusalem 80, 183, 185
John of the Cross 14
Johnson, Barry 198
Johnson, Terry 17
Jonze, Spike 20
journalism 53, 73–4, 177, 183, 200
Joyce, James 145, 166
judgment 28–32, 96–7, 100, 143, 185
Jung, Carl 184

Kafka, Franz 87, 127, 175, 180–1
Kant, Immanuel 25–6, 28–33, 39–40, 54, 62–7, 69–73, 75–6, 79, 97, 99, 137–8, 141, 143–4, 180, 184, 205
Keats, John v
Kerr, Philip 18
Khora 43–7, 49, 51, 148
Kierkegaard, Soren 14, 40
Kissinger, Henry 169–70
Kleist, Heinrich von 53–4, 57–60, 62–4, 67, 69–76, 78, 81–2, 84–7, 89–91, 94, 97–9, 121–3, 133, 195, 204–6
Kofman, Amy (Ziering) 20
Kojève, Alexander 19, 107, 109
Krell, David Farrell 16
Kristeva, Julia 15
Kurds 169–70, 178, 181
Kureishi, Hanif 18

labour 110–11, 115, 117–19, 165, 195
law 30–1, 39, 42, 59–60, 76, 78, 86, 90, 98
legitimacy 28, 65, 93, 149–51, 154, 156, 186, 201

Lentricchia, Frank   16
Lessing, George   14
Lévi-Strauss, Claude   207
Libeskind, Daniel   20
life-writing   15, 19, 40
Lispector, Clarice   84, 87
literature   1–4, 6, 14, 17–20, 40–2, 44, 47, 53–4, 62, 64, 122–3, 149, 154, 175, 181, 203
logos   42, 43, 49, 135, 144

McCarthy, Mary   17, 183
McCarthy, Tom   19
Machiavelli, Niccolò   14
machines   56, 60–1, 108, 155–6, 159–60
McMullen, Ken   179–80, 186–95
Madame de Staël   14, 40
Magdalene, Mary   15
magic   75, 148, 155
Malabou, Catherine   101–12, 174
Maley, Willy   16
Malraux, Andre   15
Manet, Edouard   186–90, 194
Mann, Thomas   69–70
Marionettes   54–62, 71, 73, 75, 81–2, 84, 89, 98, 204
markets   3, 54–8, 191, 193
Marx, Karl   38–40, 110, 140–3, 165, 176–8, 190–4
materiality   5, 17, 29, 35, 37, 39, 41, 43, 45, 48, 50, 64–5, 67, 69, 72–3, 94, 99, 104, 110, 119, 122–3, 128, 138–9, 142–8, 151, 153, 166, 176–7, 189, 193, 195–6, 198–9, 202, 204, 206–9
Mathematics   11, 29, 33–4, 64–6, 96, 205
measure   10–11, 27, 61, 139, 162, 178, 189
Media Studies   2, 8, 16, 183
Medicine   103, 160, 173
memory   91, 111–12, 129, 158
Messenger Lectures   71, 204–6
metaphor   43, 83, 87, 98, 120, 127, 148
metaphysics   32, 59, 90–1, 94, 96–7, 100, 133, 140–1, 143–4, 151, 155
metonym   93, 96, 195
Miller, J Hillis   121–4, 207
Milton, John   77, 79–81, 88, 125, 170
mimesis   43, 68–9, 72, 116

Mirabeau, Honoré-Gabriel de Riqueti   72, 74, 133
misidentification   113, 115–17, 119
misreading   54, 63, 65–6, 69, 113, 148, 205
Mitchell, Margaret   18
Mitterrand, François   172
modernity   9, 197, 203–4, 206, 208
Modjeska, Drusilla   19
Molliere (Jean-Baptiste Poquelin)   74
Montesquieu, Charles-Louis de Secondat, baron de La Brède at de   14
More, Thomas   14, 40
mourning   13, 15, 110–11, 115, 117
Murdoch, Iris   18–19
music   4, 11, 15, 26–7, 56, 156, 160, 191, 193
mysticism   4–5, 14, 38–9, 141, 145, 148, 155
myth   42–4, 47–51, 98, 104, 113, 116, 125, 127–8, 132, 135–7, 157–8

Naas, Michael   197
Nancy, Jean-Luc   15, 138–44, 146–7, 150, 158–9, 161
Napoleon III   186–7, 191–2
narcissism   86, 116–17, 121, 174
narrative   17, 19, 42–3, 47–8, 52, 59, 71–2, 104, 116, 128, 135, 153, 175, 179, 181, 183, 190, 193
National Socialism (Nazi)   17, 47, 50, 182–3
Newmark, Kevin   196–7
newspapers   57, 130
Nietzsche, Friedrich   14–17, 41, 54, 184, 202, 204–7
Nixon, Richard   170, 178
Novalis   53, 57
novels   4, 13–20, 27, 40, 53, 82, 84, 107–8, 121, 145–6, 158, 192, 200, 202

Odysseus   114
Oliver, Kelly   16
ontology   42–3
Opera   15, 54
origins   16, 32, 39, 42, 44–50, 76, 78, 83, 91, 98, 102, 105, 115–16, 127, 129, 132–5, 137–8, 142–6, 149, 154, 160, 168, 171, 180, 188–9

Paget, Sidney   196, 199, 231
painting   4, 93, 98–9, 101, 145, 167–8, 186–8, 190, 194–203, 206–8
Panenka, Antonin   178
parabasis   60, 127, 153, 158
Paradise   60, 62, 67, 75–6, 78–81, 85–6, 88, 125
paradox   57–8, 61, 82, 85, 113
paralysis   76, 89
Parker, Cornelia   18
Parmenides   140
Pascal, Blaise   14, 20, 40
pathology   111, 131
Patočka, Jan   170, 173, 175
pedagogy   9, 41, 67, 123, 157
Peeters, Benoît   166, 171, 212
Peloponnesian War   48
performance   3–4, 7, 11–12, 15, 43, 63–4, 70, 75, 151, 169–70, 179–80, 190–1, 201, 205, 216
Perry, Pinchas   184
phenomenology   92, 94, 96–7, 99, 102, 119, 122, 133
philosophy   v, 1–2, 11–21, 25–33, 37–50, 52–4, 56, 59, 62–3, 65–71, 73, 82–3, 88–9, 94–7, 100, 103–4, 106–9, 113, 117–18, 123–4, 130–3, 136, 138, 141, 148–9, 161, 165–6, 168–76, 178–9, 181–6, 195, 201, 204–5
phronesis   32, 34–7, 39, 185
Picasso, Pablo   199
Pinon, Dominique   191–2
plastic   94, 98–9, 101–12, 117
Plato   13–14, 18, 25, 40–2, 44–52, 54, 82, 95, 125, 131–5, 148
Platonism   44–5, 49
poetry   14–15, 36, 54, 151
poiesis   36–7
police   12, 171–2, 174, 176–8, 180–2
politics   2, 5, 9, 14, 26, 31, 36–9, 41, 46–8, 50, 52, 65, 75, 82, 86, 132–5, 137, 141–2, 167, 178–9, 191, 193
Poussin, Nicolas   167–70
practice-based research   1, 6–11, 18, 27, 29, 31, 38, 58, 67, 113, 124, 147, 150, 160, 166, 172, 204
Prague   171–7, 179–82
praxis   35–40, 137, 147–8

programmes   1–4, 9–10, 28, 37, 50, 56–7, 69, 73, 77, 84, 100, 123–4, 136, 138, 161–2, 186, 189
Prometheus   113, 125–37
prophecy   129–30, 167
prosthesis   59, 98–9, 100, 134
Proust, Marcel   13
psyche   148–9, 157–8
psychoanalysis   17–18, 128, 130, 168–9, 189
puppets   53–60, 84, 186
Pygmalion   113–25

quasi-transcendental   26, 150, 152
Queneau, Raymond   19

rationality   4, 6, 11, 31, 34, 36–7, 39, 42, 70–1, 77, 82, 86, 91, 96, 122–4, 141, 143, 156, 158, 180
rebellion   76, 125–9, 131, 170, 204
Redfield, Marc   196–8, 202–3, 207–9
reference   4, 27, 29–30, 34, 42–3, 47, 95, 118, 141, 143, 145, 147–8, 158, 167, 175, 178, 189–90, 200
refugees   8
Rembrandt, Harmenszoon van Rijn   98
reproduction   71, 116, 119
research   1–2, 6–11, 18–19, 27, 67–8, 93, 155
revolution   39, 72, 74, 142, 171, 183, 188, 191–4
risk   12, 28, 30, 35, 56–9, 62, 67–9, 75, 79, 81, 84, 86, 88–9, 91–3, 96, 100, 111, 130, 139, 150, 152, 157, 171, 176–7, 197–8, 205
Robespierre, Maximilien   192
Rohmer, Eric   20
romanticism   125, 131, 138, 159–60, 204, 208
Rome   40
Ross, Daniel   20
Rossellini, Roberto   20
Rousseau, Jean-Jacques   14, 15, 40, 53, 82, 95, 114, 116, 119–20, 200, 201, 204, 207
Royle, Nicholas   16
Rubenfield, Jeb   17
Rubens, Peter Paul   167
Russell, Bertrand   14
Russell, David O   20

sacrifice   62, 114, 118, 134, 170, 174, 178–9
Santayana, George   14, 18
Sartre, Jean-Paul   15, 40, 57
Satan   76–81, 87, 126
Schad, John   16–17
Schiller, Friedrich   9, 14, 40, 53, 63–72, 75–6, 79, 205
Schlink, Bernard   17
scholarship   3, 7, 12, 18–19, 196, 207, 209, 215
Science   10, 34, 36, 96–7, 102–3, 136, 160–1, 176, 184
screenplays   4–5, 17, 19, 180
sculpture   95, 98–9, 101, 114, 116
Searle, John   178
secrets   17, 54, 75, 90–1, 93, 130, 169, 174, 180–2, 191, 193
Sedgwick, Eve Kosofsky   200
Sellers, Susan   16
sensible   43, 91, 94, 100
serendipity   10, 27, 35, 189
sexual difference   116, 120, 125–6, 129, 133, 135–6
Shakespeare, William   50, 116, 140
Shelley, Percy Bysshe   125
Silesius, Angelus   141
skill   19, 34, 39, 48, 55, 87, 95, 122, 132, 134, 137, 149
Smilevski, Goce   17
Socrates   14, 20, 42, 47, 51
Sollers, Philippe   15
sovereignty   81, 140, 146, 178
Sparta   48, 50–1
speculation   2–3, 13, 15–16, 18–21, 28–9, 36–9, 51–2, 56, 104, 118–19, 121, 169, 192, 195
Spinoza, Baruch   14, 17
Spivak, Gayatri   15
staging   9, 62, 65, 68, 75, 119–20, 140, 157–8, 174, 190–1, 193, 201, 206
Stendhal (Marie-Henri Beyle)   158
Stiegler, Bernard   15, 131–7
Stone, Irving   17
Stoppard, Tom   175–6, 178–9, 186
storytelling   15, 52, 74, 93, 99, 154, 175, 183, 186
structure   1, 14, 36, 43, 45, 47, 53, 64–5, 71–2, 74, 99–100, 103, 105, 108, 120, 136–7, 175, 197

subjectivity   103–5
sublime   62, 64–7, 72, 195–6
synthesis   105, 108, 124

Tansey, Mark   166, 195–209
Tarkovsky, Andrei   20
Taylor, Astra   20
techne   32, 34–6, 83, 108, 135, 147–8, 155, 159–60
technique   9, 11, 27, 35, 89, 91, 100, 153, 157–8, 160, 178, 202
technology   123, 134, 191
techno-science   160–1
teleology   28, 71, 103–4, 106, 108
telephone   92, 151
Teresa of Avilla   14
theatre   5, 16, 54, 65, 68–9, 82, 84, 89, 99, 124, 191–2, 206
theology   14, 127, 142–5, 152
Thomas, Henri   17, 200, 202
Thoreau, William   14
Tintoretto   167
Tiresius   91
totalitarianism   61, 144, 179, 182–3
touch   66–7, 82–5, 87, 92, 94–102, 107, 113–17, 119–20, 130, 158, 161, 173, 189, 171
translation   14–15, 17, 33–4, 37, 39–40, 43, 63–4, 87, 89, 101, 103, 105, 116, 140–1, 146, 155, 179, 189, 199, 205
trauma   103, 152
tropes   48, 63, 68, 74, 90, 103, 127, 138, 142, 148
Tschumi, Bernard   20, 148
Turner, J. M. W   199
Tyson, Mike   5, 57

undecidability   13, 50, 52, 64, 155, 157, 190, 191, 203
universality   26, 31, 37, 45, 50, 82, 86, 103, 124, 141, 181, 193
universities   3, 6, 7–11, 16, 19, 25, 27, 71, 89, 92, 122–3, 150, 174, 176, 178, 181, 199, 207
university management   3, 92, 162

Valéry, Paul   15
Veneziano, Domenico   207
Van Haarlem, Cornelius   167

Venus   113–18, 120
Vernant Jean-Pierre   131, 136
Vickers, Salley   18
Voltaire, François-Marie Arouet   14, 40, 82
Von der Lippe, Angela   17
Von Trotta, Margarethe   182, 184, 186, 195

Warminski, Andrzej   204
Webster, Brenda   17
Wicomb, Zoë   19
Wilde, Oscar   30

Wittgenstein, Ludwig   16, 18–20
Woolf, Virginia   16
Wordsworth, William   138, 202

Yale University   66, 121, 196–7, 199–201, 206–7, 209
Yalom, Irvin D   17

Zeiring, Amy Kofman   20, 182
zero   19, 84, 139
Zeus   51, 125–6, 129–30, 132–5, 137
Žižek, Slavoj   15, 20
Zola, Emile   190, 194

www.ingramcontent.com/pod-product-compliance
Lightning Source LLC
Chambersburg PA
CBHW051520230426

43668CB00012B/1680